KT-228-632

Contents

CONTENTS

PART III PLACES OF RESISTANCE

PART IV POLITICS AND POSITION

CONCLUSION

WITHDRAWN

3/97 LR/LEND/001

UNIVERSITY OF
WOLVERHAMPTON

Harrison Learning Centre
Wolverhampton Campus
University of Wolverhampton
St Peter's Square
Wolverhampton WV1 1RH
Wolverhampton (01902) 322305

Telephone Renewals: 01902 321333
**This item may be recalled at any time. Keeping it after it has
been recalled or beyond the date stamped may result in a fine.**
See tariff of fines displayed at the counter.

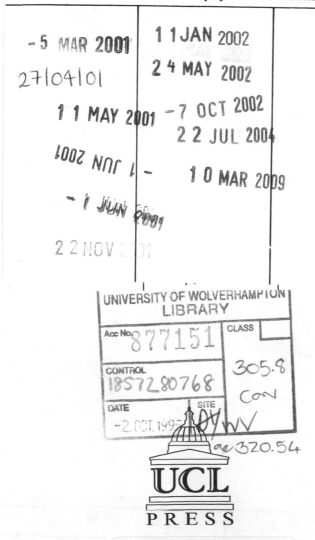

- 5 MAR 2001   1 1 JAN 2002

27|04|01   2 4 MAY 2002

1 1 MAY 2001   - 7 OCT 2002

                 2 2 JUL 2004

- 1 JUN 2001

                 1 0 MAR 2009

- 1 JUN 2001

2 2 NOV 2001

UNIVERSITY OF WOLVERHAMPTON
LIBRARY

Acc No. 877151   CLASS

CONTROL   305.8
1857280768   Con

DATE   SITE
- 2. OCT. 199   WV

ac 320.54

UCL
PRESS

WP 0877151 0

© Peter Jackson, Jan Penrose and contributors 1993

This book is copyright under the Berne Convention.
No reproduction without permission.
All rights reserved.

First published in 1993 by UCL Press.

UCL Press Limited
University College London
Gower Street
London WC1E 6BT

The name of University College London (UCL) is a registered
trade mark used by UCL Press with the consent of the owner.

ISBN:
1-85728-076-8 HB
1-85728-077-6 PB

A CIP catalogue record for this book
is available from the British Library.

Typeset in Palatino.
Printed and bound by
Biddles Ltd, King's Lynn and Guildford, England.

Preface

The essays in this book share a commitment to the idea that "race" and "nation" are social constructions rather than naturally occurring phenomena. These are powerful ideas because their legitimacy is rarely called into question: they are taken for granted, unexamined, beyond inquiry. By subjecting conventional definitions of "race" and "nation" to critical scrutiny, we hope to demonstrate their mutability as social constructions. In doing so, we introduce new ways of thinking about human difference that are not grounded in biological notions of "race" and that do not automatically regard nations as the fundamental unit of society.

The resilience of racist and nationalist ideologies is closely related to their ability to assume different shapes from time to time and from place to place. Taking examples from Australia, Britain, Canada and the United States, the essays in this volume demonstrate some of the continuities between the form of racism and nationalism in different contexts. At the same time, however, they also highlight the existence of significant differences, reflecting the particular ways that these ideologies are articulated with the societies in which they occur. Besides the application of social construction theory to particular empirical materials, the following chapters are also united in their adoption of a geographical perspective concerning the spatial constitution of social life, the territorial expression of racism and nationalism, and the variation of such ideologies from place to place.

Most of the essays were originally presented at a special session of the 1992 Annual Meetings of the Association of American Geographers in San Diego. One paper (by Heléne Clark) was given at a different session in the AAG meetings and another paper from the original session (by Melissa Gilbert) was later withdrawn. One final paper (by Susan Smith) was not presented at the AAG meetings but was included at a later stage. The San Diego meetings provided an excellent opportunity for the authors to meet one another, to share ideas and to comment on each other's papers. This has greatly added to the sense of a common endeavour, provided a comparative dimension to our thinking, and contributed to the coherence of this volume.

The AAG session attracted a large audience, generating a lively debate, and we would like to thank all those who took part in the discussion. After the conference, second drafts of each chapter were circulated among the authors to provide a further opportunity for mutual criticism and clarification. As editors, we provided detailed comments on these drafts and agreed a set of revisions with each author. In turn, authors were invited to comment on a draft of the introduction and we are most grateful for their responses.

The book is divided into four parts, each comprising a pair of essays, grouped by subject matter and theme. There is a separate theoretical intro-duction, with short linking sections serving as concise introductions to each pair of essays. Finally, we provide a brief conclusion, drawing out some comparative issues and highlighting some of the gaps for future research. We hope the volume will help clarify some of the highly charged issues that revolve around notions of "race" and "nation" as well as contributing to the development of a more rigorous social construction approach within geogra-phy and the social sciences.

Peter Jackson & Jan Penrose
LONDON AND EDINBURGH

Contributors

Kay J. Anderson is a Senior Lecturer in the Department of Geography and Oceanography, University College, Australian Defence Force Academy, University of New South Wales. She is the author of *Vancouver's Chinatown: racial discourse in Canada, 1875– 1980* (McGill–Queen's University Press, 1991) and co-editor of *Inventing places: studies in cultural geography* (Longman Cheshire, 1992). Her current research projects include the cultural history of Aboriginal Redfern, the changing environmental ethics of the Royal Zoological Society of South Australia, and gendered politics during Australia's "Green ban" era.

Alastair Bonnett undertook his PhD in the Geography Department at Queen Mary and Westfield College (University of London) and has subsequently held post-doctoral posts in the Geography Departments of McMaster University and the University of British Columbia. He is Lecturer in Human Geography at the University of Newcastle upon Tyne. He is the author of *Radicalism, anti-racism and representation* (Routledge, 1993). His most recent research focuses on reflexivity and the construction of "white" identity.

Heléne Clark is an Associate Director of the Housing Environments Research Group in the Graduate School and University Center of the City University of New York where she is completing a dissertation on "Environmental psychology as a critical theory of space and place". Her current research focuses on the potentials for social and political change through local spatial practices that alter people's relationships to place. She is the author of many articles on low-income housing cooperatives and other forms of local movements in New York City.

Claire Dwyer is a postgraduate student at University College London, writing a dissertation on questions of identity for young Muslim women in the UK. She taught geography at secondary school for several years before completing a Masters degree at Syracuse University in December 1991.

Peter Jackson is Professor of Human Geography at the University of Sheffield. He is the editor of *Race and racism: essays in social geography* (Allen & Unwin, 1987) and author of *Maps of meaning* (Unwin Hyman, 1989; reprinted by Routledge, 1992). His current research focuses on British and Canadian racism and on the cultural politics of consumption in north London.

Jane M. Jacobs is currently a Research Fellow in the Department of Geography, University of Melbourne. She has published on the cultural politics of heritage designations in both Australia and Britain. Her current research focuses on postcolonialism and space.

Jan Penrose teaches geography through the Centre of Canadian Studies at the University of Edinburgh. Her past research has included studies of cultural transition among the Finnish Sami and the role of Frisian nationalism in the preservation and promotion of cultural distinctiveness. She is currently working on nationalism in Quebec and is preparing a comparative study of nationalist politics in Scotland and Wales.

Susan J. Smith is Ogilvie Professor of Geography at the University of Edinburgh. She is the author of *Crime, space and society* (Cambridge University Press, 1986), *The politics of "race" and residence* (Polity Press, 1989) and several studies of housing and health, and social policy.

Introduction:
placing "race" and nation

PETER JACKSON & JAN PENROSE

Ideas about "race" and nation are among the most powerful sources of human identity and division within the contemporary world, as recent events from Serbia to South Africa amply confirm.[1] Indeed, both "race" and nation are so rooted in the way we think about the world that we tend to take the categories themselves for granted. Yet it is precisely through their apparent "naturalness" and immutability that racism and nationalism do their ideological work, often with dire consequences for human lives. Drawing on case studies from Australia, Britain, Canada and the United States, this book attempts a critical interrogation of the notions of "race" and nation, seeking parallels and differences between the ideologies of racism and nationalism in different places. Demonstrating that "race" and nation mean quite different things in different places underlines the notion that both concepts are *social constructions*, the product of specific historical and geographical forces, rather than biologically given ideas whose meaning is dictated by nature.

Before turning to the case study material, we will briefly outline our understanding of the theory of social construction. This is followed by an overview of the shifting meaning of some of our key terms: "race", nation and place, a process which provides an initial demonstration of their constructedness. We will then attempt to sketch the current "state of the art" in geographical studies of "race" and nation before outlining some of the intellectual and political problems that have begun to emerge as we move away from essentialist notions of "race" and nation to embrace a constructionist perspective.

1

The "theory" of social construction

At its simplest, social construction theory is concerned with the ways in which we think about and use categories to structure our experience and analysis of the world. Social construction theory rejects the longstanding view that some categories are "natural", bearing no trace of human intervention. There are two assumptions at play here, neither of which can withstand critical scrutiny. The first is that humanity is separate from nature. The second is that if something is natural its legitimacy cannot be called into question. The first assumption becomes problematic when it is combined with the assumption that things "natural" are beyond the realm of human influence. "Natural" categories come to be treated as pre-given and hence unalterable. Social construction theory challenges this "essentialist" view of categories because of the way these ideas have been used to legitimize human actions that grant advantages to some categories over (or at the expense of) others. More specifically, social construction theory argues that many of the categories that we have come to consider "natural", and hence immutable, can be more accurately (and more usefully) viewed as the product of processes which are embedded in human actions and choices. Implicit in this argument is the idea that conceptions of "nature" are themselves borne of the human capacity to form notions, so that what we consider to be "natural" can and does change with corresponding transitions in human thought. As a result, the capacity for something "natural" to confer legitimacy is undermined.

As this suggests, social construction theory offers a fresh perspective on the conception, constitution and application of categories. In particular, it forces the re-evaluation of a whole range of "givens": personal, cultural or more universally human. At the same time, it challenges our complacency in accepting the inequalities which are permitted, if not encouraged, by specific kinds of categories and their application. Moreover, by enabling us to deconstruct categories which were previously viewed as indivisible and untouchable, the theory offers new opportunities for redressing human divisiveness and inequities. In other words, if we can learn how specific constructions have empowered particular categories we can disempower them or appropriate their intrinsic power, to achieve more equitable ends.

Before attempting to apply this theory, we would like to balance an elucidation of the strengths of social construction theory with a word of caution about its potential weaknesses. As a point of departure, it is important to clarify that construction theory does not deny the need for some kind of categorization. Human thought requires categories as fundamental communicative devices. Construction theory only challenges the idea that some categories are more fundamental ("essential", "natural") than others. Related attempts to demonstrate the mutability of categories introduce a potential weakness of the social construction perspective which is largely semantic. Problems can arise from the tendency to equate "construction" with "artificiality". Such an equation tends to imply that a "real" or "authentic" alternative to the "artificial" construction is possible. This is precisely what the social construction perspective is designed to overcome. While some constructions may be more defensible than others (according to our humanly constructed powers of persuasion and legitimization), no constructions are more intrinsically "real" than others. Accordingly, any application of a social construction perspective must avoid the simple identification of falseness in constructs. To do so is, however inadvertently, to perpetuate the belief that "real" categories exist *a priori* and have only to be discovered and defined. In the process, there is an added risk of antagonizing and undermining the effectiveness of groups which have mobilized around a particular construct in order to achieve redress. We return to this criticism a little later.

A second potential problem concerns the inference that if constructions are "artificial" they lack "reality" or do not "exist". Such reasoning, however faulty, can lead to the conviction that the social construction perspective lacks internal consistency because it appears to deny the existence of the very categories that form the basis of its own analysis. Accordingly, constructionists must take care to distinguish between their acceptance of the assertion that people operate *as if* categories "exist" and their rejection of the idea that this existence is grounded in "reality" as an immutable, unalterable truth. All constructions of "reality" must be seen as a product of the human capacity for thought and, consequently, are subject to change and variability.

As all of this suggests, the social construction perspective works by identifying the components and processes of category construction. The resultant knowledge can then be used to reconstruct categories in ways which allow their inherent power to be used in the pursuit of equality. Alternatively, we can use the theory to deconstruct categories such that their power to engender inequality is dissolved. In either case, the objective is not to expose the falseness of constructs but rather to expose the falseness of our unquestioning acceptance of these constructs from which their legitimacy derives. From this perspective, social construction theory can be seen to offer a radical form of analysis and exciting possibilities for envisioning societal transformation.

Putting *"race"* in its place

In its current sense of a social classification based on physical distinctions of skin-colour, hair-type and biological descent, the word "race" seems to have come into the English language from French and Italian roots in the late eighteenth century (Williams 1976: 248–50). The word was present as early as the late sixteenth century in various senses relating to human descent and to the differentiation of plant and animal species. In the mid-nineteenth century, however, the scientific study of human differentiation became radically confused with other ideas about social progress and human evolution. This confusion is commonly associated with Social Darwinism, whereby biological ideas about competition for survival *between* species were extended into social and political debates about conflict *within* species. Ideas about human achievement, social development and "progress" all became entangled with biological notions about classification, selection and hierarchy as such theorists as Francis Galton and Karl Pearson became interested in the potential of genetic experimentation (eugenics) to prevent the "degeneration" of human populations (Stepan 1982).

The intellectual context in which ideas about "race" gained scientific legitimacy must also be placed alongside the political and economic context which allowed some people to benefit from these ideas. In general, notions about the social hierarchy of human "races" served the interests of mercantile and industrial capitalism as it moved into its expansionist phase through the development of overseas empires. Many of the stereotypes that were held about Britain's growing "New Commonwealth" population after the Second World War are grounded in ideas that derive from the colonial experience abroad. This is not to say that contemporary racism is simply an inheritance of Empire but to suggest that Britain's "ethnic minorities" did not enter an ideological vacuum: they were already "racialized" on arrival in Britain as a result of Britain's colonial history (cf. Miles 1989). Similarly, Britain did not simply export its own brand of domestic racism to its overseas colonies. But there are clear continuities between British racism and the forms of racism that developed in Australia, Canada and other white-settler colonies abroad (Ward 1978, Roy 1989, de Lepervanche & Bottomley 1988).

In general, the idea of "race" has been discredited in serious scientific work genetic variations within particular "racial" groups have been shown to be practically as wide as those between allegedly different "races" (Cavalli-Sforza 1974). However, the scientific disavowal of the "racial" differentiation of human populations has not been followed by a similar repudiation of its social significance within either political discourse or popular culture. Neither has the link between academic research and racialized thinking been entirely broken, as the social sciences have replaced the natural sciences in debates about "race". Today, it is social scientific interest in the study of "race relations" which runs the risk of legitimating and perpetuating the very categories it sets out to undermine (cf. Miles 1984).

As it has become generally accepted that "races" are socially constructed rather than biologically given, research has begun to focus on the process through which specific ideologies of "race" are mobilized in particular circumstances and with what effects:

> If "races" are not naturally occurring populations, the reasons and conditions for the social process whereby the discourse of "race" is employed in an attempt to label, constitute and exclude social collectivities should be the focus of attention rather than be assumed to be a natural and universal process. (Miles 1989: 73)

This challenge has been taken up, albeit selectively, within the geographical literature (for a review, see Jackson 1989). In South Africa, for example, an impressive literature has emerged, charting the history of apartheid through the development of extreme forms of residential segregation to the present dismantling of apartheid's cruder institutional structures (Crush & Rogerson 1983, Mabin 1986, Rogerson & Parnell 1989). These researchers have achieved an admirable blending of historical and geographical accounts of the rise and fall of apartheid. Elsewhere, with significant exceptions, there has been relatively little work on the historical geographies of "race" and racism. Social geography has been preoccupied with contemporary issues, while historical geography (again with a growing number of exceptions) has been preoccupied with class structure and consciousness rather than with the constitution of "racialized" (or gendered) identities.

Much of the current debate about "race" and racism has been couched in terms of the theory of "racialization", first advanced by Robert Miles (1982) in relation to postwar labour migration to Britain and subsequently employed by many others (including Smith 1989, Solomos 1989, Anderson 1991, Jackson 1992). Rather than accepting the idea of "race" as a biological given, the theory requires us to examine the conditions under which specific processes of "racialization" have taken place. Miles (1984), for example, has argued that the Notting Hill riots of 1958 were a key moment in the definition of "race relations" as a significant political issue in Britain. Earlier groups of Irish and Jewish migrants had faced discrimination in housing and employment, but their presence did not give rise to a discourse about "race relations" in the way that this was to occur in the wake of large-scale immigration from the New Commonwealth after 1945 when "colour" came to be regarded as the prime index of "race".

The very term "New Commonwealth" both contributed to and reflected the "racialization" of British politics by introducing a new category that was ostensibly based on history and geography but which implicitly incorporated notions about "race". Attempts to implement "racially" discriminatory legislation under the protective guise of this seemingly neutral term generated new dimensions to discourse about "race" (see Smith, below). The "racialization" of British politics has now been shown to date back well beyond the early 1960s when immigration restrictions were first imposed. For example, research by Carter et al. (1987) has shown that the 1951–55 Conservative government was already considering the restriction of New Commonwealth immigration, while even the Labour government of 1945–51 was concerned about the potential extent of "colonial immigration" (Dean 1987). Popular magazines such as *Picture Post* also referred to New Commonwealth migration in a thoroughly racialized vocabulary, including its coverage of the "30,000 Colour Problems" (June 1956) currently arriving in Britain each year. It was in this period that British "race relations" came to be defined as a "social problem". As Salman Rushdie has remarked:

. . . the worst and most insidious stereotype . . . is the characterization of black people as a Problem. You talk about the Race Problem, the Immigration Problem, all sorts of problems. If you are a liberal, you say that black people have problems. If you aren't, you say they are the problem. (Rushdie 1991: 138)

Following this logic, it would be possible to trace the racialization of British politics in terms of a whole series of place-specific "problems": from Notting Hill in 1958 to the Brixton, Handsworth, Toxteth and Moss Side "riots" of 1981 and 1985. The debate about multicultural education (discussed below by Dwyer and Bonnett) also reads like a virtual gazetteer of Britain's inner cities: from Bradford and Dewsbury to Manchester and Brent.

In combination, all of these separate incidents add up to a process of racialization which, in the context of postwar Britain, can be shown to have been "structurally determined, politically organized and ideologically inflected . . . within relations of domination and subordination" (Green & Carter 1988: 23). The chapters that follow are all concerned, in different ways, with tracing the racialization process in particular circumstances and at varying scales, from the local to the national, in Australia, Britain, Canada and the United States. In each of these places, the racialization process has been associated with particular symbolic geographies, whether in the Aboriginal enclave of Sydney's Redfern district, Britain's inner cities, or the semi-ghetto of Toronto's Jane-Finch corridor. Before turning to the significance of place for studies of "race" and racism, however, let us briefly turn to an examination of another of our key terms: namely, nation.

The shifting place of nation

Nation, like the term "race", derives part of its power and resilience from ambiguity of meaning. Over time, various scholars have attempted to locate the origins of the term and to trace shifts in its meaning over time. The title of one of the most successful of these efforts, "A nation is a nation, is a state, is an ethnic group is a . . . " (Connor 1978), highlights the complexity of the task at hand. However, rather than dispelling confusion, most attempts to elucidate and clarify the meaning of the term nation have ended by confirming a multiplicity of usages or simply introducing new conceptualizations into the intellectual melee. At the risk of perpetuating the same practice here, we would like to identify three main ways in which the term nation is currently used, and then briefly highlight the implications of semantic confusion that are of relevance to ideas about social construction.

According to Williams (1976: 213), the term nation has been in common use in English since the latter part of the thirteenth century. At this time it was used primarily as a means of connoting a "racial" group and, as such, it formed part of an ageless attempt to acknowledge broad divisions in humanity. By the eighteenth century, however, use of the term nation had undergone a shift in emphasis from descriptive to prescriptive applications. In addition to defining "peoples" as large, exclusive and distinctive human groups (a euphemism for "race"), it was increasingly used to define smaller groups, each of which constituted "a people", as the fundamental, "natural" units of humanity.

Indeed, as one of the main proponents of this view, Herder (1744–1803) denied the existence of discrete "races", arguing instead that "every nation is one people, having its own national form, as well as its own language . . . " (Herder 1968: 7). According to Herder, each of these groups would devise, internally, a means of governing itself in ways which would ensure its perpetuation and development. Enlightened though they may have been, Herder's ideas were not a product of philosophy for its own sake but an attempt to challenge the prevailing geopolitical organization which marginalized his own "German nation" within a larger empire. By arguing that nations were the fundamental units of humanity and by then asserting that their survival was dependent on each nation's ability to control its own affairs, Herder was attempting to alter the system of power relations which disadvantaged his "people" and others like them.

It is from Herder, and those who shared or refined his beliefs, that we have been bequeathed the first of three prevailing usages of the term nation. In this sense, a nation is a "cultural" entity defined by attributes such as language, religion, customs or traditions, and sometimes, "race". The selective retention of "race" as a defining characteristic of "a people" indicates a fuzziness of conception which contributes to semantic confusion and facilitates the eliding of different usages of the term.

A similar blurring of meaning, combined with new ideological goals, was instrumental in the shift towards a second application of the term nation. Like Herder, Rousseau (1712–78) was searching for a way of altering what he saw as inequalities produced by the prevailing geopolitical system. For Rousseau, the solution to problems arising from self-serving empires of religion and dynasty arose from a conception of popular sovereignty. Rather than supporting government by and for a privileged few (at the expense of the mass of humanity), he believed that sovereignty should reside in the will and institutions of "the people". Even though this conception of sovereignty was not narrowly political, and even though "the people" was, abstractly, an inclusive group, Rousseau's ideas lent themselves to narrow and exclusive political applications.

It soon became apparent that, in order for "the people" to secure a claim to power, they had to be defined. Initially, this took the form of establishing new political units, called states, and ascribing citizenship to all individuals who were encompassed by them. When citizenship failed to generate a sense of unity that was essential to the survival of the new states, additional ways of legitimizing these political entities had to be found. Through processes of transmutation that accompanied attempts to implement Rousseau's ideas, notions about the distinctiveness of "a people" were used to give empirical form to democratic notions of "the people". Over time, this gave rise to a new sense of the term nation as a political entity embodied in a state. Although this concept of nation incorporated a cultural use of the term, it did so in a way that subordinated culture to politics. Political units became the "given" and culture was adapted or created to unify and legitimize their human component.

The third prevailing use of the term nation has emerged as a casual means of connoting the spatial dimension of culturally and/or politically defined nations. In this sense, it is used as a synonym for country. Here, ambiguity about the precise constitution of the entity is downplayed by emphasizing the "fact" of its existence as manifested in territorial boundaries. Unlike the other two usages, this application of the term nation was not borne of ideological motivations, but this does not mean that it serves no ideological function. Every time the term nation is used to refer to a recognizable territory, belief in the existence and, however inadvertently, the legitimacy of the entity is reinforced. In this way, it lends credence to culturally and politically derived definitions by grounding them in physical, and consequently, conceptual space.

8

As this brief overview suggests, semantic confusion arising from various uses of the term nation is associated with their interdependence; with their incorporation of similar but differentially valued components. From a social construction perspective, confusion generated by the evolving definitions and uses of the term nation reveals three important aspects of the concept. First, the fact that we can see how it has changed over time and in response to changing circumstances is a manifestation of its constructedness. Secondly, the relationship between changes in definition of the term nation and its employment as a means of altering geopolitical systems of power, is a manifestation of its ideological nature. Thirdly, the involvement of scholars in the generation, refinement and application of the term nation is a pointed reminder that we are not passive or objective observers of our world. As commentators and interpreters we are actively involved in processes of construction and we are always ideologically involved, even when we assert objectivity. Having said this, let us turn briefly to an examination of the context in which nation and "race" come together to form what is probably the most pertinent scale at which racist ideologies are articulated: the level of the nation-state.

"Race" and nation

The nation-state is a crucial locus for the articulation of racist ideologies, because of the extent to which it embodies the idea of "race" and legitimizes it through the granting or withholding of citizenship, the right to enter and remain within a country, and a host of other entitlements. The extent to which questions of "race" and racism in postwar Britain became virtually synonymous with debates about immigration is just one example of this key nexus. But there are wider links between the ideas of "race" and nation than specific empirical circumstances such as these.

Both "race" and nation lay claim to being "natural" human divisions to the extent that it is sometimes hard to imagine a world in which these distinctions would no longer be salient (see the chapter by Penrose below). Moreover, they are both notions that dominant groups regard as unproblematic for themselves. In England, for example, nationalism is regarded as a rather vulgar and immature sentiment indulged in by *other people*. Where such sentiments are expressed by the English, they are couched in the more respectable and polite language of patriotism (Taylor 1991). Similarly, many English people regard the notions of "race" or ethnicity as something that applies only to other people, to "minority" groups. Their own identities are taken for granted and thought to be unproblematic because they are so rarely

9

examined. When these identities are called into question – in the context of large-scale immigration from the New Commonwealth or by growing integration within the European Community, for example – the implicit threat can give rise to extreme responses, such as the growth of support for the National Front in the 1960s or the entrenchment of the British National Party as part of the rekindling of fascism throughout Europe during the 1980s. Much of the debate about what it means to be British has therefore been cast in terms of the rights of "minority" groups, whether in the context of immigration from without (from the New Commonwealth or, more recently, from Hong Kong) or in terms of the possibility of secession from within (by Scottish or Welsh nationalism, for example).

The debate is also raised by the problematic identity of "second-generation" descendants of "first-generation" immigrants who are British by birth and citizenship but who are still frequently regarded as outsiders. (They are rarely thought of as English, Irish, Scottish or Welsh.) As Paul Gilroy (1987) has shown, it was the apparent incompatibility between the terms "Black" and "British" that formed a crucial element in the 1983 general election and which speaks volumes about the cultural politics of "race" and nation in contemporary Britain. Indeed, racism is increasingly being disguised in cultural clothing such that it is becoming ever harder to identify particular individuals or incidents as unambiguously "racist". As one newspaper leader-writer perceptively remarked a few years ago:

> . . . race politics in Britain are increasingly conducted in a superficially non-racist code.. . . Much of what the Conservatives say about the inner cities, council housing, education and, above all, law and order, simply cannot be understood any longer without appreciating its unspoken subtext on race ("Racism: the words and the reality", *The Guardian* 15 April 1987).

The paradoxical result, as James Blaut has observed, is a world in which we now seem to have "a lot of racism but very few racists" (1992: 289).

The cultural dimensions of "race" and nation are also played out in other domains such as the fields of policing, education and religious toleration (addressed here respectively in chapters by Jackson, Bonnett & Dwyer). Each of these areas raises questions about the articulation of state and nation at various levels of political authority. Rather than pursue these issues here, however, let us conclude this discussion of "race" and nation by looking at some of the key theories that address the links between these two concepts.

The starting point for many recent theories of nationalism has been Benedict Anderson's (1983) discussion of the nation as an "imagined community". Ideologies of "race" also make appeals to similarly "imagined communities", drawing on notions of common interest between heterogeneous groups of people who may, in fact, have little in common beyond the ideological appeal of "race". As Robert Miles argues in a study of the links between "race" and nation in contemporary Britain: "racism is the lining of the cloak of nationalism which surrounds and defines the boundaries of England as an imagined community" (1987: 38). This is not to argue that "race" and nation have more in common than other dimensions of discrimination such as those that operate along lines of gender, class or sexuality.[2] By the same count, however, it does suggest that there are many parallels between the ideologies of "race" and nation that could usefully be explored through empirical research in specific places and at different times.

A second source of much contemporary research on nationalism is the provocative work of Hobsbawm & Ranger on *The invention of tradition* (1983). Their work underlines the fact that most European nations forged their identities during the nineteenth century and therefore have little basis on which to claim a settled and timeless identity beyond the vicissitudes of recent history. The comparative recency of most nation-states and the sense of mutability that this suggests has given rise, in Hobsbawm & Ranger's terms, to a tremendous investment in the "myth" of nationhood based on a series of largely invented "traditions": around the British monarchy or the symbolism of Highland Scotland, for example. Much of the current work inspired by Homi Bhabha's analysis in *Nation and narration* (1990) also raises questions about the cultural basis of national authority: how do we construct the field of meanings and symbols associated with national life, and from what sources do they derive their legitimacy? The idea of "race" demands similar ideological work to preserve a myth whose scientific basis is at least highly questionable. The British nation, for example, continues to invest in the illusion of "racial" homogeneity, despite all of the evidence to the contrary, at least at the level of symbolism and iconography where there still "ain't no black in the Union Jack" (Gilroy 1987). Ideologically, this commitment depends on sustaining what Errol Lawrence (1982: 70) has called a "profound historical forgetfulness" which has allowed politicians of both Left and Right to argue as if questions of "race" began only with the rise of New Commonwealth immigration after 1945.

Finally in this section, it is worth drawing attention to what Philip Cohen (1988) has called the "perversions of inheritance": the extent to which ideas of "race" and nation are rooted in common myths about the social significance of biological descent. Cohen's long and detailed analysis draws on a range of fascinating material, including a brilliant discussion of the "codes of breeding", contrasting immigrants who "breed like rabbits" (in the racist imagination) with the allegedly superior "breeding" and sensibilities of the English aristocracy. Cohen uses these and other examples from popular culture, multicultural education, history and politics to show the variety of scales at which ideologies of "race" are articulated, from the level of the nation-state down to the "nationalism of the neighbourhood" and what he calls the "popular sovereignties" of place (p. 33). While Cohen himself goes on to explore the intersection of territoriality and public propriety in London's East End (Cohen 1993), his line of reasoning can be applied more generally as we now intend to show.

The significance of place

Recent years have seen a revival of interest in the concept of place, breaking free from the concept's earlier associations with a rather self-indulgent and uncritical humanistic geography. In contrast to the humanistic celebration of a unique "sense of place" (Relph 1976), a variety of authors have begun to explore the way that particular places take on their specific identities from the local incorporation of a range of processes operating at a much wider scale. Taking the example of Kilburn in west London, Doreen Massey (1993) illustrates the blending of the global in the local, striving for a more progressive sense of place than the rather backwards-looking notion of a lost "authenticity" that characterized an earlier generation of humanistic research.

Massey is not alone in trying to recuperate a critical notion of place that is consistent with current theoretical concerns.[3] John Eyles (1985) has drawn on autobiography as well as more conventional geographical sources in an ambitious attempt to explore the inter-relationships between place, identity and material life. Allan Pred (1984) has attempted to theorize place as "historically contingent process" within the more general framework of structuration theory, illustrating his approach through an empirical study of rural Sweden at the turn of the nineteenth century (Pred 1985). Pred treats place as involving the appropriation and transformation of space and nature, inseparable from the reproduction and transformation of society.

More recently, too, Ron Johnston (1991) has made a case for the centrality of place in the study of human geography. His argument is prefigured in important respects by Nicholas Entrikin's (1991) careful retheorization of the concept of place, in which he argues that place represents both a context for action and a source of identity, poised precariously "in between" subjective and objective realities. John Agnew has also drawn attention to the mediating rôle of place, both in the substantive sense of mediating between state and society (Agnew 1987) and methodologically, in bringing together geographical and sociological imaginations (Agnew & Duncan 1989). For Agnew and Duncan, the concept of place:

. . . serves as a constantly re-energized repository of socially and politically relevant traditions and identity which serves to mediate between the everyday lives of individuals . . . and the national and supra-national institutions which constrain and enable those lives. (1989: 7)

In the chapters that follow, place is rarely addressed with such theoretical formality. Yet it is a crucial element in all of our arguments about the social construction of "race" and nation. By demonstrating the existence of a plurality of *place-specific* ideologies of "race" and nation rather than a monolithic, historically singular and geographically invariant racism or nationalism, the constructedness of "race" and nation is starkly revealed. At the same time, the constructedness of place is revealed through its capacity to be moulded according to the dictates of particular racisms and nationalisms. As the chapters that follow illustrate, particular notions of "race" and nation are articulated by different groups of people at different times and at different spatial scales, from the global to the local. In each case, the idea of "race" or nation is part of a broader set of ideologies and social practices. For, as Stuart Hall has recognized: "There have been many significantly different *racisms* – each historically specific and articulated in a different way with the societies in which they appear" (Hall 1978: 26).

Beyond essentialism: the politics of position

As these preliminary remarks suggest, the geographical study of "race" and racism has come a long way since the pioneering studies of ethnic segregation and spatial sociology by Ceri Peach and his collaborators (Peach 1975, Peach et al. 1981, Jackson & Smith 1981). Among the most notable developments we would highlight a growing concern for *the politics of "race"* (especially in the field of housing and residential segregation); an increasing sensitivity to *questions of representation* (including the rôle of dominant groups in the ideological construction of various racialized Others); and a belated acceptance of what we can learn about ways of thinking about "race" from with the wide range of *feminist perspectives* about other allegedly "natural" differences concerning our sexed bodies and gendered selves.

Underlying these developments has been a growing insistence on problematizing the very idea of "race" (Jackson 1987) rather than simply mapping the categories that are recorded as "fact" in population censuses and other official statistics. Forcing ourselves to confront the problematic character of "racial" difference has had a profound effect on the conduct of empirical research, shifting the focus from an external analysis of various racialized Others onto an interrogation of our own rôles as academics, sharing many of the privileges of a bourgeois, racist, heterosexist and patriarchal society. As indicated above, one strategy for confronting this problematic positioning of self and Other has been a determined effort to throw off the cloak of scientific objectivity and to explore the consequences of our partiality: to accept that knowledge is situated and to take responsibility for our own positioning with respect to the various Others about whom we write. Drawing inspiration from recent feminist theories about standpoint and perspective, we have found it helpful to be explicit about the "politics of position" and the implications this has for our academic work (cf. Jackson 1993, Penrose et al. 1992).

Having said this, it remains all too easy to portray recent intellectual history as a triumphal progress away from static notions of "race" as a universal, biologically determined and historically invariant phenomenon towards more subtle conceptualizations that are time- and place-specific. Such an account of the triumph of social constructionism over essentialism is, however, intellectually and politically naive. To begin with, the idea that knowledge itself (and hence particular concepts such as "race" or nation) is socially constructed is by no means a recent discovery. The idea was given eloquent expression in the 1960s in the context of phenomenological debates about the sociology of knowledge. Such theorists as Berger & Luckmann (1967), drawing on the work of philosophers of social action such as Alfred Schutz, came to exert a direct influence on social geography (including studies of "race" and racism) through the work of David Ley and other self-professed "humanistic" geographers. Ley's (1974) monograph on Philadelphia's Black inner city reveals this influence in its interest in external media stereotypes about the ghetto as well as through the analysis of conflicting internal "definitions of the situation" (expressed through the work of graffiti artists and the geography of gang violence).

The political attractions of a social constructionist perspective can also be deceptive. By suggesting the arbitrariness and mutability of the concepts of "race" and nation, their fixity and inevitability are effectively destabilized. In the process, dominant ideologies are opened up to change and transformation. However, such benefits can come at a considerable cost, as recent debates in African–American literature clearly reveal. For example, literary critics such as Henry Louis Gates Jr (1986, 1988) have been chastised because of their rejection of a biological basis of "racial" difference, and their alternative assertions that such apparently "natural" distinctions are achieved through a variety of textual strategies which actively produce, rather than passively report, racialized difference. The insistence that "race" is an arbitrary signification with no biological essence has led to the accusation that

Gates and his followers are denying their very identity as Black scholars and effectively denying such an identity to others by labelling it essentialist. In his defence, one could argue that Gates' position need not invalidate political organization around the notion of "racial" oppression, although it might cast doubt on those who seek to mobilize around the notion of "race" itself. In contrast, the charge of political nihilism cannot be so easily denied. Here, the parallels with recent feminist debates are particularly instructive.

Feminists have objected that the "crisis of representation" within anthropology (Marcus & Fischer 1986) has replaced the privilege of a single (male) ethnographic authority with a relativist notion of "many voices" at the very time when women were first coming to voice. Those who champion plurality and polyvocality as strategies for ethnographic writing begin to look much less heroic when their implicit denial of the authority of particular (female) voices is noted. The charge that relativism is recognized as a problem by dominant groups only when the universality and hegemony of their particular viewpoint is challenged has been made from various quarters including feminist epistemology and postcolonial studies (cf. Penrose et al. 1992).[4] For example, Sandra Harding (1987: 10) argues that in these circumstances the accusation of relativism is a sexist response, attempting to preserve the legitimacy of patriarchal concerns in the face of contrary evidence, while Nancy Hartsock expresses a more general suspicion:

. . . it seems highly suspicious that it is at this moment in history, when so many groups are engaged in "nationalisms" which involve redefinitions of the marginalized Others, that doubt arises in the academy about the nature of the "subject", about the possibilities for a general theory which can describe the world, about historical "progress". Why is it, exactly at the moment when so many of us who have been silenced begin to demand the right to name ourselves, to act as subjects rather than objects of history, that just then the concept of subjecthood becomes "problematic"? (Hartsock 1987: 196)

It is no surprise, then, that the constructionist perspective within literary criticism has generated its own kind of political backlash.

A much-publicized version of this process has been the controversy generated in North America by slogans such as "It's a Black thing. . . you wouldn't understand", by debates about the relative merits of Black and White directors making movies about jazz, or about the staging of museum exhibitions about African history (Cannizzo 1991, Jackson 1991). Although these issues are not easily resolved politically or aesthetically, there is a variety of theoretical ideas that can help to pave the way towards such a resolution.

For example, some feminist and postcolonial authors have begun to articulate tentative solutions to the stark choice between essentialism and constructionism, recognizing that the attractions of the latter are not entirely unproblematic. Among these authors, Diane Fuss (1989) has argued that: "in and of itself, essentialism is neither good nor bad, progressive or reactionary, beneficial or dangerous" (p. xi). She argues that social constructionists are rarely able completely to escape the pull of essentialism, that the boundary between constructionism and essentialism is far from solid, and that essentialism can have certain tactical or interventionary value, especially in political struggles and debates. In fact, "essentialism can be deployed effectively in the service of idealist and materialist, progressive and reactionary, mythologizing and resistive discourses" (p. xii). The point, Fuss argues, is to examine how and why essentialist arguments are deployed, by whom and for what purpose, rather than simply rejecting them out of hand: "the radicality or conservatism of essentialism depends, to a significant degree, on *who* is utilizing it, *how* it is deployed, and *where* its effects are concentrated" (Fuss 1989: 20). Here, it is important to note that these are all empirical questions rather than ones on which it is possible to decide *a priori*.

These arguments for what has become known as "strategic essentialism" are well illustrated within recent studies of "race" and racism by the intense debate about "Black" as a political label that has been waged in Britain and the United States. In the United States, the language of "race" has seen a successive recuperation of previously derogatory labels by those who have been subject to such labelling. Long reviled for its demeaning associations with slavery and racist oppression, the word "Black" was rejected during the civil rights struggle in favour of the apparently more dignified term, "Negro". Then, in the 1970s, this label was in turn rejected in favour of a return to "Black" or "Afro-American". More recently, "African American" has become the preferred term, earnestly endorsed by politicians such as the Reverend Jesse Jackson and given a series of humorous twists in popular culture by influential movie directors such as Spike Lee. The Trinidadian Canadian poet, Marlene Norbese Philip, offers some tellingly ironic reflections on the politics of "Black" as she herself has experienced these debates:

> I always thought I was Negro
> till I was Coloured
> West Indian, till I was told
> that Columbus was wrong
> in thinking he was west of India –
> that made me Caribbean.
> And throughout the '60s, '70s and '80s,
> I was sure I was Black.

Now Black is passé,
African de rigueur,
and me, a chameleon of labels
　(quoted in Hutcheon 1991: 60).

In Britain, a similar sense of irony has been detected as a key component of debates about "race" in the 1980s (Ali 1991), although the politics of representation around the use of the label "Black" have been, if anything, more divisive than in North America. Advocates of the "Black" label have stressed the concept's appeal to unity among those who have suffered the common experience of racism and marginalization. Recently, however, the term has been objected to by some people of South Asian descent as a misrepresentation of their identity, particularly in relation to those of Afro-Caribbean descent. Tariq Modood has been a vociferous advocate of this position, arguing that the label "Black" ". . . requires too high a price in terms of loss of principle from anti-racists and sells short the majority of the people it identifies as "Black"" (1988: 397). The debate has been intensified by competition between groups for the allocation of state funding under various "race equality" initiatives. Modood's alternative strategy has been to emphasize "ethnic self-definition" rather than definitions based on how "Black" people are treated by others. Yet there is still a worrying tendency to assume the existence of some essential "ethnic" identity to which external appeals can be made. The extent to which "Asian" people wish to be subsumed under a common "Black" (or "Asian") identity clearly remains problematic, different people according different priority to "race", region and religion, for example. Ultimately, we would argue that no one is well served by attempts to reduce the complexities of human identity to a single "dimension", particularly since identities are as much the creation of human subjectivities, forged through the struggles of everyday life, as they are a simple matter of skin colour, place of birth or other "objective" criteria.

　　Indeed, those who previously argued for the use of "Black" as a political label – a matter of consciousness as much as colour – have begun to modify their positions. In an essay on "new ethnicities", for example, Stuart Hall (1992) identifies what he calls the end of the innocent notion of the essential Black subject:

　　What is at issue here is the recognition of the extraordinary diversity
　　of subjective positions, social experiences and cultural identities which
　　compose the category "black"; that is, the recognition that "Black" is
　　essentially a politically and culturally *constructed* category, which . . .
　　has no guarantees in Nature (1992: 254).

Hall goes on to argue that this recognition can either be viewed pessimistically as involving the collapse of an entire political world, or greeted with a tremendous sense of relief as the passing away of what once seemed a necessary fiction. It is this sense of "necessary fiction" that is implied in the idea of "strategic essentialism" – something chosen, despite its faults, for the positive political purchase it offers. In Hall's usage, the idea implies a commitment to an increasingly complex politics of position and a recognition that Black subjects cannot be represented without reference to other dimensions of class, gender, sexuality and ethnicity.

A further implication of this argument then becomes the way we theorize the links between these various bases of oppression. Until recently, it was common to speak of the double and triple oppressions of "race", class and gender as though these various "dimensions" of discrimination could be combined in some simple additive sense. Recent writings have suggested more subtle ways of thinking about the complex intersections of "race", class and gender. Discussing the various combinations of "race" and gender in historical constructions of White femininity, for example, Vron Ware (1992) has shown how our very notions of "race" are *already gendered*, just as our conceptions of gender are *already racialized*. Hence she prefers to write of the *mutual constitution* of "race" and gender, rather than implying that any one "dimension" has priority over any other. (A similar argument could, of course, be made for the mutual constitution of "race" and nation, or of each of these categories and particular places.) Here, too, the research agenda points to the need for particular empirical studies that would allow us to sketch the precise contours of these intersections in particular places, at specific times (as Clark does in her chapter).

One final reflection on the question of "race", class and gender concerns the way that dominant groups still manage to efface their own actions by implying that they are somehow outside the process of definition. The links between this tendency and the way in which we think about various dimensions of discrimination are poignantly articulated by Dionne Brand:

> I remember a White woman asking me how do you decided which to
> be – Black or woman – and when. As if she didn't have to decided
> which to be, White or woman, and when. As if there was a moment
> that I wasn't Black, as if there were a moment that she wasn't White.
> She asks me this because she sees only my skin, my race and not my
> sex. She asks me this because she sees her sex and takes her race as
> normal. (1990: 46)

It is always the subordinated Other who is designated as "ethnic" rather than the dominant self, inscribing not merely the existence of racialized difference but also its significance in terms of the differential relations of power that are brought to bear on the process of definition. Similarly unequal relations are present in the way men routinely imply that they are not gendered and that it is only women who bear the burden of their sex (McDowell 1992). One measure of the success of anti-racist and anti-sexist politics has been the gradual emergence of studies that seek to resist this characteristic forgetfulness. Gender studies has seen a recent proliferation of research on masculinities and there are parallel signs of an interest in "Whiteness" as a political construction, counter-balancing the virtual obsession with "Blackness" that dominated the "race" literature until very recently. Richard Dyer's important essay in *Screen* (1988) and bell hooks' discussion of "Representations of Whiteness" (1992) are highly suggestive avenues of research for social geographers, increasingly sensitive as the latter have become in recent years to debates in cultural studies.

Conclusion

Despite a concerted anti-racist politics during the 1980s and an increasingly politicized social scientific literature on issues of "race" and nation, there has been little evidence of the withering away of racism itself, while nationalism seems to be resurgent around the world. This partly demonstrates the hydra-headed nature of racist and nationalist ideologies and their characteristic ability to assume new shapes and guises as earlier forms are successfully resisted or reversed. James Blaut employs a similar metaphor in his recent essay on "cultural racism" where he argues that ". . . even if all of the roots are torn out, the vine will not wither: it will grow other roots, a new theory of racism, unless racism is attacked, not as theory but as practice" (1992: 298). Blaut's comment should give us pause for thought on the efficacy of academic research and writing in a world where neofascist activity is again on the rise throughout Europe. At the same time though, his analysis of racism's ability to adopt new forms in different times and places is surely a vindication of this book's central argument about the *constructed* nature of "race", place and nation.

This is perhaps one area in which geographers have as much to offer the other social sciences as our colleagues in other fields have to contribute to geographical research. The argument about "the difference that space makes" (Sayer 1985) will probably never be definitively resolved. But the debate is clearly worth rehearsing insofar as it offers even a partial resolution to the growing tensions around "race" and nation that currently beset the Western world. If the essays in this volume succeed in throwing any comparative light on these difficult issues, our efforts in bringing them together here will have been amply rewarded.

Notes

1. Throughout this book, the word "race" appears in quotation marks to distance ourselves from those who regard "race" as an unproblematic category. For a discussion of this strategy, see Gates (1986).
2. For recent work on the multiple links between sexuality and nationalism, see Morse (1985) and Parker et al. (1992).
3. Compare the recent debate between Meyrowitz (1985), Shields (1991) and others about the degree to which conceptions of place owe their origin to the experience of modernity, and the extent to which they are being transformed by the onset of postmodernity. See also John Western's account of the ambiguous meanings of "home" among a group of Barbadian Londoners (Western 1992).
4. The charge was all the more acutely felt because of the cavalier manner in which Clifford and Marcus had excluded feminist perspectives from their influential collection of essays on the poetics and politics of ethnography: "Feminism had not contributed much to the theoretical analysis of ethnographies as texts" (Clifford 1986: 19–20). Adding insult to injury, Clifford accused feminist anthropologists of not being "conversant with the rhetorical and textual theory that we wanted to bring to bear on ethnography" (p. 20).

References

Agnew, J. A. 1987. *Place and politics: the geographical mediation of state and society.* London: Allen & Unwin.

Agnew, J. A. & J. S. Duncan (eds) 1989. *The power of place: bringing together geographical and sociological imaginations.* Boston: Unwin Hyman.

Ali, Y. 1991. Echoes of empire: towards a politics of representation. In *Enterprise and heritage: cross-currents of national culture*, J. Corner & S. Harvey (eds), 194–211. London: Routledge.

Anderson, B. 1983. *Imagined communities: reflections on the origin and spread of nationalism.* London: Verso.

Anderson, K. J. 1991. *Vancouver's Chinatown: racial discourse in Canada, 1875–1980.* Montreal and Kingston: McGill–Queen's University Press.

Berger, P. L. & T. Luckmann 1967. *The social construction of reality: a treatise in the sociology of knowledge.* Harmondsworth: Penguin.

Bhabha, H. (ed.) 1990. *Nation and narration.* London: Routledge.

Blaut, J. M. 1992. The theory of cultural racism. *Antipode* **24**, 289–99.

Brand, D. 1990. Bread out of stone. In *Language in her eye: views on writing and gender by Canadian women writing in English*, L. Scheier, S. Sheard, E. Wachtel (eds), 45–53. Toronto: Coach House Press.

Cannizzo, J. 1991. Exhibiting cultures: "Into the heart of Africa". *Visual Anthropology Review* **7**(1), 150–60.

Carter, B., C. Harris, S. Joshi 1987. The 1951–55 Conservative government and the racialization of Black immigration. *Immigrants and Minorities* **6**, 335–47.

Cavalli-Sforza, L. L. 1974. The genetics of human populations. *Scientific American* September, 81–9.

Clifford, J. 1986. Introduction: partial truths. In *Writing cultures*, J. Clifford & G. E. Marcus (eds), 1–26. Berkeley: University of California Press.

Cohen, P. 1988. The perversions of inheritance: studies in the making of multi-racist Britain. In *Multi-racist Britain*, P. Cohen & H. S. Bains (eds), 9–118. London: Macmillan.

Cohen, P. 1993. *Home rules: some reflections on racism and nationalism in everyday life*. London: New Ethnicities Unit, University of East London.

Connor, W. 1978. A nation is a nation, is a state, is an ethnic group is a . . . *Ethnic and Racial Studies* 1(4), 377–400.

Crush, J. & C. Rogerson 1983. New wave African historiography and African historical geography. *Progress in Human Geography* 7, 203–31.

Dean, D. W. 1987. Coping with colonial immigration, the Cold War and colonial policy: the Labour government and black communities in Great Britain 1945–51. *Immigrants and Minorities* 6, 305–34.

de Lepervanche, M. & G. Bottomley (eds) 1988. *The cultural construction of race*. Sydney: Sydney Association for Studies in Society and Culture.

Dyer, R. 1988. White. *Screen* 29(4), 44–64.

Entrikin, J. N. 1991. *The betweenness of place: towards a geography of modernity*. London: Macmillan.

Eyles, J. 1985. *Senses of place*. Warrington: Silverbrook Press.

Fuss, D. 1989. *Essentially speaking*. New York and London: Routledge.

Gates, H. L. Jr (ed.) 1986. *"Race", writing, and difference*. Chicago: University of Chicago Press.

Gates, H. L. Jr 1988. *The signifying monkey*. Oxford: Oxford University Press.

Gilroy, P. 1987. *There ain't no black in the Union Jack: the cultural politics of race and nation*. London: Hutchinson.

Green, M. & B. Carter 1988. "Races" and "race-makers": the politics of racialization. *Sage Race Relations Abstracts* 13, 4–30.

Hall, S. 1978. Racism and reaction. In *Five views of multi-racial Britain*, Commission for Racial Equality, 23–35. London: Commission for Racial Equality.

Hall, S. 1992. New ethnicities. In *"Race", culture and difference*, J. Donald & A. Rattansi (eds), 252–59. London: Sage.

Harding, S. (ed.) 1987. *Feminism and methodology*. Milton Keynes: Open University Press.

Hartsock, N. 1987. Rethinking modernism: minority vs majority theories. *Cultural Critique* 7, 187–206.

Herder, J. H. von 1968. *Reflections on the philosophy of the history of mankind*. Abridged with an introduction by F. E. Manuel. Chicago: University of Chicago Press.

Hobsbawm, E. J. & T. Ranger (eds) 1983. *The invention of tradition*. Cambridge: Cambridge University Press.

hooks, b. 1990. *Yearning: race, gender and cultural politics*. Boston: South End Press.

hooks, b. 1992. Representations of Whiteness in the Black imagination In *Black looks: race and representation*, b. hooks, 165–78. London: Turnaround.

Hutcheon, L. 1991. *Splitting images: contemporary Canadian ironies*. Toronto: Oxford University Press.

Jackson, P. 1987. The idea of "race" and the geography of racism. In *Race and racism*, P. Jackson (ed.), 3–21. London: Allen & Unwin.

Jackson, P. 1989. Geography, "race" and racism. In *New models in geography*, vol. 2, N. J. Thrift & R. Peet (eds), 176–95. London: Unwin Hyman.

Jackson, P. 1991. The crisis of representation and the politics of position. *Environment and Planning D* 9, 131–4.

Jackson, P. 1992. The racialization of labour in postwar Bradford. *Journal of Historical Geography* 18, 190–209.

Jackson, P. 1993. Changing ourselves: a geography of position. In *The challenge for geography*, R. J. Johnston (ed.), 198–214. Oxford: Basil Blackwell.

Jackson, P. & S. J. Smith (eds) 1981. *Social interaction and ethnic segregation*. London: Academic Press.

Johnston, R. J. 1991. *A question of place: exploring the practice of human geography*. Oxford: Basil Blackwell.

Lawrence, E. 1982. Just plain common sense: the "roots" of racism. In *The Empire strikes back: race and racism in 70s Britain*, Centre for Contemporary Cultural Studies (ed.), 47–94. London: Hutchinson.

Ley, D. 1974. *The Black inner city as frontier outpost*. Washington DC: Association of American Geographers.

Mabin, A. 1986. At the cutting edge: the new African history and its implications for African historical geography. *Journal of Historical Geography* **12**, 74–80.

Marcus, G. E. & M. M. J. Fischer (eds) 1986. *Anthropology as cultural critique*. Chicago: University of Chicago Press.

Massey, D. 1993. Power-geometry and a progressive sense of place. In *Mapping the futures*, J. Bird et al. (eds), 59–69. London: Routledge.

McDowell, L. 1992. Doing gender: feminism, feminists and research methods in human geography. *Transactions, Institute of British Geographers* **17**, 399–416.

Meyrowitz, J. 1985. *No sense of place*. Oxford: Oxford University Press.

Miles, R. 1982. *Racism and labour migration*. London: Routledge & Kegan Paul.

Miles, R. 1984. Marxism versus the "sociology of race relations"? *Ethnic and Racial Studies* **7**, 217–37.

Miles, R. 1987. Recent Marxist theories of nationalism and the issue of racism. *British Journal of Sociology* **38**, 24–43.

Miles, R. 1989. *Racism*. London: Routledge.

Modood, T. 1988. "Black", racial equality and Asian identity. *New Community* **14**, 397–404.

Morse, G. L. 1985. *Nationalism and sexuality*. Madison: University of Wisconsin Press.

Parker, A., M. Russo, D. Sommer, P. Yaeger (eds) 1992. *Nationalisms and sexualities*. London: Routledge.

Peach, C. (ed.) 1975. *Urban social segregation*. Harlow, England: Longman.

Peach, C., V. Robinson, S. Smith (eds) 1981. *Ethnic segregation in cities*. London: Croom Helm.

Penrose, J., L. Bondi, L. McDowell, E. Kofman, G. Rose, S. Whatmore 1992. Feminists and feminism in the academy. *Antipode* **24**(3), 218–37.

Pred, A. 1984. Place as historically contingent process: structuration and the time-geography of becoming places. *Association of American Geographers, Annals* **74**, 279–97.

Pred, A. 1985. *Places, practice and structure: social and spatial transformation in southern Sweden, 1750–1850*. Cambridge: Polity Press.

Relph, E. C. 1976. *Place and placelessness*. London: Pion.

Rogerson, C. & S. Parnell 1989. Fostered by the laager: apartheid human geography in the 1980s. *Area* **21**, 13–26.

Roy, P. E. 1989. *A White man's province: British Columbia politicians and Chinese and Japanese immigrants, 1858–1914*. Vancouver: University of British Columbia Press.

Rushdie, S. 1991. The new empire within Britain In *Imaginary homelands: essays and criticism, 1981–1991*, 129–38. London: Granta (originally published in 1982).

Sayer, A. 1985. The difference that space makes. In *Social relations and spatial structures*, D. Gregory & J. Urry (eds), 49–66. London: Macmillan.

Shields, R. 1991. *Places on the margin: alternative geographies of modernity*. London: Routledge.

Smith, S. J. 1989. *The politics of "race" and residence*. Cambridge: Polity Press.

Solomos, J. 1989. *Race and racism in contemporary Britain*. London: Macmillan.

Stepan, N. 1982. *The idea of race in science: Great Britain, 1800–1950*. London: Macmillan.

Taylor, P. 1991. The English and their Englishness: "a curiously mysterious, elusive and little understood people". *Scottish Geographical Magazine* 107, 146–61.

Ward, W. P. 1978. *White Canada forever: popular attitudes and public policy toward Orientals in British Columbia*. Montreal: McGill–Queen's University Press.

Ware, V. 1992. *Beyond the pale: White women, racism and history*. London: Verso.

Western, J. 1992. *A passage to England: Barbadian Londoners speak of home*. Minneapolis/London: University of Minnesota Press / UCL Press.

Williams, R. 1976. *Keywords: a vocabulary of culture and society*. London: Fontana.

PART I
CONSTRUCTING
THE NATION

The two chapters in this part explore the ways in which the assumed "natural-ness" of nations grants them an appearance of neutrality and inviolability, encouraging the reproduction of hegemonic power in ways that are seldom questioned. Through a critical examination of the construction of particular nations, these two chapters reveal the power of nations as spaces for the reproduction of hegemony and the extent to which that power can be resisted.

In the first chapter, **Jan Penrose** explores the complex intersection of social constructions in shaping and protecting the legitimacy of the nation. She argues that the pervasive acceptance of *general* categories (such as "nation") sets the parameters within which power can be legitimately contested. Within these parameters, debate is confined to a largely self-perpetuating discourse. When applied to the "nation", the acceptance of the *general* category establishes a definition, a logic and a rhetoric of nationalism to which *specific* nations must conform if they are to be seen as legitimate. In practice, this mean that while *specific* nations can be challenged, the concept itself is rarely challenged.

Taking the example of Scottish nationalism, Penrose goes on to show that the reification of categories such as "nation" has important consequences for those who are attempting to use such constructions to alter existing power relations. She argues that new constructions of *specific* nations can be used to effect change in specific contexts, but that this always comes at the cost of reproducing what are ultimately restrictive *general* categories. Moreover, because the *general* category of "nation" is reliant on other social constructions (for example, territorial boundaries, "race", sexuality and gender), the benefits of changing power relations in one context will be restricted by the reproduction of hegemonic relations in these other related contexts.

In her chapter on immigration and nation-building, **Susan Smith** provides a vivid illustration of the capacity of categories to regulate political discourse. Here, assumptions about the "naturalness" and neutrality of nations are shown to influence the formulation of immigration policies which actively reinforce hegemonic visions concerning who and what the nation is, could or should be. As Smith demonstrates, the social and economic selectivity of immigration policies reflects (and is legitimized by) an assumption that there is a pre-given nation to which immigrants must conform. Where this process involves a belief in an inherent or immutable national character, nationalism has the capacity to legitimize racism.

Through an examination of British and Canadian immigration policies, Smith challenges the assumption of immutability by revealing the responsiveness of policies to changing constructions of the nation. Comparing recent developments in Canada and Britain, Smith illustrates the different ways in which immigration policy can serve the changing goals of nation-building. She shows how the construction of such "imagined communities" are used to determine the permeability of the boundaries of the nation-state: as power shifts and perceptions of "national" needs change, immigration policies are employed to redefine the imagined community.

CHAPTER ONE

Reification in the name of change:
the impact of nationalism on
social constructions of nation, people and place
in Scotland and the United Kingdom

JAN PENROSE

Introduction

At its conception, this chapter was intended to have pursued an interest in
the rôle that nationalism, particularly nationalist rhetoric, played in the
construction of nations. I was concerned with the processes of social construction and with the reasons behind the promotion of particular visions of specific nations. Since then, my interest has expanded to include the capacity
for social constructions to be used as a means of instigating change. In other
words, rather than focusing on the tendency for socially constructed categories to *maintain the status quo*, I have become increasingly interested in the
possibilities of using established categories to *bring about changes* in the
distribution of power. This subsequent interest is a logical consequence of
the first, for the fundamental objective which underlies nationalist promo-
tions of a specific nation is a desire to influence the distribution of power.
Whereas recognized nations use their self-construct to maintain the existing
power structure, aspiring nations promote an alternative construct in an
effort to change the power structure in ways which favour them. All
nationalists want the nation which they represent to be recognized as
legitimate and to be awarded the power which this legitimacy bestows.

Here, I will argue that entrenched social constructions can be used to
bring about positive changes in the distribution of power, but that the immediate cost of such changes is likely to be the reification of categories that

continue to be applied in restrictive ways. This is because the accepted rhetoric of nationalism perpetuates a reliance on destructively discrete categories by defining the ways in which nations must be constructed. In so doing, it controls both membership in any specific nation and the access of such nations to formalized power structures. At the same time, I will emphasize the dependency of the social construction of nation on social constructions of people and place. Although the discussion of this relationship can only hint at the complexities which ensue from the intersection of socially constructed categories, it will support my contention that the use of the socially constructed category of nation to change the distribution of power leads to the reification not only of nation, but also of people and place.

The chapter is divided into two main sections. In the first, I present five theoretical assertions that form the basis of my argument. In the second, some of the practical manifestations of these assertions are illustrated by drawing on a case study of nationalist politics in the United Kingdom and Scotland. The chapter concludes with a consideration of the costs and benefits of employing social constructions to challenge inequity and injustice.

The argument: reification as the price of change

The assumption which underpins the following argument is that both the *general* category of "nation" and *specific* nations are not natural entities but social constructions.[1] By this I mean that the socio-cultural–political units which are commonly referred to as "nations" are not immutable "givens" but the product of human thought and action. The existence of nations is not a truth that human beings have *discovered* but a conceptualization of the world that we have *created*. Part of the power of this creation is that it can be advanced convincingly as something "natural". By conceiving of nations as "natural" and by promoting them as such, processes of construction, of human intervention, are obscured and the motivations behind such constructions are removed from the realm of discussion. In this way, people whose motives have been fulfilled by a particular national construction are protected and people who have been disadvantaged are denied recourse.[2] As this suggests, nations are ideological. They embody political and cultural plans and incorporate the means for putting these plans into operation while protecting them from alternative visions or objectives.

The conviction that the *general* category of nation is a social construction rather than a "natural" phenomenon is substantiated by my first assertion that: **social constructions of *specific* peoples and places play a critical rôle in** generating, refining and maintaining the social construction of the *general* category of nation. I make this assertion because, since the concept of nation was originally advanced in the eighteenth century, it has consistently had three main components.[3] The first is *a distinctive group of people*, although, over time, conceptions of what constitutes a distinct group of people have varied. For some, tangible characteristics such as language, religion, cultural practices or physical and/or behavioural traits, have been the defining features. For others these tangible characteristics are simply *expressions* of human groupings, the origins of which lie deeper in abstruse realities such as a "national soul", "national consciousness" or "national identity". For others still, the simple fact of citizenship in a state has been seen as the defining characteristic of the distinct group of people who are central to the nation. Regardless of the basis of definition, these conceptions of the *general* category of nation all concur in their assumption that the discrete groups of people who underlie *specific* nations are "natural" and immutable, if not God-given.

The second component of the generally accepted concept of nation is *a distinctive territory or place*. Discrete regions have tended to be seen as the "natural" divisions of the world's surface and each legitimate nation is seen to occupy one of these regions. Here again, recourse is made to a particular idea of what constitutes the "natural": it is often the *existence* of topographical features, rather than *human selection* of these features, that is seen to be the determining factor in defining the boundaries between groups of people. Even where human intervention in the creation of borders is accepted, the idea that nations can exist without a coherent territory is generally viewed as impossible. The fact that few people can conceive of a nation that does not occupy or lay claim to a particular place is a manifestation of the centrality of place to the conception of nation. Just as the division of humanity into discrete groups of people is seen as "natural", so too have we accepted as "natural" the idea that such groups necessarily inhabit discrete regions.[4]

The clear-cut conception of the *general* category of nation as a "natural" phenomenon is reinforced by its third, and perhaps most important, component: the conception of *a mystical bond between people and place*. This bond is itself seen as "natural" and its identified function is to meld, "naturally", the other two components of "people" and "place" into an immutable whole. This immutable whole is called a nation.

The fact that the concept can be deconstructed to reveal universally accepted components demonstrates that the *general* category of nation is a social construction. In other words, the fact that we can see how the category has been constructed reinforces our conviction that it is a construction and not a "natural" entity. The reality of construction processes at work is even more clearly manifested by the fact that the accepted components of nations are not accurate reflections of experience: even cursory consideration reminds us that human groupings are neither discrete, nor homogeneous, nor immutable, and that association with a particular place is not essential to the retention of group identity. Moreover, we can see that the *general* category of nation has consistently, by its very definition, explicitly included social constructions of "people" and "place". The existence of the *general* category of nation requires the existence of categories of people and place. For all of these reasons, it seems logical to assert that social constructions of people and place play a critical rôle in generating, refining and maintaining the social construction of the *general* category of nation.

This leads to my second assertion that: **the social construction of *specific* nations is necessary because the *general* category of nation is the central organizational unit of the current world order. This means that the convincing construction of a *specific* nation is an essential pre-requisite to successful assertions of a right to power**. The first part of this assertion is validated wherever we care to look. From our reverence, however tempered, for institutions such as the United Nations (in which only recognized nations have a right to representation), through the overwhelming concentration of power in national rather than other levels of government, to our active promotion and unconscious responsiveness to national symbols, our whole world is structured around the *general* category of the nation. The institutionalized dominance of nations in the current world order means that access to power has become virtually conditional upon nation status. This second part of the assertion is demonstrated by the often desperate attempts of newly asserted nations to receive the blessing of "international recognition". The importance of this kind of recognition to the independence movements in the Baltic states is but one example which demonstrates that external confirmation of nation status is not an aesthetic or superficial consideration. However, recognition as a legitimate nation requires that all three components of the *general* category of nation be demonstrably extant. Accordingly, *aspiring* nations must promote a vision of themselves as a people bonded to a particular place that can justifiably claim a legitimate right to power. Here, it is important to clarify that, while I regard the power which nation status bestows as hegemonic, I do not see it as omnipotent or inviolable. As a nation, the people who occupy a particular territory are granted a right to control their own affairs. This right is usually embodied in a state that is granted control over resources as well as the capacity to establish institutions of government, law and education through which power is exercised. However, this situation does not preclude external and/or internal challenges to the legitimacy of a *specific* nation; to a prevailing construction of a *specific* nation; or to the ways in which rights of self-determination are applied by those who dominate any given nation at a particular point in time (cf. Penrose 1994). As this suggests, nation status grants a right to power but this power remains fluid and dynamic, and is exercised in and through continuing negotiations and contestations.

The connection between the effective construction of a nation and a right to power is a product of the ideology of nationalism. At its simplest, nationalism combines the assumed "naturalness" of nations with the conviction that government should be by and for "the people". As an ideology, nationalism advances the argument that any *specific people* can only follow its "natural" course of development if these people are in control of their own territory and their own affairs. In this way, the existence of a nation is intrinsically linked to the right to self-determination. If the nation defines both "the people" and the territory of the new geopolitical unit (the "nation-state"), then demonstration of the existence of a nation is a pre-requisite to successful assertions of a right to power. In other words, a nation composed of a distinctive people bonded to a distinctive place must be shown to exist before power can be contested legitimately (cf. Giddens 1985).

The need for *specific* nations to demonstrate that they exist *as nations* reaffirms the power vested in the *general* category of nation as the cornerstone of geopolitical organization. In other words, the *general* category of nation is reified by the attempts of *specific* groups of people occupying *specific* places to demonstrate that they constitute an example of this *general* category. By attempting to replicate the accepted components of "a nation", rather than challenging the validity of these components, nationalist movements contribute to the reinforcement of a system which invests power in the constructed category of nation. The pervasiveness of our acceptance of the category of nation and the concomitant investment of power in it places nationalist movements in a paradoxical position. They are forced to frame their claims to a right to power in terms which have previously marginalized the people who they represent and which will continue to marginalize other people who do not fit the new nationalist construct of a nation.

As this suggests, the need to promote a convincing rendition of a nation also highlights the constructedness of the *general* category. This is because efforts to show that a nation exists inevitably reveal the impossibility of reproducing the category in its pure conceptual form. No alleged nation, either recognized or aspiring, can demonstrate unequivocally that it comprises a discrete and uniform people who are bonded to a discrete and uncontested territory. Pluralism, not homogeneity, is the fundamental human characteristic of the countries which make up our world. Similarly, the boundaries that

31

divide these countries from one another remain fundamentally arbitrary and, hence, changeable, protected as they are only by the strength of historical precedent and/or military might (and not by "natural right"). Under these circumstances, the only option is to construct a nation, and the power of the *general* category dictates that this construction must be founded on assertions of human and territorial distinctiveness as a "natural" state of affairs.

Clearly, the irreconcilability between the general definition of nation and the conditions that prevail in practice becomes highly problematic for those attempting to acquire or maintain power on nationalist grounds. Nevertheless, the strictures of nationalism prevail, and efforts to surmount the insurmountable seek recourse in the art of rhetoric. Rhetoric is used to convince us of the existence of something that is not and, in this instance, cannot be there. To achieve this end, nationalist rhetoric reasserts the "naturalness" of the nation it represents, often through references to the historical longevity of human occupation of a particular place. Assumptions of "naturalness" are also sustained through mutually reinforcing processes of treating the nation as a "collective individual" and as a "collection of individuals" (Handler 1988: 39–46). However, given that the elucidation of specific national characteristics or qualities has the capacity to alienate people who form part of a potential support base, nationalist rhetoric tends to confine itself to *general assertions* that the nation in question actually *exists*. If something can be named, and is widely recognized by that name, then any questioning of its existence tends to dissolve before it needs to be actively countered.

However, at the same time the political expediency of vagueness is countered by the need to demonstrate distinctiveness. To find an effective compromise between these conflicting demands, nationalists tend to employ two additional rhetorical tactics. Rather than precisely defining the basis of human and physical uniqueness, nationalists identify broad areas of distinctiveness, usually accompanied by an adjective that connotes its nationalness. The result is a constant reiteration of not just the existence but also the uniqueness of the specific nation: the American National Anthem, English culture, the Finnish language, the Tibetan landscape, French cuisine.[5] Our experiential knowledge of the existence of tangible things such as the American National Anthem subtly diverts us from questioning the existence of the American nation. Similarly, even though most of us cannot define English culture at all (let alone in a universally acceptable manner), we accept that such a thing somehow exists. What is more, we use this acceptance as a basis for substantiating our belief in an English nation.

The assertion and reiteration of broad areas of distinctiveness is complemented by an additional rhetorical tool which I call "the foil of other". To avoid the hazards attendant on the precise definition of what the nation *is*, nationalist rhetoric frequently asserts the existence of a nation by document-ing what it is *not*. Almost invariably this involves direct comparisons with other groups of people, often focusing on those who are seen to be prohibit-ing the achievement of national or nationalist goals. Here, the specifics that are lacking in self-definition appear in abundance: for example, Canadians can assert that they are not loud and brash like the Americans; Bretagnes can insist that they are untouched by French snobbery; or Sami can argue that Finnish regimentation and reserve are alien to them. Although such declar-ations tell us little about the people who make them, they serve the dual function of reinforcing our belief in the existence of these people and entrenching our belief in their distinctiveness. The most astute aspect of such rhetoric is that it inherently precludes dissension. Those who believe are reassured and those who are not convinced can have their disbelief turned against them as evidence of their exclusion from the nation – anyone who belongs will understand.

Alone and in combination these various applications of rhetoric contribute to the social construction of *specific* nations. Such construction is vital for two reasons. First, because nations cannot exist in their accepted conceptual form, they must be created to approximate this form as closely as possible. Secondly, there is no alternative to attempted replication of the conceptual form as long as the world system continues to view nations as the only rightful repositories of power. Thus, the convincing construction of a *specific* nation remains a pre-requisite to successful assertions of a right to power.

This leads to my third assertion that: **the relationship between recognized nation status and power means that the successful construction of a** *specific* **nation can instigate change in the distribution of power**. In other words, if an aspiring nation can convince people – both "inside" and "outside" – that it constitutes a legitimate nation which has been denied its right to power, then this nation may be able to achieve "nation-state" status and the access to globally recognized power which this status bestows. Here again, contem-porary examples abound. In the case of the Baltic countries, a redistribution of power in favour of "insiders" has been effected through convincing dem-onstrations of the existence of nations which have been repressed (if not oppressed) by an "outside" nation (in this case, "the Russians"). Interna-tional recognition of the legitimacy of Baltic claims to nationhood and the attendant right of self-determination has proven tantamount to club member-ship, and Estonian, Latvian and Lithuanian representatives can now congregate in the halls of the United Nations or march into the Olympic Stadium under their own national flags. Few would deny that this kind of change in the distribution of power is positive, at least insofar as it reduces the exploitation of regions and people by larger entities that do not have the interests of these "people" and "places" at heart.

However, and this is my fourth assertion: **because socially constructed nations rely on social constructions of people and place to be seen as legitimate, inequalities based on social constructions of people and place will be perpetuated *within* newly empowered "nation-states"**. As discussed above, it is impossible to divide people and territory into discrete units because the boundaries are always fluid. Individuals have multiple or divided loyalties, and rights to particular areas of land are frequently contested. However, the successful construction of a nation requires that this fluidity be denied. This means that the individuals and places which do *not* fit into the newly recognized nation's self-construction will continue to be marginalized.[6] Moreover, it is conceivable that the refinement and maintenance of "nation-state" status will engender a solidification of the newly developed social constructions of "people" and "place". Once a nation has been defined successfully, pressure to conform to the definition may increase. Consequently, the nation's capacity or willingness to tolerate internal differences may be reduced.

In the early 1990s, elements in the fragmenting entity which we used to call the nation of Yugoslavia provide vivid and horrifying illustrations of the cruelty, injustice and inequality that can ensue from employing a construction of nation to gain access to power. All of the boundaries of the emerging nation-states are contested and, even if boundaries could be agreed upon, none of these new entities would encompass a discrete group of people. Rather than acknowledging the impossibility of replicating the conceptual construct of a nation, newly acquired power is used to create what nature could never provide. Attempts to maintain or expand national borders are considered a "natural" course of action and the use of violence rather than diplomacy is a distressing illustration of the negative consequences that can ensue from employing the concept of nation to effect change. Even as these borders shift, the new "nation-states" pursue policies which will *make* their human composition fit the national territory. Thus, the Serbs enforce policies of "ethnic cleansing", concentration camps are established to remove (if not eliminate) people who do not fit the various new national constructs, and the thousands of people who do not fit into any of the neatly constructed categories (e.g. Muslims or people of mixed allegiance) are despised and oppressed by all sides. In each of the emerging "nation-states" the conflict between the need for cultural "purity" and the reality of cultural pluralism have engendered gross violations of the human rights of those who do not fit the new national mould. Here, the construct of nation has been used to effect a redistribution of power, but in the process, the category of nation has been reified and this has engendered the solidification of associated constructions of people and place.

This brings me to my fifth and final assertion: **the capacity for the continued application of the concept of nation to reify constructions of "people" and "place" suggests that, until the concept of nation is successfully challenged, the inequalities arising from social constructions of "people" and "place" (the legitimizing cornerstones of nations) will not be eliminated.** Here, the complexities of intersecting social constructions become manifest. The intimate relationship between nation, people and place means that the use of any of these categories to effect change is likely to entail a reification of all the categories concerned. If a group of people unite to counter a category that has oppressed them, the position of the people involved may improve, but, in the process, the category that unites them is reified. A change in the distribution of power may be effected, but the root of the problem, the undesirable association of power with value-laden categorizations, remains unchallenged. Reification of the belief that humanity can be divided into discrete groups of people contributes, however unwittingly, to a reinforcement of our association of groups of people with particular places. Similarly, attempts to alter conditions in a particular place cannot proceed without the precise definition of the place concerned, and such actions are seldom advanced without reference to, if not the involvement of, specified groups of human beings. Ultimately, both of these kinds of processes involve the entrenchment of the categories of people and place, fortifying the cornerstones of the concept of nation.

The interconnections between these three categories means that *all* of them must be challenged before the destructive and limiting capacities of *any* of them can be curtailed. Having said this, I have chosen to focus on the category of nation for two reasons. First, unlike the categories of people and place, the category of nation is seen as the sole rightful repository of power in the current world order.[7] Secondly, unlike the other two categories, nation is directly dependent on social constructions of people and place. It is for these reasons that I argue that the concept of nation must be successfully challenged before it is possible to eliminate the use of social constructions of people and place as "natural" entities which legitimize claims to power.

Social constructions of nation, place and people in Scotland and the United Kingdom

Thus far, I have provided a theoretical outline of my argument that entrenched social constructions can be used to bring about changes in the distribution of power, but that the immediate cost of such changes is likely to be the reification of undesirable and restrictive categories. In the remainder of this chapter, I will provide empirical substantiation of my position by showing how the unquestioning acceptance of the *general* category of nation has dictated the parameters for contesting power within the United Kingdom. More specifically, I will show that "Scottish" *and* "British" reliance on the concept of nation (in strategies for asserting or defending, respectively, a right to power) has already contributed to the reification of this concept and of its attendant categories of people and place. The section concludes with a consideration of the potential impact of Scotland's continued attempts to achieve power through the construction of a convincing nation.

The pervasiveness of nationalist rhetoric: the nation as object and context of resistance
No matter where we look, there is very little evidence that the concept of nation *is* being challenged. In the United Kingdom, nationalist rhetoric continues to define what constitutes a valid geopolitical unit as well as the framework within which power can be contested legitimately. In other words, the nation is consistently both the object and the context for debating the distribution of power. This is evident in the attempts of supporters of British nationalism to maintain the Union in its current form. It is also evident in the attempts of Scottish nationalists to transform the distribution of power through the promotion of an independent Scottish nation.[8] In both cases, the legitimacy of *specific* nations is challenged, but in the process the *general* category of nation is constantly reified.

The centrality of nationalist rhetoric to the attempts of recognized nations to resist aspiring nationalist movements within their borders is frequently overlooked.[9] This, in itself, is a measure of the deep entrenchment of our acceptance of nations as "natural". Even though the United Kingdom of Great Britain and Northern Ireland achieved its current boundaries only in 1921, the geopolitical entity, both the state and the nation, is ascribed with an historical longevity and continuity that goes back to time immemorial. In the United Kingdom, the acceptance of the status quo gives Unionists an advantage in continuing debates about the distribution of power. This is because acceptance of the existence of the nation means that we do not notice the nationalist rhetoric which is constantly creating and refining it. When we look for it, however, this rhetoric is easy to find.

In the United Kingdom, Unionist rhetoric downplays the prominence of the English and the South East within the current national construct by arguing that the cultural and geographical concentration of power works well in the interests of *all* of the United Kingdom and its citizens. Not surprisingly, this position has been consistently supported by the Conservative Party, in power since 1979. One of its representatives, the Scottish Secretary, Ian Lang has tenaciously held to this line even in the face of outright derision from other Scots.[10] A recent "special issue" of the Scottish Conservative paper reported his position as follows:

> . . . in whatever form, separation is the "common enemy". He stressed that Scotland has "flowered and flourished" within the United Kingdom, and added that the sense of Scottish identity is stronger today than ever before because of Scotland's successful rôle within the Union. The Scottish Secretary said "we don't need a separate Scotland to prove that we are Scottish". (Scottish Conservatives 1992: 2)

In the same breath as Lang tacitly acknowledges Scotland's distinctiveness and asserts his *own* Scottishness, he also manages to credit this to its membership in the Union. While the logic cannot bear too much thought, the audacity of the rhetoric makes it worthy of applause. By incorporating the potentially rival nation into the Union, it is devalued and disempowered: Scottishness is not denied, but it is transformed into something that can only be realized within the United Kingdom.

Using a different tack, a speech by the Transport Secretary, Malcolm Rifkind, commands support for the Union by stressing the cultural and territorial unity of the United Kingdom.

> . . . the relationship of Scotland, England and Wales is far deeper than that of the two halves of Germany, a country which has opted to unite rather than separate. He [Mr Rifkind] said ours is a Union based on a shared culture, language and political institutions. Mr Rifkind added: "We remain destined to share a small island in the North Sea. To subdivide would be an act of monumental folly". (Scottish Conservatives 1992: 2)

In contrast to Lang, Rifkind implicitly argues against Scottish distinctiveness by highlighting the commonalities of all members of the United Kingdom. By accentuating human and territorial unity, his comments constitute a reassertion of the established national construct. Here, the social construction of "people" is the British, who share culture, language and political institutions, and the social construction of place is the *natural* unit of an island or the British Isles.[11]

In both instances, however, and in virtually all of the Unionist rhetoric, the political community and membership in this community (namely, the state and citizenship in this state), are privileged over cultural group (or alternative nation) membership. The established nation challenges the aspiring nation by incorporating the latter's differences into an overriding entity and then generating new allegiances to that entity. The capacity for Union nationalists to achieve this is enhanced by their access to institutions through which power is exercised and by the comfort associated with the status quo. Power enables the established nation to posit itself as the protector of Scottishness and to back this up persuasively with the strategic distribution of funds and support. The longer this situation prevails, the deeper it becomes entrenched; as the status quo it is perceived as desirable because it is known.

The various defences of the Union do *not* challenge the legitimacy of nations as the rightful repositories of power. Rather, such arguments reify the nation by relying on the accepted criteria for defining a nation to build a case. It is *because* the United Kingdom can assert itself, and be recognized, as a nation that it can claim a legitimate right to power over all of its territory and citizens.

The pervasive acceptance of nationalist rhetoric is also evident in Scotland's challenge to the legitimacy of the United Kingdom's national construct. Scottish nationalism's argument against the current construction of the British nation does *not* question the legitimacy of the *general* category of nation as the appropriate repository of power. On the contrary, its argument reinforces the legitimacy of this *general* category. It does so by asserting that the current distribution of power is wrong *because* it denies the distinctive Scottish nation its "natural" right to protect itself by controlling its own affairs.

Where British nationalists accentuate Scotland's incorporation into the British nation, Scottish nationalists accentuate Scotland's distinctiveness from the rest of Britain, especially England.[12] However, without the power of the status quo, Scottish nationalists must work hard to demonstrate that they represent the interests of a legitimate nation. In so doing, they are constrained by the dictates of accepted nationalist rhetoric. This means they must show that Scotland is a clearly delineated territory occupied by a discrete group of people who possess a long-standing "natural" bond to "their" land. In other words, Scottish nationalists must convince people – both inside and outside of the area called Scotland – that a legitimate Scottish nation exists.[13] Belief in the existence of a Scottish nation is a pre-requisite to attempts to achieve a share of power for this nation.

Here, the important point is that Scottish nationalists are compelled to do the impossible if they hope to achieve a devolution of power from the United Kingdom to Scotland. Even as regions and inhabitants of the Borders, the Islands and the Highlands struggle to assert identities that are distinctive from that of the dominant Lowlands, and even as the overall level of cultural pluralism increases, nationalists must convincingly demonstrate that Scotland is a unified (if not uniform) nation.[14] The practical impossibility of this task forces nationalists to resort to the kind of rhetorical strategies discussed in the first half of this chapter.

Scottish nationalists, regardless of their specific political leanings, promote Scotland and its people as "natural" entities; they assert the nation's existence; they hint at distinguishing features; and they refine the overall picture by distancing the Scottish nation from that of the English. One example which brings together several of these rhetorical devices is nationalist appropriation of the Battle of Bannockburn (1314), which saw Robert the Bruce secure the independence of Scotland by defeating English forces. In 1930, a proposal to develop the site of the battle was countered with a scheme to ensure its historic preservation as a Scottish national monument. The *general* nationalist rhetoric which underlies the *specific* resistance to the destruction of a "national" symbol is unmistakable:

It is unthinkable that the Battlefield of Bannockburn, hallowed ground, where Scottish freedom was won for all time, at present a beautiful open space, and the Mecca of our countrymen and our kith and kin from overseas, should now be built over and obliterated . . .

The Battle of Bannockburn was the greatest event in Scottish History. This scheme to preserve the Battlefield inviolate in perpetuity is not put forward from the point of view of glorification of military prowess, but as a tribute to that spirit of Scottish independence, grit, and determination typified by the word "Bannockburn" – a spirit which has ever proved dominant for Justice and Freedom. (*The battle of Bannockburn* 1930)

Here, a symbol of broad but unspecified appeal is drawn into nationalist rhetoric as a means of asserting the existence of a distinctive nation. In the process, assumptions about the "naturalness" of the nation are reinforced. In drawing on a shared cultural heritage, large numbers of people are invited to recognize their affinity with this nation. When affinity is recognized and adopted as part of a personal identity, demonstrations of the existence of the nation are strengthened. By incorporating such symbols into its rhetoric, nationalism reinforces perceptions of both the tangibility of the nation and of the need to defend it – a need which can be met solely by granting the nation control over its own affairs.

Although the precise focus of Scottish nationalist rhetoric varies according to context, it is all designed to challenge the prevailing nationalism of the United Kingdom by constructing and promoting an alternative nation. Ultimately, all assertions and "proofs" of the existence of a unique nation are incorporated into a defence of the right to self-determination. Although complex and not without contradictions, aspiring nationalism challenges the existing nation by using accepted rhetoric as a means of claiming rights that the established nation once claimed for itself. In the process of contesting power, the *general* category of nation and its attendant categories of people and place are constantly reified.

The effectiveness of rhetorical constructions and
their capacity to instigate change in the distribution of power

The success of Scottish nationalism's promotion of a distinctive nation is evident in at least three ways, each of which has the capacity to alter the distribution of power. First, a widespread belief in Scottish distinctiveness is reflected in both the ability and the willingness of individuals to describe Scottish identity in their own words. In the spring of 1990, I conducted postal surveys among members of the Scottish National Party (SNP) and among a sample of Scotland's population at large. In both instances over 75 per cent of the respondents (a total of over 500 individuals) backed up their professed belief that Scotland had a unique identity by attempting to articulate this identity in their own words.

As a manifestation of the successful promotion of a Scottish nation, these figures speak for themselves. However, the responses also confirm two important aspects of the social construction of nations. First, while there is some repetition of particular characteristics (e.g. "dour" or "proud"), these responses do not reflect anything even approaching uniform agreement about the nature of Scottish identity. Even though most respondents are united in their sense of being Scottish, their convictions about what this actually entails vary dramatically. Some of the descriptions of Scottish identity constitute perfect replications of the *general* conceptual category of nations:

> [Scottish identity] is based on *history* – on the development of the nation-state, maintaining its independence against aggression and contributing to European cultural and intellectual development – and on the highly distinctive social, literary, religious, legal institutions of Scotland, which have fundamentally shaped the national character even when they superficially appear to be eroded. (SNP Survey: 51)

> The belief that an individual is part of a group of people with a common cultural heritage, a shared historical experience, a defined geographical area, recognizable institutions, distinctive and shared attitudes (SNP Survey: 15).

On the other hand, some of the descriptions reflect the impossibility of reproducing the conceptual category in practice by highlighting internal differences within Scotland. For example:

With the many regional differences in Scotland coupled with the influx of "White settlers" it is difficult to establish a single Scottish identity (SNP Survey: 42).

No one composite identity – varied mixture e.g. chip on the shoulder type (Glasgow, drunken variety!), clever, quiet type (often in business), enterprising type (often emigrates!) (SNP Survey: 183).

There is no *one* Scottish identity – but several, e.g. the people in Grampian have little in common with the people of Glasgow (General Survey: 434).

Even though the latter group of responses explicitly reject the notion of a *uniform* Scottish identity, the very fact that they have attempted to describe Scotland's unique identity is a reflection of their belief that such a thing somehow exists. Perhaps more telling still is the pervasive use of other stereotypes, a practice which implicitly reinforces the idea that people can be divided into discrete groups. Moreover, these responses perpetuate the conviction that these discrete groups are intimately, "naturally", associated with particular places. The lack of uniformity in descriptions of Scottish identity reflects the impossibility of replicating the *general* category of nation within *specific* nations. At the same time, however, the reliance of these same responses on the assumed "naturalness" of discrete peoples and places highlights the prevailing dominance of this *general* concept of nation as the "natural" state of affairs.

The second aspect of the social construction of nations revealed by my survey responses is the tendency to elide culture or citizenship with "race". This is reflected in the following descriptions of Scottish identity:

A hardy independant [sic] race at present held back by being shackled to England (SNP Survey: 136).

A race of people who have since recorded times developed their own language, cultivated their own land, fished their own seas, forged their own clans and developed their own arts (SNP Survey: 245).

The similarity between definitions which employ the term "race" and those which employ the term "people" indicates that the two terms are commonly used to refer to the same phenomenon. Moreover, both usages draw on and reify assumptions of "natural" divisions in humanity. While "race" is more likely than "people" to imply visible difference, both terms rely on the assumption that it is possible to identify distinctive social characteristics that are biologically inherited. Given the impossibility of identifying Scots (or any other group, for that matter) on the basis of physical characteristics, the use of visible difference to determine group membership can only be exclusionary. The confusion that results from eliding culture or citizenship and "race" is also likely to exacerbate the negative repercussions of employing a construction of nation in the contesting of power (cf. Williams 1976: 250).

At an informal level, the inculcation of individual belief in the existence of a Scottish nation has a subtle but pervasive capacity to affect the distribution of power within "Scottish" society. This can be manifested positively in the support of "Scottish" businesses or charities and, if the vision of the nation is a tolerant one, individual actions can lead to the creation of a just and egalitarian society. More commonly, however, and as the earlier descriptions of Scottish identity suggest, individual conceptions of Scotland are constrained by the same kind of assumptions that make nationalism such a powerful ideology. The belief that Scots are a discrete group of people, or that they comprise discrete groups of people, who are invested by the laws of nature with a right to live in Scotland, makes derogatory references to groups such as "White settlers" part of common parlance. Here, it is ostensibly audible difference, as revealed by accent, that forms the basis of discrimination. At the same time, though, the designation "White" is clearly being used to distinguish groups of immigrants on the basis of colour (read "race"). As such, the designation of "White settlers" opens the door to other designations based on destructive categories of "race" and the potential for the solidification of a narrow and exclusionary construction of a Scottish nation is increased. Clearly, the way that people think about themselves has a tremendous impact on the ways in which they think about others and the combination of these conceptions is instrumental in determining the distribution of power within any society.

On a more formal level, individual beliefs in a Scottish nation have the capacity to effect changes in the distribution of power by generating convictions that propel people into public life. More commonly, though, the formal expression of a belief in Scottish distinctiveness is manifested in political activism or voting behaviour. If individuals value their Scottishness above other political concerns, or if they feel that their Scottishness is somehow threatened, they may support a political party or movement that is committed to promoting or protecting this Scottishness. This leads me to the second manifestation of the successful promotion of a Scottish nation.

One of the most tangible indications of the convincing construction of a Scottish nation is the continued existence of the Scottish National Party. The very presence of a political party whose *raison d'être* is the achievement of independence for a Scottish nation indicates that substantial numbers of people are satisfied that such a nation exists, or that it should exist. The SNP has the capacity to effect changes in the distribution of power in two ways. First, and most directly, an electoral victory would constitute a clear mandate to begin negotiating the secession of Scotland from the United Kingdom.

Secondly, and less obviously, the party, by its very presence, can alter the political agenda such that the Scottish demands are granted increased priority. Although other political parties may be anxious to interpret electoral support for the SNP as a protest vote, evidence suggests that this is not the case (Brand 1987: 343). Given that votes gained by the SNP are translated directly into votes lost by other parties, it is reasonable that other parties attempt to reverse this trend by responding to the issues that are seen to have reduced their support. In the case of losses to the SNP, the efforts of other parties to recoup votes necessarily involves paying increased attention to conditions within Scotland and to the position of Scotland within the United Kingdom. In other words, the very presence of the SNP forces other political agents to promote at least some of the interests that the party has introduced into the political arena. In this way, the SNP has the capacity to change the distribution of power, and it can do so to a degree that is, proportionally, much greater than its actual electoral support.

This introduces the third manifestation of the successful promotion of a convincing Scottish nation: namely, the Campaign for a Scottish Assembly. This Campaign would be unimaginable without a deeply entrenched belief in Scottish distinctiveness, and the Union Government would not be entertaining discussions about devolution if it did not fear a complete loss of power through what it perceives as the greater evil of Scottish independence. As this suggests, the Campaign can be seen as the culmination of a process which sees individual belief in a Scottish nation translated into the creation and growth of a nationalist political party. This, in turn, has spawned a willingness in the encompassing nation to negotiate (and thereby limit) the transfer of power.[15]

Having said this, it is important to acknowledge that the Campaign for a Scottish Assembly also reveals two of the inherent difficulties of using the category of nation to effect change. First, widespread variation in conceptions of what actually constitutes the Scottish nation are paralleled by equally varied opinions regarding the most desirable future for Scotland. To the SNP and its supporters, the idea that a Scottish nation can be best served as part of the Union is tantamount to a betrayal of that Scottish nation. Accordingly, it can be argued that the SNP had little choice but to decline any involvement in discussions concerning a Scottish Assembly. The fact that debate has continued without the participation of the SNP is a pointed reminder that the concept of nation can be incorporated into power struggles in a variety of ways. Here again, the range of possibilities allows both tolerant applications of the concept of nation as well as restrictive ones. In both cases, however, the *general* conceptual category and its attendant categories of people and place are likely to be reified.

The pervasive capacity for the concept of nation to confine debate to a self-perpetuating discourse is equally apparent in the second difficulty which the Campaign for a Scottish Assembly has revealed. The fact that discussions about Scotland's future need to be legitimized by the recognized nation, and that they must follow rules and regulations that have been designed to preserve that nation, is a sobering reminder of the hegemonic power of the recognized nation. This leads to a paradox which ensures the perpetuation of nationalism, or at least a nationalist frame of reference, at every turn. For Scotland to contest power, nationalism dictates that a Scottish nation must be shown to exist but, when this has been demonstrated, the power which nationalism has already invested in the United Kingdom is used to control expressions of Scottish nationalism. Regardless of how power is ultimately divided, the basis for effecting a division will be one that ensures the survival of the concept of nation and that entrenches its position as the sole rightful repository of power.

All three manifestations of widespread acceptance of the existence of a Scottish nation incorporate a capacity to use the constructed nation as a lever in continuing contestations of power. Moreover, every employment of the concept of nation to encourage a devolution of power from the United Kingdom to Scotland can be defended insofar as it reduces "external" control of the Scottish people(s) and of the area(s) which support(s) them. However, even this general idea of external control is dependent on boundaries between "inside" and "outside" and, as the preceding discussion has shown, it is precisely these kinds of boundaries that form the basis of the concept of nation. As it is currently constructed, the category of nation can be used to effect change only by perpetuating visions of people and place as discretely bounded entities. This, in conjunction with the constraints of a pervasive nationalist frame of reference, means that any change in the distribution of power is limited to a redistribution *between* nations. Even where it is used to effect the kind of change which challenges injustice and inequality, the concept of nation is always reified.

As the preceding discussion has also shown, the reification of the Scottish nation necessarily entails the reification of conceptions of a distinctive group of people who are "naturally" bonded to a distinctive place. Even where the constructed nation permits individuals who are not born into the nation to become members of it, admission to the nation requires conformity to that nation's self-definition. For those individuals who do not, cannot, or will not, fit the mould of the Scottish nation, a redistribution of power to this nation will not increase their access to power. On the contrary, it is likely to engender a solidification of the categories which already leave them isolated within Scottish society. As long as the nation is seen as the rightful repository of power, and as long as the nation is built around social constructions of uniform "people" and place, the application of the concept of nation may produce changes in the distribution of power, but it will not change the intolerance of difference which leads to the marginalization of particular individuals and groups.

Conclusion

In this chapter I have advanced the idea that entrenched social constructions can be used to bring about positive changes in the distribution of power. At the same time, however, it seems that any benefits ensuing from such a transition are countered by the negative repercussions of continuing to use restrictive, value-laden categories. In the case of the category of nation, this means that the successful promotion of a national construct can lead to the transfer of power to the *specific* nation involved, and the wise use of this new-found power can improve the lives of those within the newly established nation. However, this process of change has negative repercussions on two levels. On a *general* level, any use of the category of nation contributes to the reification of that category and of its attendant categories of people and place. By using the nation as a legitimate means of obtaining power, the idea that nations are "natural" repositories of power remains unchallenged and any transfer of power remains confined to a potentially growing but ultimately unbroken chain of nations. This produces a paradoxical situation in which the use of a category that gave rise to resistance in the first place is reified by those who considered themselves oppressed by its application.[16] The net result is a world order which continues to be organized around a restrictive concept, and its supportive ideology, which bears little resemblance to empirical conditions.

On a second, *specific* level, the use of a national construct to effect change means that restrictions inherent in the *general* category are transposed to a different, usually smaller, geographical scale. Neither the restrictions, nor the inequalities which they generate, are eliminated. To promote and to secure recognition of the new nation, component categories of people and place need to be solidified. Sadly, experience suggests that this process is more likely to replicate past injustices than to eradicate them. For individuals who are allied with the previously encompassing nation the result is marginalization in ways which effectively reduce their access to power. For individuals who fail to conform to either the old or the new national construct, the result is, at best, continued marginalization and alienation. It is at this *specific* level that the reification of the nation's attendant categories of people and

45

place becomes most pronounced. The net result is the perpetuation of an unequal distribution of power within the new nation.

The processes that work to ensure the reification of the concepts of nation, people and place are both indicative of, and conditional upon, a deep entrenchment of categories as part of our world-view. Acceptance of categories is reinforced continually by reliance on them as organizational and communicative devices. With categories so deeply engrained that they have become nearly indispensable, it becomes very difficult to challenge those that are seen to promote an undesirable state of affairs. In the case of nation, this problem is compounded by an inability to conceive of an alternative way of managing the world (even assuming that such a reorganization would be tolerated by those who are advantaged under the current system).

The combination of a deeply entrenched system of categories and the lack of a workable alternative to this system leaves little option but to pursue changes from within. Where nations are concerned this has to involve undermining the relevance of the cornerstone categories of people and place. As *individuals*, we can do this by changing the ways we refer to and describe both ourselves and others, eliminating references to categories that have no relevance to the information which we are trying to convey. As a *society*, we can subvert the notion of discrete groups of people by defining ourselves as heterogeneous and our composition as ever-changing.[17] Where there is no longer a separate group of people to define, boundaries lose their power to delimit. As a *nation*, we can undermine the rigidity inherent in the *general* construct by redistributing power in ways which bring responsibility for decisions into line with the context of their impact. By making local, regional *and* international bodies responsible for decisions which affect the people that they represent, the current concentration of power in "the nation" can be altered. In doing so, processes which reify our perception of the nation as the sole rightful repository of power can be subverted. If the nation is deprived of its intrinsic and exclusive right to power, at least some of the incentive for reproducing nations composed of a distinct people bonded to a distinct place will be eliminated.

These ideas are general, and their refinement – let alone their application – constitutes an enormous task. What they suggest, however, is that, where categories cannot be avoided, their meanings and functions can be altered in ways which reduce their power to engender inequality. Categories can be used to effect positive change but they can only do so if we are prepared to alter the categories at the same time. Only by simultaneously employing the concepts of nation, people and place to redefine one another in ways which reflect heterogeneity and fluidity can we hope to reduce the inequality that these concepts have so consistently generated.

Acknowledgements

I am grateful to the Social Sciences and Humanities Research Council of Canada and to the Canadian High Commission in London for financial support which made possible some of the research presented here. I would also like to thank Kay Anderson, Peter Jackson and Susan Smith for their constructive and stimulating comments on an earlier draft.

Notes

1. The ideas which support this starting point are being developed in a working paper entitled "Nationalist rhetoric and the social construction of nations" and will not be pursued here. However, the argument which follows provides indirect substantiation of the claim that both "nation", as a category, as well as *specific* nations are social constructions.
2. Moreover, the successful promotion of nations as "natural" entities means that resistance to one construction necessarily involves the creation of a counter-construction.
3. For a discussion of the origins of the concept of nation see Penrose & May (1991), and for an overview of the development of the term "nation" see Hobsbawm (1990, especially pp. 1–44).
4. While most groups of people associate themselves with specific, clearly delineated regions, exceptions can be found in transient groups such as Gypsies and in trans-humant groups such as Inuit. It is worth noting, however, that the power of territorial affiliation to confer cultural, and hence political, legitimacy is reflected in the fact that the lack of a definitive "homeland" has been used to deny groups rights to which they would otherwise be considered entitled.
5. It is worth noting that our acceptance of, and our assumed comprehension of, these terms is yet another manifestation of the absolute dominance of the *general* category of nation as the fundamental organizational unit of our world.
6. Here, it is important to note that, even though the self-constructions of nations are multi-faceted, they retain the capacity to exclude as long as they incorporate discrete territories and people.
7. The individual is the only other unit that is commonly ascribed a right to power. However, this is limited to the right to determine one's own affairs, with the added qualification that the enacting of this right should not infringe on the rights of others. Furthermore, all individuals (in theory, regardless of their social position) are constrained by the laws of the nation-state to which they belong and/or by international law, devised through co-operation between nation-states.
8. The term "Scottish nationalists" is used to connote *all* people who support a redistribution of power towards Scotland, either through devolution or independence. Where the Scottish National Party (SNP) is being referred to it is explicitly identified.
9. This point has been raised in various ways by: Blaut (1988), Hobsbawm (1990, especially p. 11), Newman (1987) and Taylor (1991).
10. In *The Scotsman* Debate held in Edinburgh on 18 January 1992, Ian Lang was greeted with loud boos and heckling from the audience, but when he asserted that "Scotland has prospered under the Union", the audience response was one of laughter.

11. As Kay Anderson has noted, this comment begs an explanation of Britain's policy in Northern Ireland.
12. I am grateful to Susan Smith for reminding me that many Scottish nationalists view the entire concept of "British" as the cloak of "Englishness". In other words, "British" is seen as little more than a euphemism for "English" which, by its all-encompassing nature, fulfils the dual function of obfuscating English dominance within the nation at the same time as it protects it.
13. Demonstration of the existence of a nation is a pre-requisite for debates about whether or not any particular group of nationalists actually represents the interests and aspirations of the people whom they purport to represent. Such debates fall outside the scope of this chapter.
14. At the very least, nationalists must demonstrate that differences between Scotland and the rest of Britain are greater than those which exist within Scotland.
15. It is important to note that processes of change are frequently marked by temporary compromises which are part of the continuing negotiation of power. In the case presented here, a new institution called a Scottish Assembly does not conform with either British Unionist or Scottish Independence visions of a legitimate nation or, consequently, their views on the appropriate distribution of power.
16. A similar situation arises when people organize themselves as "races" in an effort to resist racist oppression. To some extent, such actions inadvertently reflect the success of racism.
17. Clearly, groups which have recently begun to challenge derogatory and disadvantageous portrayals of themselves through the promotion of new self-defined constructions may resist this course of action, at least in the short term. In the long term, however, the kind of societal redefinition which I propose here offers one of the few conceivable means of reducing individual discrimination based on group affiliation.

References

Anderson, B. 1983. *Imagined communities: reflections on the origin and spread of nationalism.* London: Verso.

The battle of Bannockburn dated Stirling November 1930, Scottish National Library, document 5. 5501.

Blaut, J. 1988. *The national question.* London: Zed Books.

Brand, J. 1987. National consciousness and voting in Scotland. *Ethnic and Racial Studies* 10, 334–48.

Giddens, A. 1985. *The nation-state and violence.* Cambridge: Polity.

Handler, R. 1988. *Nationalism and the politics of culture in Quebec.* Madison, Wisconsin: University of Wisconsin Press.

Hobsbawm, E. J. 1990. *Nations and nationalism since 1780.* Cambridge: Cambridge University Press.

Newman, G. 1987. *The rise of English nationalism: a cultural history, 1740–1830.* New York: St Martin's Press.

Penrose, J. & J. May 1991. Herder's concept of nation and its relevance to contemporary ethnic nationalism. *Canadian Review of Studies in Nationalism* 18, 165–78.

Penrose, J. 1994. "Mon pays ce n'est pas un pays" full stop: the concept of nation as a challenge to the nationalist aspirations of the Parti Québécois. *Political Geography*, in press.

Scottish Conservatives. 1992. All-party chorus condemns separation. *The best future for*

Scotland (February), p. 2.
Taylor, P. J. 1991. The English and their Englishness: "a curiously mysterious, elusive and little understood people". *Scottish Geographical Magazine* 107, 146–61.
Williams, R. 1976. *Keywords: a vocabulary of culture and society*. London: Fontana.

CHAPTER TWO
Immigration and nation-building in Canada and the United Kingdom

SUSAN J. SMITH

Introduction

Notwithstanding romantic ideas about the boundedness of space, the fixity of place and the reality of "race", the world is on the move. The impetus for this mobility comes from a series of economic and political restructurings accompanying the rise and fall of colonialism, the maturation of industrial capitalism and the advent of the postmodern world. These restructurings have been uneven on a world scale, and they have helped generate successive waves of migration as labour adjusts to the changing needs of capital, and as nations adjust to the political realignments of postcolonialism. International migration in the late twentieth century is thus regulated by the internationalization of the labour market, the restructuring of world politics and, crucially, the enacting of immigration legislation.

When governments regulate the movement of people across political boundaries – determining who can enter their jurisdiction and on what terms, and deciding who must leave and when – they work with a concept of what their nation is and/or should be. Immigration policy and nation-building therefore must be two sides of a single coin. Immigration controls, which are always socially and economically selective, may be regarded as one expression of a political idea of who is, or could be, eligible to receive the entitlements of residence and citizenship. The symbolism of nationhood which is encapsulated in this kind of legislation is, as Breton (1984) illustrates, an essential dimension of its social and political reality. Today, immigration controls, at least as much as territorial extent, are an indicator of where the boundaries of a nation-state lie.

Currently, the direction of intercontinental migration is almost entirely determined by the immigration policies of the developed world. These countries have an ageing population and low, often decreasing, rates of population growth. Nevertheless, their policies are designed to regulate the inflow of workers, asylum seekers and their families from the less developed countries, in order to meet certain social and economic goals of the receiving society. To this end immigration policies do not simply inform nation-building on a regional scale; they sustain regional inequalities on a world scale.

This chapter compares the immigration legislation enacted through the global restructurings of the past half century by two developed countries which are differently positioned in the world order, and whose experiences illustrate the different ways in which immigration policy serves the aims of nation-building, and contributes to a divided world.

Comparing Canada and Britain

The case study countries are Canada and Britain. In one sense, they are so different that comparisons seem impossible and contrasts appear meaningless. Demographically and economically, the two nations are poles apart (Richmond 1979), and as Reitz (1988) notes, their immigration policy "has served different goals, was governed by different political relationships, and employed different legal and administrative rules" (p. 117). More productive comparisons, it might be argued, would be between Canada and Australia – two federations, both seeking selectively to increase the size of their populations, and both committed not only to promoting immigration but also to developing multiculturalism (Atchison 1984, 1988, Hawkins 1989, Richmond 1991) – or between Canada, the United States and South Africa – three "Anglo-fragment" societies which can be analyzed in terms of plural society theory (Baker 1979).

Nevertheless, Canada and Britain have interlinked, if distinctive, histories in the process of world development, and their immigration strategies began with certain common goals. Crucial ties between the economies and political cultures of the two nations arose when Britain's place at the centre of the industrial revolution was complemented by Canada's rôle in receiving the export of surplus labour. Palmer (1990) charts the rise and fall of the principle of Anglo-conformity which these early links established, and which underpinned so much of Canada's early public policy, including, as this chapter shows, its immigration policy. However, as Britain surrendered first

Empire for Commonwealth and then Commonwealth for Europe, and as Canada fell increasingly under the influence of the USA, the content of the two nations' immigration programmes appeared to diverge.

The main points of contrast are illustrated in Figure 2.1. To summarize, Britain has only ever seen itself as a country of emigrants, has never welcomed immigrants and rarely accommodates them in significant numbers. British immigration policies thus express and shape a vision of nationhood based on ideas about an inherent, immutable national character, which is ascribed through birthplace and lineage and whose strengths and future depend on preserving the integrity of geographically bounded traditions. Canada, on the other hand, celebrates its identity as a nation of immigrants whose past and future rest on the attraction of new settlers. "Canadians", argues the Economic Council of Canada (1991), "are proud of their heritage as a nation built on immigration" (p. ix). Here, immigration has a rôle in "economic development, future population planning, and the continuing process of Canadian nation-building" (Immigration Canada 1989: 3). In this context, to speak of the impact of migration is "in a sense to speak of all that is Canadian" (Hersak & Thomas 1988: 17). The vision is of a nation emerging from the gradual accretion of the right kinds of peoples, who acquire their national identity by living in Canada and contributing to a Canadian way of life.

Figure 2.1 Traditions of control: Britain and Canada.

	Britain	Canada
Origins of nationhood	History, tradition and stability	Immigration and change
Achieving national identity	Ascribed through birthplace and lineage	Acquired/achieved through residence in Canada and participation in Canadian life
Rôle of immigration legislation	Control entry to protect the national spirit, using the principle of exclusion	Regulate entry to construct a Canadian future, using the principle of selection
Key immigration debate	The immigration status of citizens	The citizenship status of immigrants
Consequence of policies	Citizenship for some but not others, despite economic costs	Citizenship for sale, irrespective of cultural conformity

Neither of these self-images is entirely accurate, yet both generalizations contribute to the "imagined" communities which Satzewich (1991) shows can become an important variable in determining the permeability of the boundaries of the nation-state. In practice, British society has been moulded as much by immigration as by natural increase; and the Native Peoples of Canada have a fundamental claim to Canadian territory and identity. But these claims have not secured space on the agenda underpinning immigration control; and they are not the views that have shaped the immigration debates.

For the past thirty years, therefore, Britain's immigration policy has centred on the theme of exclusivity. As Miles (1990) points out "There is considerable political investment in the conviction that Britain is a culturally homogeneous society whose island status has protected it from 'invasions' of various kinds over many centuries, and that its future is dependent upon the maintenance of vigilance at the borders in order to guarantee this homogeneity in the future" (p. 283). Immigration legislation has, in short, served the project of nation-building by protecting the integrity of a national character which is thought of as founded on tradition and grounded in experience. It has helped develop a sense of self which, by anchoring lineage and tradition to territory, privileges birthplace and descent and looks to the future as an extension of the past. From the perspective of British nationhood immigration policy has a protective rôle.

For Canada, on the other hand, immigration policy serves a more constructive rôle: it is the very tool of nation-building. The immigration programme is expanding, and its rôle is to regulate, rather than restrict, access to Canadian territory. Its hallmark is selectivity rather than exclusivity through policies which aim to compensate for the greying of the nation, to promote the country's domestic interests, to enrich its bilingual character and to foster a strong economy. Canadian immigration policy has therefore served the interests of nation-building by selecting for the skills and talent that contribute to a vision of what Canada could be. This sense of self is about capturing lineage and tradition – whatever its origins – and harnessing it to the needs of a territorially based economy.

As a consequence of the different values placed on the immigration process, British debate has centred on the question of immigration *control*, and is underpinned by the principle of exclusionism, while Canadian debate has hinged on immigration *regulation* and is informed by the principle of selectivity. Britain has effected policies which exclude certain groups (in practice, non-Whites of New Commonwealth origin) irrespective of economic costs or formal citizenship status. Canada, on the other hand, has moved to a position where it selects for capital and entrepreneurial skills irrespective of perceived cultural conformity.

This chapter considers what these different emphases mean for actual and potential migrants, and for the countries that they are moving to. To this end, the essay reviews the various policies which have developed in the past half century in response to labour migration, refugee migration, and the process of family reunion.

Labour migration: constructing the nation

Labour migration is an expression of interdependence between the political economics of sending and receiving societies. The varying pattern of labour migrations must be set, therefore, in the context of successive waves of economic restructuring and political reordering.[1] The most appropriate way to examine the changing rôle of labour migration in relation to the task of nation-building is therefore chronologically.

Labour shortage and the postwar reconstructions: a dilemma shared
During the 1930s, Canada and the UK felt the full force of the recession: for Britain this vindicated the anti-immigration tradition; for Canada it interrupted the settlement process as attempts were made to safeguard existing jobs and to remove unwanted burdens on the welfare services (Elliott 1979).[2] Canada imposed strict immigration controls during the years of the Second World War, and (despite having accommodated significant numbers of refugees) experienced net outmigration during that period. Likewise, even as late as the mid–1940s, Britain saw itself as a net exporter of population. Both countries were, therefore, largely unprepared for the labour demands of postwar reconstruction, and both experienced labour shortages during the 1950s and early 1960s. The solution in both cases was to import workers from overseas.

The policies pursued to encourage labour migration reflect the position of the two nations in the world order. For Canada, the aftermath of the war marked a significant step in the transition from not just a colony but also an outpost of the British Empire, to fully independent nationhood. A Canadian Citizenship Bill was introduced in 1946, confirming that "the British Empire . . . of which many Canadians felt their country to be an integral part, was itself on the decline and could therefore contribute less to Canadians' sense of collective identity" (Breton 1984: 37). For Britain, on the other hand, the shift was from colonial core, via the creation of the Commonwealth, to the periphery of the European community. These divergent trajectories required two ostensibly different approaches to nation-building and these are etched into the immigration regulations of the time. The differences arise primarily because while Canada, freed from its formal attachment to Britain, was able to use legislative measures to preserve a Eurocentric character, Britain, in the interests of sustaining a precarious relationship with the New Commonwealth, was forced to adopt an ostensibly more liberal position.

Canada's period of Anglo-conformity, therefore, went hand in hand with an explicitly racialized immigration agenda. In the early years of this century, ". . . a group's desirability as potential immigrants varied almost directly with its members' physical and cultural distance from London (England), and the degree to which their skin pigmentation conformed to Anglo-Saxon White" (Palmer 1990: 194). Palmer identifies a hierarchy of preferred immigrants from British and American (most preferred) through other North and West Europeans, Central and East Europeans, Jews and Southern Europeans, to East and South Asians (least preferred). Of all groups, observe Francis et al. (1988), Canada preferred British immigrants, because, it was argued, it is easier to transplant immigrants onto "similar soil". Therefore, "if additional people were needed to build a greater Canada, many sectors of Canadian society hoped they would be of British stock" (Dirks 1977: 53). As Avery's (1988) work shows, "The Canadian consensus seems to have been that Orientals and Blacks were unassimilable. Their future in the country, to the extent that they were thought to have one at all, was that of the most grinding labour" (p. 7). These "undesirable" immigrants were therefore limited by a series of legal and administrative measures,[3] implemented on the assumption that those "who were culturally or racially inferior and incapable of being assimilated either culturally or biologically would have to be excluded (Palmer 1990: 96).

North American Blacks were excluded, for instance, on the grounds that the cold winters made Canada climatically unsuitable for them (Troper 1972) and climatic unsuitability was a statutory reason for barring non-Whites until as late as 1953 (Kallen 1982). Francis et al. (1988) show that even in 1952 this view prevailed, citing a government minister's remark that "it would be unrealistic to say that immigrants who have spent the greater part of their life in tropical or subtropical countries become readily adapted to the Canadian mode of life" (p. 404). Likewise, a head tax was used to regulate Chinese immigration, an agreement was made with Japan to limit emigration to Canada, and a "continuous journey" stipulation in the immigration regulations effectively debarred East Indian settlers in the early 1900s.[4] Canada in the 1930s and 1940s could, as Abella & Troper (1986) show, be seen as a nation characterized by racism, xenophobia and anti-Semitism.

Some regulations were changed in 1949. For instance, France was added to Britain and the USA on the list of preferred immigrant countries, South Europeans were admitted and, for the first time, some Asians were allowed to sponsor their families. But for the most part, between 1945 and 1962, immigration to Canada remained selective by "race" and region and, albeit in the context of an overall increase in immigration,[5] aimed to limit the entry of non-Europeans (Finkel 1986). The tacit assumption was that the migrants intended to stay and become part of the Canadian nation (Satzewich 1990), and that, therefore, they should be carefully selected to conform to the ideals of Canadian nation-building. These ideals were still rooted in the sentiments expressed by Exton Lloyd, who asked in 1928 "Shall Canada develop as a British nation within the Empire, or will she drift apart by the introduction of so much alien blood that her British instincts will be paralysed?" (Exton Lloyd, 17 August 1928). As Prime Minister King noted, even in 1947 the Canadian people did not wish mass immigration "to make a fundamental alteration to the character of the Canadian population". This kind of reasoning, coupled with the assumption that immigrants would stay for good, is what underpins the "racially" selective legislation that persisted for so long.

Britain's attempt to wrest Commonwealth from Empire, on the other hand, made explicitly exclusionary legislation as impossible as statutory anti-racism throughout the 1950s. Britain saw itself as a world leader in tolerance, understanding and generosity to its subjects. Indeed in 1948 a new nationality act was passed which explicitly reaffirmed the rights of all British subjects (i.e. citizens of the present and former British Empire) to freedom of movement within the Commonwealth.[6] In practice, however, New Commonwealth migrants were accepted only as a last resort; they were actively discouraged by a range of quasi-legal administrative controls, and even those who came were not expected to stay (Smith 1992). British politicians were, it seems, every bit as selective as their Canadian counterparts, their only "comfort" being that they saw their immigration programme as short-lived, and they believed that those who settled would "having helped our productivity and output . . . go back to the Colonies and be a nucleus of productivity there" (Harold Davies, Hansard 1946–47, Vol. 441, col. 1415).

Between 1945 and 1962, the immigration regulations of Canada and the UK were, in theory, quite different: Canada's were explicitly selective (of Anglo-Europeans) and largely excluded non-Whites; Britain's rested on the assumption of free entry and settlement for British subjects throughout the world. In practice, however, the effects of these policies were remarkably similar. Both were designed to attract migrant labour and both actively resisted (to a limit imposed by the economy) the entry of significant numbers of non-Whites from the New Commonwealth countries. Both were implementing a strategy of nation-building founded on the principle of "racial" difference and shot through with the presumption of White supremacy. The difference was that Britain was receiving British migrants with an inviolable right to settle; Canada had no such constraint and unequivocally viewed settlement as a privilege, not as a right. As a consequence, Britain encouraged the view that immigration would be short-lived and temporary, and resisted non-White migration covertly, while Canada was in a position – in a world where the principle of anti-racism had scarcely appeared in the political arena – to be explicitly selective, and openly to resist non-White immigration. Legislation passed in 1962 marked the beginning of a period which, by 1968, was to see almost a complete reversal of these rôles.

The 1960s: immigrant threat and legislative response

In 1962, Canada's Conservative government replaced ethnicity and country of origin with education and training as the criteria for entry. This was an explicit attempt to "deracialize" the selectivity which had previously been explicitly built into the immigration programme. In the same year, Britain's Conservative government passed the Commonwealth Immigration Act, limiting, for the first time, the settlement rights of British citizens living overseas. The timing, implementation and effects of this Act marked a clear step in the direction of exclusionism with a racist bias.

In Canada the change came about because of the pressures first for bi-culturalism and then multiculturalism.[7] French Canadians' demands for equality in the nation-building process spilled into other areas of social and civic life, and in 1960 the Bill of Rights was introduced (something Britain has never entertained), signalling a rejection of discrimination by reason of "race", national origin, colour, religion or sex.

In Britain a contrary change was facilitated by the Notting Hill riots and a recession in the car industry (Smith 1989), but it was demanded primarily by the call of Europe. Britain first applied to join the EEC in 1962. Entry was unlikely to be granted to a Community that saw a common labour market as one of its ultimate goals if some security against the mass migration of British citizens from the New Commonwealth was not provided. The Commonwealth Immigration Act provided the requisite security (although at that stage, Britain's attempt to enter Europe failed).

In 1967, Canada took further steps to "deracialize" its immigration laws, with the introduction of a points system. In 1968, Britain took a further step in the opposite direction, by revoking an earlier agreement to admit Ugandan Asians with British passports. In 1971 the government also introduced a patriality clause into the Immigration Act which further limited the settlement rights of British citizens without a family origin in the UK.

By the beginning of the 1970s, the two countries thus perceived themselves to be moving along different paths to nation-building. Canada saw itself as a nation emerging from the spatial convergence of anyone who possessed the skills, personal character and financial attributes required to develop a buoyant economy and a stable society. (As early as 1966 governmental documents had recognized that a substantial, continuing inflow of immigrants was required to sustain economic growth and maintain a national identity separate from that of the USA (Taylor 1987)). Britain, on the other hand, was progressively closing its doors to anyone without a demonstrable claim to Anglo-Saxon heritage: a new vision of nationhood was under construction and it was clearly detached from the old visions of "multiracial" Empire and multicultural Commonwealth. Whereas Canada was orientating its legislation to allow economics to determine who came and how many; Britain was pursuing a political goal irrespective of economic repercussions.[8]

In practice, however, the differences were not always as marked as the formal shift of emphasis might suggest. Immigration to Canada declined into the 1970s and Canadian parliamentary debates on immigration during that decade have much in common with their British counterparts which developed during the 1960s. Both centred on the importance of controlling the origin, characteristics, numbers and destinations of immigrants. The relevant British debates are summarized in Smith (1989). They exaggerate the size of the immigrant population and depict the neighbourhoods they settled in as an environmental hazard, a drain on welfare services, and a threat to the British way of life. The identified way of tackling this threat to the cultural landscape was to remove its source (immigration) and lessen its visible impact by dispersing the settlers.

Some of these themes were picked up in the Canadian immigration debate of July 1977, when David MacDonald (Egmont) compared an earlier vision of immigration as "one of the important characteristics, one of the really hopeful aspects, of the unfolding history of this country" with the current view that "immigration is now rather like a genie out of the bottle . . . something that is perhaps somewhat dangerous to the development of Canada" (Vol. 8, 1977: 7871). Immigration was constructed as a threat to resources, prompting Jake Epp (Provencher) to urge that "we must lose some of the attitudes we have had about Canada – that Canada is a vast land and that we can accept people without any further view as to the distribution of the population, the demand on natural resources, housing, transport, education . . . " (Vol. 8, 1977: 7884). Benno Friesen (Surrey – White Rock) took up the theme, arguing ". . . If we are to preserve an attractive country, we must preserve the characteristics which made it attractive and which we enjoy today. In order to do this we must maintain a sensitive control of immigration flow . . . the first principle is that of preserving the wellbeing of Canada" (Vol. 8, 1977: 7983). Ian Watson (Laprierie) agreed, asserting "I do not want to open the doors wider than they are now open . . . if we are to maintain the present high quality of life in Canada and our present living standards, we shall have to think seriously about slowing down the growth of our population" (Vol. 8, 1977: 7969).

The plea to limit numbers was augmented by Lloyd Frances (Ottawa West) who argued that, if immigrants were to be admitted, they should certainly be dispersed. He shared "the fears of those who point out that our immigration has been heavily concentrated in the cities", claiming that this "has added to our housing problems and to the social services that are requested". Consequently "[An] attempt to direct immigration to the slower growth areas in Canada seems to me to be a reasonable thing to do". He goes on, "I am not persuaded that it is a violation of human rights to say to those who choose to come to Canada that they are requested to spend a certain period of time in one of the slower growth areas". This, he thinks, could ensure that "they would not all go, in overwhelming numbers, to the urban centres where the problems of urban life are magnified as a result" (Vol. 8, 1977: 7970). Attempts to insert a clause that would award extra points to migrants who were willing to live away from the larger metropolitan centres for six months were defeated. Nevertheless, the idea attracted support on the grounds that it could not be criticized as a human rights violation in the context where, as Ian Watson put it "the granting of immigration status is a privilege and is not, as some would assert, the right of any person coming to this country" (Vol. 8, 1977: 7969).

Until the mid–1970s, then, the policies for regulating labour migration into Canada and the UK were different in principle, but similar in practice. It is only with the advent of neo-conservatism towards the end of the 1970s that the first real divergence became apparent. Ironically, it was under ostensibly similar political regimes, that the two nations were to develop very different immigration policies. Selectivity and exclusivity were to hang, for the first time, around quite different principles.

The 1980s: exclusion vs selection

In the early 1980s, the fears of British and Canadian politicians, and of their voting publics, were translated into further immigration restrictions:[9] indeed the recession of the early 1980s cut immigration to both societies to their lowest levels for 20 years. However, in Canada, unlike Britain, this period of restriction never affected those wealthy immigrants who were prepared to invest in the nation's future and, as the decade progressed, Britain retained its exclusionism while Canada substantially revised it.

In the mid–1980s, in the wake of evidence concerning the "shrinking and greying" of the population,[10] Canada took steps actively to increase its immigration levels, and to persuade Canadian citizens of the wisdom of this move.[11] Accordingly a series of reports emphasizing the positive contribution made by migrants to the national future was published. In 1986 the Demographic Review was set up and it produced three key reports on immigration, which were unanimously supportive of the rôle of immigration in shaping the Canadian past, present and future (see Ebanks 1990).

The 1986–87 annual report, prepared by Employment and Immigration Canada, went on to refer to a growing awareness that immigrants are a spur to economic growth and development, and related studies showed immigration to be a net generator of employment (Samuel & Conyers 1986). In 1989, the same body announced "we have sufficient evidence to dispel some common myths about immigration's economic impacts" (1989a: 5): migrants do not monopolize social assistance; they contribute more than average in taxes; they are generally well educated and well qualified, and they do not take jobs from established Canadians. Indeed, they "fill gaps in our labour market and they create jobs through their consumption of goods and services and their entrepreneurial and investment activities" (1989a: 6). Some studies also demonstrated that immigrants bring money with them with the net effect that the economy grows, per capita wellbeing is unaffected, and any costs associated with immigration are entirely short-term (Employment and Immigration Canada 1989b; see also Akbari 1989, Samuel & Woloski 1985). From the mid–1980s, then, the Canadian government began to expand its immigration programme, based not only on consultation with the provinces (since 1982) but also on discussions with 500 non-governmental organizations. From a low point of 85,000 admissions in 1985, annual increases were planned to reach 175,000 by 1990.[12]

This programme was viewed by the government as an economic necessity, and, as Malarek (1987) points out, amid a wide range of consultations "the issue of just who will be allowed to immigrate to Canada is being side-stepped by politicians, who are afraid of what they will hear. They are afraid of a racist backlash" (p. 69). And, indeed, the plans to expand immigration were not received without public reservations. An opinion survey conducted in the late 1980s showed growing opposition to rising immigration and a clear preference for continuing selectivity in the Canadian nation-building programme (Angus Reid Group 1989). Canadians are more likely to accept immigrants who contribute to the country's growth and prosperity or who come to be reunited with close family member. There is concern, too, about the changing composition of the migrant groups, which were once dominated by North Western Europeans but which are now increasingly from the developing world.[13] Even the Economic Council of Canada's generally positive review of the impact of *New faces in the crowd* (1991) concluded with the observation that "Canadians have no special exemption from the virus of prejudice and intolerance . . . [therefore] . . . Cautious expansion should be our watchword".

It seems, in short, that immigration is currently acceptable to the Canadian public as long as the programme is effectively managed from the standpoint of Canada's needs. The government has tried to meet this requirement, without either compromising the economy or pandering to exclusionism, in two ways. First, in 1989 it introduced a five-year strategic planning cycle for immigration levels (building on the unusual clause in Canadian legislation which requires non-governmental and provincial consultation to precede the setting of immigration targets). Secondly, it confirmed its commitment to selectivity, along the lines set down in the 1976 Immigration Act.[14] This selectivity has been promoted above all by a vigorous business migration scheme, and the prominence of this scheme within the overall immigration programme confirms that potential to generate income, wealth and jobs is the criteria by which Canadian migrants are selected.

The points system has always massively favoured business and entrepreneur class entrants (Segal 1990), and subsequent legislation (in 1984 and 1986) has accentuated this trend. Indeed, Canada has made it so easy for investors to immigrate that the government has been accused of selling citizenship to those who can bid successfully for it, and denying it to those who cannot. However, as Nash (1988a) shows, entrepreneurs rather than investors now make up the biggest proportion of the business immigration programme, and by the mid–1980s, this stream was dominated by entrepreneurs from Hong Kong. In relation to this migrant stream, Canada can be criticized for its selectivity as much as Britain can for its exclusivity. Nash (1991) thus argues that the economic benefits to Canada of targeting Hong Kong settlers is working to the detriment of Hong Kong itself: the lure of easy money is preventing countries such as Canada from pledging their faith to the future of Hong Kong.

In Canada, then, immigration policy has harnessed the practice of labour migration to the principles of the free market and to the ideals of the enterprise culture. Immigration policy is thus economically selective, and more sensitive to the colour of money than to that of skin. In this sense, current immigration policies – the product of a Conservative government – are allied more with neo-liberalism (Stasiulis 1991) than with the moral authoritarianism that is also a part of neo-conservatism. Entirely the opposite may be said of Britain.

By 1976, Britain had tightened its immigration laws to reduce immigration to a trickle. A pattern of strict exclusionism was established and this has never changed. Indeed the prospect of an open labour market within Europe has served to draw the boundaries around the continent even closer, and Britain has been no exception. British citizenship is not for sale; after 1981, it was not even available as a right to many of those who had previously possessed it. For British policy-makers, who were still busy wresting nationhood from Commonwealth, the promise of economic benefits could not off-set the concern for cultural heritage. Even migration from Hong Kong was resisted, so that few passports were issued, and even fewer actually taken up (Findlay 1992). Indeed, the Thatcher government passed unnecessary and symbolically restrictive legislation which served largely to bolster national pride and undermine the status of "visible minorities". Here, immigration policy was allied to the moral authoritarian strand of neo-conservatism, which is prevalent in so many other areas of British political life.

Today, then, Britain and Canada both operate neo-conservative immigration policies. However, their effect is quite different and there are marked contrasts in the relationship between immigration policy and economic migrants in the two nations. This difference is rooted in the different priorities for immigration policy and in two different strategies for nation-building. In Britain, the emphasis remains on the exclusion of non-Whites, irrespective of the economic costs; in Canada, the emphasis is on selecting those with capital and entrepreneurial skills, irrespective of cultural conformity.

Refugee migration: personal needs vs collective identity

An examination of responses to what has become the world's major international migration stream – refugee migration – confirms the distinctions between Canadian selectivity and British exclusivity, although it also raises some uncomfortable points of convergence between the two nations' strategies.

Canadian governments frequently and proudly refer to the country's long tradition of humanitarian settlement. Certainly, refugees have found their way to Canada in various waves since the late eighteenth century. Initially, refugees were desirable settlers from the perspective of politicians, "especially in the years when hardy 'peasant' folk were in fashion" and where "sparseness of settlement enabled non-English and peculiar sects to reside unseen by those opposed to that type of migrant". By the 1920s, however, "refugees were a nuisance: just additional numbers of the undesirable 'non-preferreds' seeking entry to Canada" (Dirks 1977: 43). It is hardly surprising, then (though not undisturbing), that Canada's main achievement at the outset of the period discussed in this paper was in keeping its doors firmly closed to refugees from a war-torn Europe. When they finally were admitted, it was cautiously and selectively. Refugee intake was geared to the needs of industry and qualified by the government's undertaking to ensure that those admitted would make good citizens and not fundamentally alter the character of the population (Purves 1990). Discussing this undertaking, Francis et al. (1988) cite the words of John Holmes, an external affairs officer, who noted that refugees were being selected "like good beef cattle, with a preference for strong young men who could do manual labour and would not be encumbered by ageing relatives" (399–400).

Nevertheless, Canada steadily increased its refugee intake, and the 1976 Immigration Act made, for the first time, comprehensive provision for the selection of refugees from abroad and for the determination of refugee status for those who applied for asylum from within Canada.[15] By 1980, Canada had become the country with the highest ratio of refugees to population (1:324, compared with 1:374 in the USA, 1:780 in France and 1:1783 in Norway). Since then the figure has steadily risen. Canada is currently one of the largest contributors to the United Nations High Commission for Refugees. On the basis of this openness and support for the world's refugees, the Canadian people were awarded the Nansen medal in 1986.[16]

Canada is a signatory (albeit a late one[17]) to the United Nations convention on refugees, which signals its willingness to play a part in solving the world refugee crisis by, where appropriate, offering asylum to those defined as refugees under that convention.[18] However, under the 1976 Immigration Act, Canada retains its discretion to be selective when enacting its humanitarian programme through a commitment to accommodate not just convention refugees but also people in "refugee-like" situations. These are identified in law as "designated classes".[19]

By combining convention refugees and designated classes under the same heading of humanitarian migrants, Canada has been able to exercise considerable selectivity over who is admitted.[20] The result, illustrated in Figure 2.2, is that most of the humanitarian intake is selected from those areas with least refugees; and that the majority of those selected are economically active men (the intake of women – who comprise the majority of refugees – and of sick or disabled refugees is disproportionately low).[21] As a consequence, it has been suggested that ease of entry to Canada via the humanitarian route is inversely proportional to the human needs of those seeking asylum (Nash 1989a).

This degree of selectivity (under a programme that is supposed to be the least selective of the migration streams), is possible because, traditionally, the main route for refugees into Canada is via a refugee determination process which takes place overseas. First, therefore, the prospects of selection depend on proximity to an immigration office. These are not evenly distributed, and the unevenness is partly what accounts for the under-representation of refugees from the major refugee source areas. The message for refugees seeking protection is, in the critical words of David Berger (Laurier) "Do not disturb. Don't call us, we'll call you" (1987, Vol. 4: 4524).

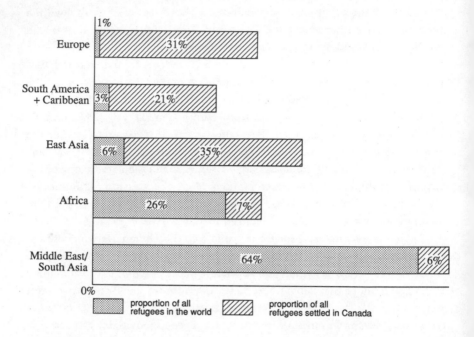

Figure 2.2 Origin zone of refugees in all countries and in Canada.

Secondly, and related to this, is Whitaker's (1987) observation that Canada's immigration programme may have become colour-blind to race, but in terms of refugee settlement, it is certainly not blind to *political* hue, to the extent that the immigration programme has "proscribed certain kinds of political views and certain kinds of political associations" among prospective entrants (p. 302). This is consistent with the treatment of refugee immigration in government policy papers which see it as a process which, although humanitarian, should also serve foreign-policy objectives (Purves 1990).

Thirdly, as Malarek (1987) points out, the policy of sending teams abroad to hand-pick settlers tends to result in the recruitment of those "who fit Canadian views of who deserves our help" (p. 103). Immigration officers have considerable discretion when evaluating refugees' motives and their potential to settle in Canada. This practice was criticized in Parliament in the immigration debate of June 1990 by Dan Heap (Trinity–Spadina) who, discussing the process of recruitment by Canadian consular officers from refugee camps, noted "strong indications that in fact refugees from those camps are selected first for their supposed economic benefit to Canada. . . .

Only secondly are they selected for their need." (Vol. 131, 1990: 12755)

Fourthly, this stipulation that refugees should be selected on the basis of their ability to settle in Canada has meant that "in our quest for refugees who will not be a burden on the Canadian economy, economic consider-ations far outweigh humanitarian concerns" (Malarek 1987: 102). A relaxed points system is therefore applied to refugee applicants in order to select those who are best able to care for themselves and their family and to adapt to a productive rôle in Canada (Weinfeld 1988).[22]

The overwhelming impression is, as David Berger (Laurier) noted in a stormy Parliamentary debate during August 1987, that "the Government does not want refugees to make claims in Canada. It wants to select refugees abroad", through a process which arises "more out of our need for immigra-tion than out of our concern for the plight of refugees" (1987, Vol. 7: 8039). Through its process of recruiting refugees from overseas, Canada can there-fore control both the numbers and type of people admitted under its human-itarian programme. Currently, the aim is to freeze admissions of government assisted refugees (those selected abroad) at 13,000 p.a. until 1995, and a reduction is also anticipated (from 24,000 to 15,000) of privately sponsored refugees.

Because of this emphasis on overseas selection, the Canadian polity has taken a tough line against refugees who attempt to gain entry not by the normal route (of contacting a refugee determination officer overseas) but by finding their way to Canada prior to requesting asylum. Although the gov-ernment anticipates a five-fold increase in refugees landed in Canada (from 5,000 to 25,000 p.a. to 1995), the reaction against this entry route has all the characteristics of the "moral panic" originally identified by Hall et al. (1978) as a response to perceptions of deviance and disorder. As Weinfeld (1988) has observed, a consequence of Canada's lack of preparation for this dimension of the refugee crisis is that "occasional boatloads of refugees have triggered bouts of national hysteria" (p. 19).

Two events precipitating such hysteria in the late 1980s had a decisive effect on Canada's refugee policy, and in doing so exposed its continuing rôle in the rhetoric of nation-building. These were the arrival in Nova Scotia of boats carrying 155 Tamil refugees in August 1986 and 173 Sikhs in July 1987. As Malarek (1987) shows, the Tamils hit the headlines because their original story – of being cast adrift from a German freighter which had picked them up from the south coast of India – proved untrue. They had in fact been smuggled to Canada from a German refugee camp. The *Montreal Gazette* identified them as the "tip of the iceberg" (14 August 1986: A1), and later ran a story headed "The Tamils. Are we a soft touch?" (16 August 1986: B1). This sentiment was echoed in Parliament by Mary Collins (Capilano) who was concerned that "Canadians honestly feel, given the instances that we have had in the past year, that Canada is becoming a patsy, an easy mark internationally" (1987, Vol. 7: 8064). Although the Tamils (who were genuine refugees) were allowed to stay, the mass media complained that they had jumped the queue, and that such tolerance would fuel a backlash against the immigration programme. "Many Canadians", claimed a Toronto pollster through the pages of the *Montreal Gazette*, "see the country changing before their eyes, and they don't like it" (19 August 1986: B2).

Scarcely had the Tamil panic subsided from the pages of the popular dailies, when the Maritime Police arrested two men implicated in the landing of 173 Sikhs, again in Nova Scotia. This exploded into the headlines and prompted the Minister for Immigration to request the recall of Parliament to "deal with an issue of grave national importance". Justifying the recall to disgruntled MPs he went on, "A serious problem – the growing number of migrants who are entering Canada by posing as refugees – has reached critical proportions". Public concern, he argued, is well founded "since organized attempts to evade the immigration laws of this country are absolutely unacceptable." (Vol. 7, 1987: 7910)

The House went on during the remainder of August to debate two crucial changes to the immigration legislation: Bill c–55 to tighten controls on access to Canadian territory, and Bill c–84 to establish "tough deterrents to stop the increasing number of illegal aliens posing as refugees from entering Canada" (EIC 1987, cited in Nash 1989a: 34). Between them, these Bills aimed to deter carriers from transporting refugees to Canada, reduced the rights of refugees to stay in Canada while their claim was assessed, and provided for the swift deportation of anyone thought to be a threat to security. "We want refugees to know that we have an open door policy" observed Ted Schellenberg (Nanaimo–Alberni), "but that that back door is closed. We do not welcome people who arrive by stealth or individuals who bring the murderous hatreds with them" (1987, Vol. 7: 8015).

In the Canadian example, these moral panics served to reinforce the selectivity of the refugee settlement programme. The argument that dominated political and popular rhetoric was that refugee migration is only a problem when it lacks order. Order, it seems, implies an organized queuing system, geared to Canada's own economic and cultural needs, accessed from outside the national territory, and resulting in "a controlled, predictable movement which allows Canada to select the cream of refugees" (David Berger, Laurier, 1987, Vol. 6: 7356). This is the way that the immigration debate has responded to what Jim Manley (Cowichan–Malarat–The Islands) identified as "a fear of being overwhelmed by refugees . . . a fear of many Canadians that our traditional values will be swamped by an influx of people from different cultures" (1987, vol. 7: 8150). This fear that "We've lost control of our border" (*Globe and Mail* headline 27 February 1991: A4) continued to be addressed in the round of immigration measures announced in summer 1992 which are designed "to more effectively select those who come to Canada, to better protect Canadian society . . . [and] . . . to streamline our world-class refugee determination system" (Bernard Valcourt, Immigration Minister, cited in *Canada News*, July 1992: 1).

In Britain, parallel events and sentiments have confirmed the exclusivity of a settlement programme which has produced an immigrant population of overwhelmingly European origin. Every British Immigration Act between 1968 and 1988 has been motivated by attempts to restrict refugee access (even when those refugees have been British citizens). As a consequence, refugee migration is less significant in Britain than in Canada and it forms only a tiny proportion (2 per cent p.a.) of the British total (Fig. 2.3). Although this British exclusionism is part of a wider programme of control being put into place by the European Community (Baldwin-Edwards 1992, Joly 1989, Widgen 1989), Britain has played a leading rôle in forging this consensus (Kaye 1992), and now receives fewer requests for asylum, in absolute terms and per head of the population, than most of its European neighbours. Indeed, Britain has gone further than many European counterparts in developing a set of policies in which, across the board, "the emphasis is on restriction and exclusion rather than on rational and humane immigration policies, or on providing more effective support to refugees" (Castles 1991: 3). Thus, notwithstanding the extent to which "the boundary of 'our' economic and political field has been extended, necessitating an extension of the boundary of the 'imagined community' beyond that of each nation-state to Europe" (Miles 1991: 27), in recent discussions on the Maastricht treaty, immigration control has emerged as "one of the key issues on which Britain wishes to maintain independent policies from Europe in order to 'double-bolt' the doors against immigrants" (Findlay 1992: 7).

Thus, although the advent of 1992 and the Single European Act has prompted Britain to relax its attitude to economic migrants from the EC, who can enter alone or with their families, with or without a job, irrespective of their likely income, and with a wide range of social entitlements, this stands in stark opposition to policies for asylum seekers who face pre-entry visa controls and hostility from carriers, who must prove, ironically, that their motivation is *not* economic, and who are constantly under threat of deportation (Joint Council for the Welfare of Immigrants 1989). In opening its doors to the EC, Britain seems to have accepted that immigration can be a good thing, but, in subscribing to the policies of "fortress Europe", current legislation confirms that the relationship between immigration control and nation-

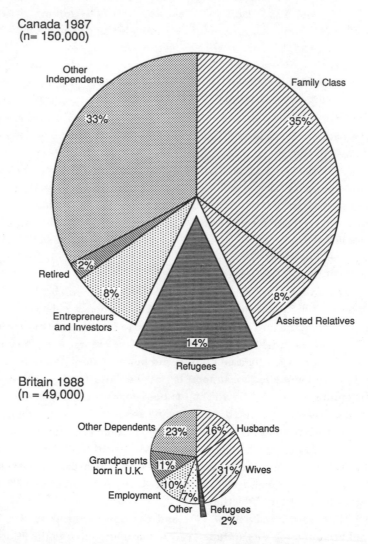

Figure 2.3 Type of immigration to Britain and Canada.

building is substantially the same as in the earlier phase of labour migration.

Canadian and British refugee settlement policies differ in some key respects. These differences arise because, while Canada sees immigration generally as the key to economic success and simply wishes to ensure that the right kinds of people are selected, Britain regards immigration as a threat to social and economic wellbeing (despite Ashford's (1981) and Findlay's (1992) illustrations to the contrary). Nevertheless, the two sets of policies have much in common, and share some similar aims. These are:

- To limit the access which refugees have to Canadian or British territory. The principle tool here is the imposition of carrier liability regulations, which both countries have enacted despite an executive order of the UN Commission on Refugees which states that "the obligation to examine the claims of asylum seekers cannot be delegated by States to private companies such as transport carriers".

- To define tightly who is and is not a refugee. In the British case the objective is to exclude as many as possible; in the Canadian case it is to preserve possibilities for selectivity.

- To process those who do arrive as quickly as possible. To this end both countries have developed fast-tracking procedures. In Canada these act primarily to admit rapidly those who obviously are refugees; in Britain they function to expel rapidly those who "obviously" are not refugees. During the waiting period, therefore, refugees in Canada are better protected than those in Britain, largely as a consequence of the fact that Canada possesses a charter of human rights.[23]

Thus, although Britain and Canada are both committed to accommodating the needs of refugees, they treat refugee migration like all other forms of settlement and manage it in ways that maintain the traditions of exclusivity and selectivity which are so important to each country's conception of nationhood. Despite the difference in emphasis, moreover, there is one way in which the net effect of these selective and exclusionary policies are the same. Even as it opens its frontiers to labour migration within the European Community, Britain joins with its neighbours to ensure that there is less and less scope for Third World refugees to find a home there. And while Canada has progressively increased its humanitarian intake, it has done so within a framework that allows politicians to select settlers more for their capacity to meet the demands of the Canadian economy than for their own human needs. The policies employed to limit refugee admission thus contribute not only to the construction of nationhood but also to the partitioning of a starkly divided world. Alongside a barrage of fiscal and trading arrangements which, on a global scale, currently keep poor places poor, are a set of immigration policies epitomized by those adopted in Canada and Britain which symbolize a desire to keep poor people in their place (Smith 1992). The net effect is to keep Britain White, Canada rich, and the world divided.

Nation-building and family life

Britain and Canada both ostensibly place importance in their immigration policies on the process of family reunion. This is in line with political convictions about the rôle of the family as the building block of nationhood. The methods by which family reunion is secured provide a third illustration of the distinction between Canadian selectivity and British exclusivity.

The Canadian Minister for Immigration (Barbara McDougall) announced to Parliament in October 1989 that family reunification "remains the cornerstone of the current immigration policy", and public opinion polls show that this kind of immigration is generally favoured by the Canadian public (Angus Reid Group 1989). Canada readily allows family reunion within Canada itself, and actively encourages sponsorship. Indeed, there are no limits placed on family immigration: the level per year reflects how much sponsorship there is from existing settlers. The assumption is that the "right" people were chosen for settlement originally (under the independent, business or refugee programmes) and that their family is therefore also among the preferred classes for Canadian nation-building. Although there is some tension in allocation of targets between this ("dependent") group and the more productive "economic migrants", the evidence all suggests that immigrating dependents adjust well and find a place in the economy (Samuel 1988a, 1988b).

In contrast, British policy for family reunification has encouraged and often required this reunification to occur not within Britain itself but rather within in the country of origin. The emphasis here is on excluding people whose family background is not spatially rooted in the UK. If people whose family history is lodged overseas wish to reunite their family, they must do so by returning to their roots, not by bringing those roots to Britain.

Thus, where migrants wish to be joined by their fiancee or spouse, they are subject to humiliating interviews to ensure that the marriage (rather than some other motive) is the "primary purpose" of their attempt to settle in Britain. Families are no longer allowed to immigrate if they, or their sponsor, are likely to have to make recourse to public funds (e.g. social security, housing benefit and so on) in order to support them. People who leave the country on long visits to families overseas find it difficult to re-enter or claim permanent residence in Britain. Even those whose entry is technically guaranteed (e.g. East African Asians waiting in India), face long queues at the few points of access in the origin zones.

The similarity between British and Canadian policy here is that the "families" eligible for reunion must all conform to the heterosexual norm. The only partners eligible for entry are those bound by marriage to a person of the opposite sex. The national identities constructed through immigration legislation are thus gendered as well as racialized, and they contribute to what might be called the sexing of space.

In Britain, this sexing is explicitly patriarchal, since men have more *de facto* rights than women to have their spouse join them (Leigh 1986). It is also Eurocentric, and because of the kind of family it portrays as the norm, it has always favoured migrants from Europe over those from the New Commonwealth. This preference persisted through the immigration debates of the late 1980s. MPs argued that family reunion should occur overseas on the assumption that "If two parties to a marriage share a common language, surely it is more appropriate, more humane and more enlightened for the happy couple to settle in the land of their common language" (Hansard 1988: 1459, col. 421). This kind of argument, as Miles (1989) shows, has been used time and again "to support the introduction of yet further restrictions on the entry to Britain of dependants, wives and husbands of earlier migrants from the New Commonwealth or of their British born children. " (p. 49). Even, perhaps especially, in the sphere of family reunion, therefore, the interdependency between immigration legislation and ideas about nationhood is confirmed.

Conclusion

The case studies of Canada and Britain provide some important insights into the relationships between immigration control and nation-building. Their common experience confirms that, because immigration legislation is selective, it has a symbolic as well as a practical rôle. This selectivity ensures that nations are only partly described by lines on a map: they are bounded, too, by the policies and practices which regulate access to territory. At a time of unprecedented global mobility, spatial boundaries may no longer be significant for what they physically contain, but they are increasingly important for who they symbolically exclude.

Despite common origins, the form and consequences of the relationships between immigration control and nation-building in Canada and Britain are in one sense quite different. British immigration policies speak of an enduring national character formed in antiquity, anchored to territory, and accessed by lineage. The legislation which results has typically placed the preservation of (a particular type of) society before the wellbeing of the economy. Canada, on the other hand, has a self-identity driven by immigration and shaped by policies which favour capital and entrepreneurial skills irrespective of cultural conformity. British debate has thus hinged on the question of immigration *control* and is underpinned by the principle of "racial" exclusivity, while Canadian discourse has centred on ideas about *regulation* and is guided by the principle of economic selectivity.

Despite these local differences, some effects of the two forms of immigration legislation are strikingly similar. They are both about the construction of not only distinctively and differently bounded nations but also a fundamentally divided, and unyieldingly heterosexual, world. The geographical boundaries of nations define the spaces in which people must live, and to which they must gain access if they are to exercise certain rights and entitlements. Immigration policy uses ideas about the link between people and place to ration these resources and, in the end, to segregate the wealthy from the poor on a global scale. Viewed from this perspective, both countries have put the parochial aims of nation-building before a more universal code of human rights.

Acknowledgements

The ideas developed in this chapter formed part of my unpublished inaugural lecture at the University of Edinburgh on 15 October 1992. I am grateful for the assistance provided by the Canadian High Commission in London, and for information and discussion provided by the Ministère des Communautés Culturelles et de l'Immigration de la Gouvernement du Québec and by the Parti Québécois. Thanks are also due to the helpful and resourceful staff of the National Library in Ottawa, and to Professor Audrey Kobayashi for providing a range of documents and source materials on immigration to Canada. I am especially grateful to Jan Penrose for many hours of discussion and debate.

Notes

1. Some key changes over the past 30 years are discussed by Castles (1991).
2. At this time, Canada's immigration legislation (dating from 1919) provided for the deportation of non-citizens on relief.
3. A review of the use of Canadian law to legitimize racist exclusionism is provided by Kobayashi (nd).
4. In 1908, measures were introduced to refuse entry to immigrants who arrived "otherwise than by continuous journey from the countries of which they were natives or citizens". The only company which provided one continuous journey from India was prohibited by the Canada government from selling through-tickets (Bolaria & Li 1988).
5. A stated aim of the 1952 Immigration Act was to increase the size of the population.
6. This was an important pre-requisite of securing India's place in the Commonwealth (Moore 1987).
7. A Royal Commission on Bilingualism and Biculturalism was appointed in 1963 largely in response to the Quiet Revolution which had begun to transform the province of Quebec.
8. It has been argued that, by limiting immigration during this period, Britain lost ground economically to the rest of Europe, which maintained a more buoyant labour recruitment programme (Freeman 1979).

9. In May 1982 a freeze was imposed on the entry to Canada of selected workers.
10. Since the early 1970s, Canadian fertility levels have been below replacement value.
11. The Immigration Act 1976 demanded the setting of immigration levels with a view to gearing immigration not simply to the economy but also to fulfilling demographic requirements. However, until the mid–1980s, what actually happened was "a continuation of a short-term "tap-on, tap-off" approach to immigration planning based on fluctuations in unemployment levels" (Employment and Immigration Canada 1987: 10).
12. The latest targets were announced in a press release documenting a speech to Parliament by Minister of Employment and Immigration, Barbara McDougall. The aim, she declared, was to raise immigration to its postwar high and to "sustain our conviction that immigrants make a valuable contribution to Canada, enriching our society, our economy, and our tradition of tolerance that is the envy of the world". Immigration revamp. *Canada News* (July 1992), 1–3.
13. In 1960, the "traditional" source countries (of White caucasian migrants) made up 90 per cent of the immigration flow; these countries now account for less than one-third of new landings.
14. This requires immigration legislation to promote (among other things) Canada's domestic and national interests, enrich its bilingual character, and foster a strong economy.
15. This Act distinguished (in a way that British legislation never has done) refugee migration from other forms on the grounds that the motivations, standards and procedures that may be necessary for the general immigration programme could be inhumane when applied to refugees.
16. It was awarded to the people as a whole, reflecting the importance to the refugee programme of the sponsorship initiative, whereby groups of 5 or more people can sponsor a refugee whose status has been confirmed by an officer abroad.
17. Canada signed in 1969, after a delay caused entirely by "the issue of our continued sovereignty to exercise our own choice in whom we would and would not accept" (Weiner 1988: 234).
18. Namely people eligible for asylum under previous treaties and conventions, people who have fled their countries owing to "a well founded fear of persecution" (by reason of race, religion, nationality or political opinion) and are unable or unwilling to take up protection from their home government, or to return to their country of origin.
19. Paragraph 114 (1) d) and e) of the 1976 Immigration Act allows the government to designate classes of persons whose admission can be in accordance with "Canada's humanitarian tradition with respect to the displaced and persecuted". Currently there are three designated classes: political prisoners and oppressed persons (restricted to citizens of Chile, El Salvador and Guatemala); self-exile persons (former residents of the Soviet Union, its European satellites and Albania, but with no new admissions after 1 September 1990); Indo-Chinese (limited to Cambodians from 1 September 1990).
20. The government aims to assist only those refugees abroad who cannot avail themselves of voluntary repatriation or local integration. "Refugees selected abroad by Canada are, therefore, those who legitimately require third-country resettlement" (Employment and Immigration Canada 1989: 4).
21. Canada does have programmes to admit refugees with special needs, viz. the Tuberculosis Programme for Refugees, the Joint Assistance Programme and the Handicapped Refugee Programme. Intake is limited, however, because receiving provinces (who will be responsible for welfare costs) must agree to the

admission.

22. One consequence is that, on the whole, refugee migrants have prospered economically after settlement within Canada (Samuel 1984).

23. In 1985, in *Harbhajan Singh et al. vs The Minister of Employment and Immigration*, the Supreme Court ruled in favour of the appellants to the effect that, under the Canadian Bill of Rights and the Canadian Charter of Rights and Freedoms, anyone who succeeds in gaining access to Canadian territory has the right to an oral hearing and the right to stay in Canada until it has occurred.

References

Abella, I. & H. Troper 1983. *None is too many*. Toronto: Lester Publishing.

Adachi, K. 1991. *The enemy that never was*. Toronto: McClelland & Stewart.

Akbari, A. H. 1989. *Net impact of different immigrant groups on Canadians. Some evidence from the 1956–80 cohort*. Ottawa: Employment and Immigration Canada.

Angus Reid Group 1989. *Immigration to Canada: aspects of public opinion*. Winnipeg: ARG (for Employment and Immigration Canada).

Ashford, D. E. 1981. *Policy and politics in Britain*. Oxford: Basil Blackwell.

Atchison, J. 1984. Patterns of Australian and Canadian immigration 1900–83. *International Migration* 22, 4–32.

Atchison, J. 1988. Immigration in two federations: Canada and Australia. *International Migration* 26, 5–32.

Avery, D. H. 1977. The immigrant industrial worker in Canada 1896–1919: the vertical mosaic as historical reality. In *Identities: the impact of ethnicity on Canadian society*, W. Isajiw (ed.), 15–33. Toronto: Peter Martin Associates.

Avery, D. 1979. *Dangerous foreigners*. Toronto: McClelland & Stewart.

Baker, D. C. 1979. Ethnicity, development and power: Canada in comparative perspective. In *Identities: the impact of ethnicity on Canadian society*, W. Isajiw (ed.), 109–31. Toronto: Peter Martin.

Baldwin-Edwards, M. 1992. Recent changes in European immigration policies. *Journal of European Social Policy* 2, 53–6.

Bevan, V. 1986. *The development of British immigration law*. London: Croom Helm.

Bolaria, B. S. & P. S. Li 1988. *Racial oppression in Canada*. 2nd edn. Toronto: Garamond Press.

Breton, R. 1984. Multiculturalism and Canadian nation-building. In *The politics of gender, ethnicity and language in Canada*, A. Cairns & C. Williams (eds), 27–66. Toronto: University of Toronto Press.

Cappon, P. 1975. The Green Paper: immigration as a tool of profit. *Canadian Ethnic Studies* 7, 50–54.

Castles, S. 1991. Migrations and minorities in Europe: perspectives for the 1990s: Twelve hypotheses. Paper presented to the conference on Racism and Migration in Europe. Warwick: Centre for Research on Ethnic Relations.

Chodos, R., R. Murphy, E. Hamovitch 1991. *The unmaking of Canada*. Toronto: James Lorimer.

Department of Manpower and Immigration 1974. *The immigration programme*. Canadian immigration and population study, Vol. 2. Ottawa: Information Canada.

Dirks, G. E. 1977. *Canada's refugee policy*. Montreal: McGill–Queen's University Press.

Ebanks, G. E. 1990. Immigration: its nature and impact. *Canadian Studies on Population* 17, 13–17.

Economic Council of Canada 1991. *New faces in the crowd: economic and social impacts of immigration*. Ottawa: Canadian Communications Group.

Elliott, J. L. 1979. Canadian immigration: a historical assessment. In *Ethnic groups in Canada*, J. L. Elliott (ed.), 51–76. Scarborough Ontario: Prentice-Hall

Elliott, J. L. & A. Fleras 1990. Immigration and the Canadian ethnic mosaic. In *Race and ethnic relations in Canada*, P. Li (ed.), 51–76. Toronto: Oxford University Press.

Employment and Immigration Canada 1987. *Demography and immigration in Canada: challenge and opportunity*. Ottawa: Immigration Policy Development Immigration Group.

Employment and Immigration Canada 1989a. *Immigration to Canada: issues for discussion*. Ottawa (public affairs and immigration policy branch).

Employment and Immigration Canada 1989b. *Annual report to Parliament on future immigration levels*. Ottawa.

Findlay, A. 1992. *The economic impact of immigration to the United Kingdom: trends and policy implications*. APRU Discussion Paper 92/5, Glasgow University.

Finkel, A. 1986. Canadian immigration policy and the cold war, 1945–1980. *Journal of Canadian Studies* 21, 53–70.

Foot, D. K. 1986. Population ageing and immigration policy in Canada: implications and prescriptions. Employment and Immigration Commission Working Paper 1. Ottawa.

Francis, R. D., R. Jones, D. B. Smith 1988. *Destinies. Canadian history since confederation*. Toronto: Prentice-Hall.

Freeman, G. P. 1979. *Immigrant labour and racial conflict in industrial societies*. Princeton, NJ: Princeton University Press.

Girard, R. 1988. Refugee determination in Canada. In *Human rights and the protection of refugees under International Law*, A. Nash (ed.), 273–6. Montreal: Canadian Human Rights Foundation/Institute for Research on Public Policy.

Hall, S., C. Crichter, T. Jefferson, J. Clarke, B. Roberts 1978. *Policing the crisis: mugging, the state, and law and order*. London: Macmillan.

Hawkins, F. 1988. *Canada and immigration: public policy and public concern*. 2nd edn. Montreal & Kingston: McGill–Queen's University Press.

Hawkins, F. 1989. *Critical years in immigration: Canada and Australia compared*. Montreal & Kingston: McGill–Queen's University Press.

Hersak, G. & D. Thomas 1988. *Recent Canadian developments arising from international migration*. Ottawa: Employment and Immigration Canada.

Howith, H. G. 1988. *Immigration levels planning: the first decade*. Ottawa: Employment and Immigration Canada.

Hughes, D. R. & E. Kallen 1974. *The anatomy of racism: Canadian dimensions*. Montreal: Harvest House.

Immigration Canada 1989. *Immigration to Canada: Economic aspects*. Ottawa: Employment and Immigration Canada (public affairs and immigration policy branch).

Immigration Canada 1990. *Report on the consultations for immigration 1991–1995*. Ottawa: Public Affairs Division and Immigration Policy and Programme Branch.

Joint Council for the Welfare of Immigrants 1989. *Unequal migrants*. CRER Policy Papers in Ethnic Relations 13, University of Warwick.

Joly, D. 1989. *Harmonising European asylum policy*. CRER Policy Papers in Ethnic Relations 15, University of Warwick.

Kallen, E. 1982. *Ethnicity and human rights in Canada*. Toronto: Gage.

Kaye, R. 1992. British refugee policy and 1992: the breakdown of a policy community. *Journal of Refugee Studies* 5, 47–67.

Kobayashi, A. 1990. Racism and the law in Canada: a geographical perspective. *Urban Geography* 11, 447–73.

Leigh, S. 1986. Family resettlement problems. In *Towards a just immigration policy*, A. Dummett (ed.), 169–75. London: The Cobden Trust.

McLaren, A. 1990. *Our own master race*. Toronto: McClelland & Stewart.

Malarek, V. 1987. *Heaven's Gate. Canada's Immigration Fiasco*. Toronto: Macmillan

Marr, W. 1985. The Canadian temporary visa programme as an alternative to the European guest worker scheme. *International Migration* 23, 81–395.

Miles, R. 1989. Migration discourse, British sociology and the "race relations" paradigm. *Migration* 6, 29–53.

Miles, R. 1990. Whatever happened to the sociology of migration? *Work, Employment and Society* 4, 281–98.

Miles, R. 1991. The articulation of racism and nationalism: reflections on European history. Paper presented to the conference on Racism and migration in Europe in the 1990s, Kenilworth, September.

Moore, R. J. 1987. *Making the New Commonwealth*. Oxford: Oxford University Press.

Nash, A. 1988a. Our enterprising immigrants. *Policy Options Politique* (December), 19–23.

Nash, A. 1988b. *Human rights and the protection of refugees under International Law*. Nova Scotia: Canadian Human Rights Foundation / Institute for Research on Public Policy.

Nash, A. 1989a. *International refugee migration and the Canadian public policy response. Discussion paper* 89. B. 1. Ottawa: Studies in Social Policy.

Nash, A. 1989b. We can meet the refugee challenge. *Policy Options Politique* (September), 21–6.

Nash, A. 1991. The Hong Kong brain drain. *Options* 12, 21–23.

Palmer, H. 1990. Reluctant hosts: Anglo-Canadian views of multiculturalism in the twentieth century. In *Readings in Canadian history post-confederation*, R. D. Francis & D. B. Smith (eds), 192–209. Toronto: Holt, Rhinehart & Winston.

Platt, C. 1990. The Immigration Act 1988. CRER Policy Papers in Ethnic Relations 16, University of Warwick.

Proudfoot, B. 1989. The setting of immigration levels in Canada since the immigration act, 1976. *British Journal of Canadian Studies* 4, 233–56.

Purves, G. 1980. *Humanitarian immigration and Canadian immigration policy*. Ottawa: Library of Parliament, Research Branch.

Reitz, J. G. 1988. The institutional structure of immigration as a determinant of inter-racial competition: a comparison of Britain and Canada. *International Migration Review* 22, 117–46.

Richmond, A. H. 1979. Immigration and racial prejudice in Britain and Canada. In *Two nations: many cultures*, J. L. Elliott (ed.), 290–310. Scarborough Ontario: Prentice-Hall.

Richmond, A. H. 1988. Caribbean immigrants in Britain and Canada: socio-economic adjustment. *International Migration* 26, 365–86.

Richmond, A. 1991. Immigration and multiculturalism in Canada and Australia: the contradictions and crises of the 1980s. *International Journal of Canadian Studies* 3, 87–110.

Robinson, G. (ed.) 1991. *A social geography of Canada*. Toronto: Dundurn Press.

Samuel, T. J. 1984. Economic adaptation of refugees in Canada: experience of a quarter century. *International Migration* 22, 45–55.

Samuel, T. J. 1988a. Family class immigrants to Canada 1981–84. Part 1. Labour force activity aspects. *International Migration* 26, 171–86.

Samuel, T. J. 1988b. Family class immigrants to Canada 1981–1984: Part 2. Some aspects of social adaptation. *International Migration* 26, 287–99.

Samuel, T. J. & T. Conyers 1986. The employment effects of immigration: a balance sheet approach. Employment and Immigration Canada, Working Paper 1. Ottawa.

Samuel, T. J. & B. Woloski 1985. The labour market experiences of Canadian Immigrants. *International Migration* 23, 225–50.

Satzewich, V. 1990. Rethinking post–1945 migration to Canada: towards a political economy of labour migration. *International Migration* **28**, 327–46.

Satzewich, V. 1991. Capital accumulation and state formation: the contradictions of international migration. In *Social issues and contradictions in Canadian society*, B. S. Bolaria (ed.), 91–107. Toronto: HBJ Holt.

Segal, G. 1990. *Immigrating to Canada*. 9th edn. Vancouver: Self-Counsel Press.

Smith, S. J. 1989. *The politics of "race" and residence*. Cambridge: Polity Press.

Smith, S. J. 1992. Where to draw the line? Inaugural Lecture, University of Edinburgh.

Stasiulis, D. 1991. Symbolic representation and the numbers game: Tory policies on "race" and visible minorities. In *How Ottawa spends*, F. Abele (ed.), 229–67. Ottawa: Carleton University Press.

Taylor, C. 1987. *Demography and immigration in Canada: Challenge and Opportunity*. Ottawa: Canadian Employment and Immigration.

Torvato, F. & S. S. Halli 1983. Ethnicity and migration in Canada. *International Migration Review* **17**, 245–67.

Troper, H. M. 1972. *Only farmers need apply*. Toronto: University of Toronto Press.

Weiner, G. 1988. Canada's refugee policy. In *Human rights and the protection of refugees under international law*, A. Nash (ed.). Ottawa: Institute for Research on Public Policy.

Weinfeld, M. 1988. Immigration and Canada's population future. Working Paper on Social Behaviour (no number), Department of Sociology, McGill University, Montreal.

Whitaker, R. 1987. *Double standard*. Toronto: Lester and Orpen Dennys.

White. P. M. & T. J. Samuel 1991. Immigration and ethnic diversity in urban Canada. *International Journal of Canadian Studies* **3**, 69–85.

Widgen, J. 1989. Europe and international migration in the future. In *Refugees and international relations*, G. Leesher & L. Monahan (eds), 49–61. Oxford: Oxford University Press.

Wydrzynski, C. J. 1979–80. Refugees and the Immigration Act. *McGill Law Journal* **25**, 154–92.

PART II
CONSTRUCTIONS
OF ABORIGINALITY

The chapters in Part II are concerned with groups who fall outside hegemonic definitions of the imagined national community but who challenge their exclusion, calling into question the legitimacy of those who wield such power. Both chapters focus on the political significance of territory, and question the neutrality of conventional modes of representation (in newspapers, official reports and geographical mapping).

In her chapter on Redfern, an Aboriginal housing enclave in Sydney, **Kay Anderson** explores the ways in which constructions of Aboriginality intersect with constructions of particular urban places in mutually reinforcing ways. The chapter reveals the constructedness of categories and their capacity to shape concrete experience. Those who were anxious to invalidate Aboriginal claims used pejorative names and stigmatized characteristics to construct a negatively racialized place. Those who supported Aboriginal claims invoked equally essentialist but positively valued constructs as a strategy for promoting their reformist vision of the relationship between people and place. The Redfern case study reveals how constructions of identity and place grow out of asymmetrical power relations. In this particular case, Aboriginal claims to territory were simultaneously contested *and* endorsed by European authorities, acting at different scales according to changing political agenda.

The interconnections between "race", place and nation are central to **Jane Jacobs's** chapter, which shows how spatial representations help to reinforce hegemonic constructions of the nation. The priority accorded to conventional cartographic representation forces Aboriginal people to adopt alien conceptions of themselves and of their relationship to the land in order to secure a place within this static conception of the nation. Maps and mapping come to serve as means of inscribing political domination in ways that homogenize, unify and flatten out the complexities of human experience.

For Aboriginal Australians, the relationship between spatial representation and power means that land-rights claims must be asserted in terms of a fixed and "authentic" identity that can be precisely located in specifically defined areas. As Jacobs demonstrates, this requirement can be subverted by conforming with the need to produce maps while simultaneously changing their form. By replacing solid lines with hazy borderlands, and pinpoints with smudges, Aborigines have portrayed themselves as fluid in time and space. In so doing they are able to challenge hegemonic constructions of nation and identity.

CHAPTER THREE

Constructing geographies:
"race", place and the making of Sydney's Aboriginal Redfern

KAY J. ANDERSON

Introduction

Since April 1973, when the tiny pocket of the Sydney suburb of Redfern was set aside by the Commonwealth government of Australia for Aboriginal residential use (see Fig. 3.1), the area has been transformed by a range of languages into a district of national distinction and notoriety. For many White and some Black Australians, Redfern promptly became a "slum", a "ghetto", with physical and social problems wrought by racial tensions and the "breakdown" of traditional Aboriginal culture in the city. It was a perception sponsored by all agencies of the White media which began to filter "Aboriginal Redfern" through a screen of racialized representations of the kind that today surround Brixton in London, England, or parts of South Central Los Angeles in the United States. For some Black and White activists, on the other hand, Redfern assumed other meanings in the struggle to acquire the area for Aboriginal residence. Redfern became a sphere of indigenous protest, an heroic site of resistance to European culture and colonialist control. Situated at the very core of metropolitan Australia, Redfern held out the promise of being a "heartland" of Black Australian affairs.

The narratives surrounding this urban space have not only afforded Aboriginal Redfern cultural distinction, however, but have also shaped the area's concrete experience and relations. Indeed, as we shall see in this chapter, imaginative projections about "race" and place informed the wider

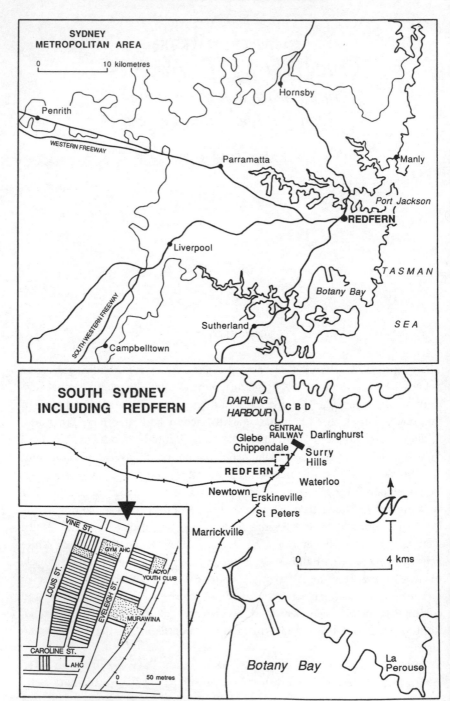

Figure 3.1 Location of Sydney's Redfern and terraces owned by the Aboriginal Housing Company (1992).

institutional processes that brought the settlement into being. The cognitive operations performed on "Redfern" in the early 1970s entered formal politics at all three levels of Australian government, where they were assimilated into more inclusive political agenda. In this chapter I seek to demonstrate the institutional "translations" undergone by place representations in the period leading up to the establishment of the settlement in 1973. More specifically, I attempt to uncover the connections between place/"race" images and the political projects out of which this district evolved. In so doing, the chapter brings into view, through an Australian case study, the intersection of racialized languages (imposed by powerful groups) and discourses of resistance (invoked by minorities to renegotiate power relations) in the socio-political construction of place.

Since the late 1960s, challenges to colonialist control have been increasingly evident in the White hinterlands of imperialism, including Australia, where the contestation between settler–invader and indigenous populations has been progressively destabilizing the authority of the Anglo cultural framework imposed in 1788. By 1992, the Aboriginal land rights movement had effected the return of some 12 per cent of Australia's land (Young 1992), while at the same time throwing into moral and legal question the past two centuries of European land ownership and use. It seems clear that the re-colonization of territory by indigenous people holds a very real capacity to transform the deeply institutionalized relations of dominance and subordination handed down by 200 years of dispossession. Significantly, this challenge acquired a major part of its impetus at the core of European, urban, capitalist Australia. In 1973 the Commonwealth of Australia, overriding opposition from lower levels of government and local White residents, granted an Aboriginal Housing Company in Sydney's suburb of Redfern the funds to purchase a row of (approximately forty) Victorian terraces for Black housing. The struggle at Redfern in the early 1970s was an important moment in Australia's cultural relations, repositioning certain European players and demonstrating the political significance of territory – and the rhetorical contests surrounding it – in the renegotiation of dominance. The story of this place-based agitation forms the basis of this chapter.

Geography and the study of localities

Localities open windows onto the complex interactions that connect the spheres of politics, culture and economy. Researchers have begun to demonstrate this in many useful forays – mostly in the United Kingdom – into the local impacts of deindustrialization (see, for example, Massey 1984, Cooke

1989). There, the concern has been to examine from a realist perspective the "spatial ranges of the many causal elements that impinge on a chosen area" (Bagguley et al. 1990: 10). However, despite the attempt of some scholars in that tradition of locality research to examine people's experience of restructuring (see, for example, Bagguley et al. 1990, ch. 4), that tradition of work has largely neglected the manner in which localities are *constituted* by subjects who perceive, represent and over time construct them. The research has focused on the production of (predefined) places, as if the fundamental determining processes are economic, and as if the process of *place-making* can be wholly captured by measuring statistical changes over time in labour forces, gender relations, market pressures, and so on. Yet as Jackson (1991) argues, the decisions and practices of manufacturers, labourers, executives – and indeed all agents – are "culturally encoded" with definitions of, and languages about, places, identities, work and family. These notions do not inhabit a free-floating world of ideas and speech, but rather inform the very processes out of which are "made" – morphologically and cognitively – the places that have been the subject of investigation (see also Paasi 1991, Pratt 1991, Smith 1992). Research that opposes the ideological and material spheres in the study of localities, therefore, often depends upon a false dichotomy.

The Aboriginal settlement in inner Sydney, so remarked upon in Australian society today, emerged in 1973 out of a matrix of intersecting pressures in Australia's colonial encounter. The dimensions of this matrix can be illuminated by a constructionist research strategy that seeks to uncover the contextualized process through which that locality was produced as a "fact", a process in which the relations between ideologies, material conditions and practices were thoroughly interconnected. With regard to ideologies surrounding the proposal for Black housing in Redfern in 1972, we shall see how distinctive constructions of an "Aboriginal place" did not lie fallow in people's minds but became political instruments in the hands of social actors, most notably Black and White activists, politicians, bureaucrats, the police, unions, resident action groups and others. Those who envisaged the housing project (romantically) as a "Black commune" became engaged in conflict with those who saw it (defensively) as a "Black ghetto", in a battle not simply of verbal quibbles and imaginative projections, but for practical and political control over a contested piece of metropolitan land.

Just as due attention must be paid in the historical analysis of Redfern to the functions and purposes of the diverse representations of Aboriginal housing, so were there decisive material contexts for housing concerns in inner Sydney in the early 1970s. Capitalist modes of control had, since the late nineteenth century, progressively transformed the productive basis of

Aboriginal economy and society in New South Wales, leaving many Aborigines without a resource base and dependent on urban industrialists for unskilled employment. This was the circumstance of many Aborigines in Redfern in the post- Second World War period. Not only were they, and their urban counterparts elsewhere, the most legally and culturally stigmatized members of Australian society in the late 1960s (and arguably still today), they were also the country's poorest inhabitants according to every indicator of economic wellbeing (Lipmann 1970). The material circumstances of Sydney's Aborigines in the late 1960s were desperate (see Scott 1973) and, in many senses, the campaign for improved housing at Redfern constituted the mobilization of an underclass to secure greater control over the conditions of its existence.

But the local agitation for housing in inner Sydney in the early 1970s was leverage for a far more ambitious anti-hegemonic struggle on the part of local Aborigines and their non-Aboriginal allies. The campaign was directed not just at securing shelter for a group of local Black squatters, but also at gaining access to collective control over a piece of strategically located territory awaiting redevelopment according to capitalist modes of urban transformation. We shall see that the quest for a place at the heart of metropolitan Australia in the early 1970s signalled a bold intervention in a capitalist, colonialist regime – one fuelled by an oppositional culture and a resurgent language of struggle and resistance.

Localities such as Aboriginal Redfern, then, are "complex amalgams" (Dear 1988) whose critical analysis is helpfully undertaken following Abrams' (1982) project for historical sociology, "in process, in time". Following the realist approach mentioned above, to conceptualize localities as unidimensional byproducts of economic regimes would seem to be as restricting as the approach growing out of some branches of cultural studies that places/ landscapes are mere "texts" to be "read" for their cultural meaning (see, for example, Relph 1987, Tanaka 1984). It seems more helpful to conceptualize localities as concrete and symbolic forms undergoing continuous construction and transformation in structured circumstances. Embedded within the making of localities (such as Aboriginal Redfern) are interlocking semiotic *and* material processes, whose complex interactions need for their adequate theorization to be problematized and historicized. Thus framed, locality studies have the potential to illuminate the interacting spheres and phases in the structuring of social relations.

Racial discourse: emancipatory and defensive idioms

The seizure of "Aboriginality" for political purposes on the part of both advocates and critics of Redfern's housing project, reveals an interesting conjuncture in the history of, and theorizing about, cultural relations in British settler societies. Elsewhere, I have demonstrated for a Canadian city the connection of the locality called "Chinatown" to an ethnically based hegemony that grew out of a global imperialist regime and a long tradition of Orientalist learning (Anderson 1991). While emphasizing the changing forms of Chinatown's racialization over time, that story also specified the constitutional limits to hegemonic practices in Vancouver and the strategies of people of Chinese origin in managing their "racial" classification. It is useful, however, to examine further the paradoxical manner in which at certain moments in the negotiation of power relations marginalized peoples appeal to the racialized identities assigned them; that is, certain groups engage a "strategic essentialism" (Alcoff 1988, Pettman 1992) through which to articulate their opposition and secure reforms. This process re-inscribes difference and enjoins a range of influences in the continuing construction of racialized identities.

Such a calling up of difference occurred in Sydney's Redfern in the early 1970s when, as stated above, the local campaign for housing was transformed by certain activists of (diverse) indigenous origins and non-Aboriginal backgrounds into a "pan-Aboriginal" struggle against "White" Australia. The referent for this campaign was not some permanent foundation of Aboriginal identity[1] – a stable heritage handed on from the past – but instead a cultural and political invention invoked to serve contemporary purposes. At a time when the status and conditions of Australia's first settlers was coming into view on the national political agenda – in 1967 a referendum determined that Aborigines would for the first time be counted as Australian citizens – the activists harnessed an ideology of "Aboriginality" infusing it with oppositional value in part through claims to territory.[2] The effort met with success, as we shall see, when in April 1973 one of Australia's first "land rights" victories was proclaimed at Louis and Eveleigh Streets in Sydney's Redfern.

Yet, at the same time, the struggle over housing in Redfern reactivated a different – although in the history of Australia's cultural relations more enduring – project of domination on the part of certain Europeans. While politicians in the distant capital in Canberra traded in high-sounding rhetoric about "Aboriginal self-determination", seeking to contain the emerging oppositional voices in Aboriginal affairs, authorities closer to the scene in New South Wales and Sydney sought to obstruct the campaign for Black housing. Politicians and officials in local and state governments drew on an established (pejorative) set of images of Aboriginality, not out of any simple "prejudice", but in order to win the support of local White residents. Here again, then, concepts of Aboriginality were politically sponsored and manipulated. Media and police surveillance also relied upon such stigmatized characterizations of Aboriginality, helping to construct a negatively racialized Redfern that has not eroded with time.

The continuities and discontinuities with the past suggest that, by the 1970s, "Aboriginality" was providing a medium for the construction of new levels of resistance to White Australian hegemony, while simultaneously structuring a persistent racist targeting. Versions of Aboriginality were being (selectively) chosen and ascribed, through a complex interplay with a state which was itself divided by scale and function. The contradictions were also evident in relation to place politics. Spatial concentration at Redfern afforded a territorial base for the advancement of Aboriginal affairs, while at the same time rendering residents vulnerable to racist currents in the dominant culture. I shall demonstrate, then, that Aboriginal Redfern was constructed out of multiple and contradictory discourses and practices, the deconstruction of which clears the way for a non-essentialized theorization of not only Aboriginal identity but also of the place "Redfern".

In what follows, I offer a preliminary phase in the development of such a theorization of Redfern by examining the emergence of the Aboriginal settlement in inner Sydney in the early 1970s. The story relies on previously undisclosed primary sources, collected from three levels of government, and interviews with key actors still alive today.[3] Whereas elsewhere I document in detail the sequence of the conflict over housing (Anderson 1993), here the story is condensed to present the early struggles over the meaning of Redfern, struggles over the right to construct Redfern according to particular versions of it, and Redfern as contestable space. While ambitious questions concerning the significance of this place-based action in the transformation of Australia's hierarchical social relations must await a later stage of research (addressing phases of Redfern's structuring into the present), some conceptual implications are drawn together at the end of this chapter. It begins with some background about Aborigines in Sydney in the 1960s, then proceeds to an outline of the campaign for housing in the early 1970s that drew into conflict the utopian voices of "change" and the defensive voices of White racism.

Redfern's underclass in the 1960s

During the 1930s, as the myth of White Australia flourished and rural recession in New South Wales deepened, Aborigines in reserves throughout the state migrated to Sydney in search of job opportunities and fresh beginnings (Parbury 1986). The movement set in train a flow of migrants from diverse backgrounds who were attracted to the cheap housing, unskilled employment, and transport opportunities afforded by central, working-class neighbourhoods such as Redfern. By 1971, there were between four and nine thousand Aborigines living in inner Sydney, the large majority of whom were "living in the worst housing conditions", according, in 1970, to an officer from a local welfare organization (South Sydney Community Aid, submission, 30 September 1970). In 1971, a survey by the Commonwealth Office of Aboriginal Affairs discovered problems as serious as malnutrition among the city's Aboriginal population, which were attributed to poverty and to unsanitary and crowded living conditions. Another report pointed to discrimination in the housing and rental market in its analysis of Aboriginal welfare (Laurie to Director, 20 August 1971, in Department of Aboriginal Affairs [hereafter DAA] R76/89). The attention of the first federal agency concerned with Aboriginal affairs was focused by these investigations, but, as we shall see, no formal action was taken until a new government was elected late in 1972.

Not that South Sydney's Aborigines were inclined to wait for bureaucratic interventions on their behalf. In 1971, the first Aboriginal community-based services to be established in Australia were opened in Redfern by Black and White activists, who sought to address through their own efforts the plight of inner Sydney's Aborigines. Most notably, the Aboriginal Legal Service and the Aboriginal Medical Service were set up – in the face of much opposition from the Council of the City of South Sydney (about which more later) – to manage the urgent problems of police harassment and poor health of their clientele. These agencies provided the impetus for Aboriginal assertiveness and for a collective identification with the suburb of Redfern, such that by 1972 Aboriginal activist Gary Williams could say: "Redfern is the heart and Redfern is the community. . . . At the moment, Redfern is where it is happening" (cited in transcript of radio interview, Murphy papers). However, it was the lack of access to shelter that created a generic vulnerability to colour and class-based oppression for inner Sydney's Aborigines as a group of concerned locals were to find late in 1972.

The practice of squatting in vacant premises was a popular mode of existence for many inner-Sydney Aborigines in the 1950s and 1960s. This precarious lifestyle brought them into frequent contact with not only land-interested groups but also law enforcement agencies including police and the courts. One encounter in late October 1972 saw police arrest, and charge with trespassing, a group of some fifteen Aboriginal squatters who had taken refuge in derelict premises awaiting redevelopment in Redfern's Louis Street. A bitter trial ensued and a verdict was eventually returned that would, if unchallenged, have confined the squatters to an extended period of shelter in the Redfern jail. The rest of this chapter consists of the story of this group of destitute Aborigines.

At the nearby Redfern Presbytery two young priests, who were known to the squatters' lawyer, saw an opportunity to politicize the Aborigines' plight in the context of rising concern, from some quarters of Australian society, about the status of the country's first settlers. Aboriginal demands for land rights, employment and access to education and health were also beginning to filter into media and government circles. The priests sought to connect themselves with these critiques emerging in new Left politics in the late 1960s (Docker 1988), although their immediate concern was Sydney's Catholic Church establishment, an institution which, in the priests' eyes, had become insulated from human rights concerns. The convicted Aborigines became the priests' *cause célèbre* and, on hearing the guilty verdict at the Redfern courthouse, they offered to make available the church's school hall for the temporary shelter of the homeless men. An emergency refuge supplying food, medicine, shelter and acceptance was soon opened at the hall, funded by the proceeds of a bottle collection operation that the Aborigines themselves undertook.

Before long the presbytery's unconventional hostel attracted the notice of other Aborigines and within weeks over fifty Blacks had made a new home of the church hall. The refuge also caught the attention of local White residents, however, some of whom included members of the Council of the City of South Sydney. Vocal among them were Aldermen Terry Murphy and Keith Challenger, who adopted the unorthodox arrangement at the church hall as a political mission, and set out to break the alliances being forged there. Their strategies included scrutiny of the hostel for compliance with council bylaws and within weeks council declared the hall a "danger to children and community health" and had found a pretext in the lodging house bylaw to serve an eviction notice on the Catholic Archdiocese of Sydney (Treffery, St Vincent's Church, Redfern, unpublished report, 3 November 1972, in Murphy papers). The trustees of the church were given seven days to cease residential use of the school hall, so provoking a campaign for Black housing that would defiantly bypass local (and state) government agencies and seek to attract to its cause more powerful allies in the national capital.

Politicizing difference: emancipatory idioms

The priests and Aboriginal activists who ran the hostel operation at the Redfern Presbytery knew well that they were plunged in a micro-encounter with an adversarial colonial legacy. When South Sydney councillors refused to entertain a proposal for alternative housing for the homeless Aborigines somewhere in their constituency, on the grounds that "encouragement of this nature would bring others into the municipality" (cited in report of meeting between members of council and Ingrid Sandberg and Peter Bradley, 5 December 1972, in Murphy papers), a few members of the presbytery team sought to pressurize the elected officials of South Sydney. Father J. Butcher met with the Mayor on 15 November 1972 to ask: "What is this Council going to do about this? What are politicians going to do? Rich developers are buying up land and forcing these people out . . . What is anybody going to do about the Aboriginals?" (cited in report of meeting with the Mayor and priests on 15 November 1972, in Murphy papers). Mayor Hartup insisted that the matter was one for the State Housing Commission. Two weeks later, following a visit by the priests to the housing commissioner, Father T. Kennedy told council in committee: "The Aboriginal group regards itself as one family. . . . They do not want to be broken up but want communal housing" (report of meeting between members of council and representatives of the Catholic Church, 29 November 1972, in Murphy papers).

Meanwhile, enquiries in the latter part of 1972 by the presbytery intelligence revealed that a single developer had bought a row of terraces in nearby Louis Street with a view to upgrading them for high income residential use. The possibility for a communal housing option that the vacant terraces presented was quickly absorbed by the priests and squatters who saw the potential for a territorial base from which to launch a concerted agitation. And not only did the terraces hold out the promise of bloc housing; they were also located, as one priest observed, in full view of passing White passengers to Sydney's Central Station (Ted Kennedy, personal communication, June 1991). Certainly the political significance of a Black settlement at the heart of Australia's premier city was not lost on the presbytery activists. In the ferment of the early 1970s, when communitarian thinking infused many intellectual critiques (see Munro-Clark 1986, Head & Walter 1988), the priests anticipated that a "Black commune" (in the priests' words) at this location would send a message to individualistic White Australia. The conjuncture of purposes fuelled the sense of purpose of the activists who quickly set about making strategic contacts with Commonwealth officials and the New South Wales trade union movement.

The newly formed Aboriginal Housing Committee (AHC), consisting by this stage exclusively of Aborigines, found a receptive ear in Dr H. C. Coombs, of the Sydney branch of the Commonwealth Office of Aboriginal Affairs, in an otherwise disinterested bureaucracy. Coombs's office had been formed in 1967 under the Liberal administration of Howard Holt and it had begun the task of compiling information, for the first time, on the status and conditions of Australia's indigenous population. However, following Holt's death in 1967, there had been little support for the activities of the office from Holt's successor, John Gorton, nor his Minister-in-charge of Aboriginal Affairs, William Wentworth (Coombs 1978, ch. 1). Thus, by late 1972, when a mood-swing was beginning to infiltrate Canberra's political circles, the frustrated members of the office were fully primed for action. A delegation from Redfern met with Coombs in December 1972 and there soon followed a written submission from the AHC calling for "extended housing" in Redfern (Bellear et al. to Coombs, 17 December 1972, in DAA R76/89).

Just as Redfern's destitute Aborigines were a *cause célèbre* for priests seeking distance from the conservative wing of Sydney's Catholic establishment, so did elements in the New South Wales trade union movement see an opportunity to etch their mark in the labour movement by supporting the Aboriginal oppressed. The class-based alliance was to prove particularly effective for the "Black commune" initiative. Bob Pringle, president of the radical Builders' Labourers' Federation (BLF), was especially well versed in socialist critiques of capitalism that were increasingly influential in new Left movements. In the squatters, Pringle saw an opportunity to unite the oppressed classes and support a communal project, one which afforded a "socialist alternative" to the proposed "capitalist development" for Louis Street (cited in Bellear 1976: 23). Armed with this imaginative projection, Pringle placed pressure on Ian Kiernan, owner–developer of the terraces in Louis Street, to offer his houses for the temporary occupation of the presbytery evacuees (Ian Kiernan, personal communication, June 1991). Indeed Pringle went further, threatening Kiernan with a work ban on his future terrace redevelopment project and all of the developer's other Sydney projects, if he didn't agree to release some of his Louis Street terraces. The developer eventually capitulated to pressure and signed documents freeing two of his houses for the squatters who now possessed rights to occupy the terraces and deflect police harassment.

The significance of this intervention in the trajectory of modernist, European urban transformation was not lost on the AHC, whose sense of resistance and defiance appeared to swell by the day. Bob Bellear, president of the committee, announced that Kiernan's offerings were "uninhabitable" and with the assistance of the BLF, the Plumbers' Union, and the squatters' own "mop and bucket brigade", brought up to bylaw standard two of

Kiernan's better terraces . These were in turn occupied by refugees from the church hall. The emancipatory visions of the activists, then, were not merely expressive, but also formative, of the processes out of which this place was being constructed (see Hall 1988: 27). "We are making a stand for Aboriginal land rights", announced Bellear to the press. "This will be Sydney's Aboriginal Embassy." Other houses would be "taken over", Bellear threatened, "until the Labor government gives Aborigines better homes" (*Sydney Daily Telegraph*, 30 December 1972).

The oppositional appeals from Redfern were not only heard but enthusiastically embraced in Canberra where a new Labor government under Gough Whitlam swept to federal office in December 1972. At the seat of federal parliament, the grass-roots agitation could be construed in terms of a radical reform agenda, including in the arena of Aboriginal affairs where a slogan of "self-determination" was creeping into official parlance and discrediting the older management philosophy called "assimilation". A new Ministry of Urban and Regional Affairs could also find merit in a project based on the "rehabilitation" of existing housing in Australia's cities. This was the language with which that ministry sought to distance itself from the discourse and practice of "slum clearance" prevailing in Australian planning circles since the 1950s. The Redfern agitation could thus be drawn into more inclusive political agenda and, by January 1973, Gordon Bryant (Minister for Aboriginal Affairs) saw fit to view for himself the efforts of the local "mop and bucket brigade".

By the time of Bryant's visit, some forty-five Aboriginal members of the clean-up campaign were occupying three of the developer's houses (*Sydney Daily Telegraph*, 2 January 1973). The Minister gave the activists a favourable hearing and, before leaving the site, encouraged the housing committee to lodge a formal application for Commonwealth funding for a "co-operative housing scheme" in the block bound by Louis, Caroline, Eveleigh and Vine Streets. This it did, as well as recruiting an architect who, like other actors we have seen, sought to legitimize his involvement in language consistent with his day and, more particularly, his profession. Colin James, a graduate of Harvard University, appealed to the rhetoric of "self-help" in extending his support to the AHC. "Surely the way out is to get them together so that they can provide their own help", he said. "It is very natural for Aborigines to share their resources", said James, whose design proposed, despite the diverse regional and ethnic origins of Redfern's Aborigines, to combine all the backyards of the terraces in the block into a communal area (cited in transcript of settlement meeting, 25 March 1973, in Murphy papers). Thus inscribed within the proposal were idealizations of Aboriginality that equated it with tradition – a form of racialization that belongs to the "European's spiritualizing gaze" in the words of Rowse (1988: 271) and to which the Black activists in Redfern keenly subscribed. (By 1980, when tenant complaints about violence and vandalism in the area were increasing, a set of tall, corrugated iron fences were restored to each backyard – demonstrating, among other things, the multiplicity of constructs of Aboriginality among Black, as well as between White and Black, Australians).

However, what, in the eyes of the visiting federal minister, might have been a noble badge of indigenous courage in Redfern was a more ominous signal for other government officials. The unannounced ministerial visit from Canberra bristled the vigilant aldermen at the Council of the City of South Sydney. Within weeks, they were rallying their own campaign of resistance that invoked (negative and pejorative) constructs of Aboriginality and Redfern, deriving from quite different discursive sources from those we have met to date.

Politicizing difference: repressive idioms

If Aboriginality offered a source of political and cultural distinctiveness to the Redfern activists, so did it afford the medium through which critics defined and targeted them. The critics' version of Aboriginality departed widely from the resurgent Aboriginality being invoked by the activists, but it was one no less strenuously called up and wielded. For the Labor aldermen who formed a majority on the South Sydney Council, and in particular Terry Murphy and Keith Challenger, the proposal to house Aboriginal squatters foreshadowed a "ghetto" which would "encourage Aboriginal people who are disadvantaged to come into South Sydney which lacks suitable accommodation" (cited in minutes of meeting between Bryant and representatives of AHC, unions, and council, 23 February 1973, in Murphy papers). The council set about obstructing the project, first, by requiring Ian Kiernan (the owner–developer) to clean up the buildings used by the squatters and, secondly, by approving Kiernan's application for renovations to the Louis Street properties on the sole condition that each of the premises provide for single family housing.

The major effort of the aldermen, however, was directed at rallying the opposition of local non-Aboriginal ratepayers. At least two of the councillors did not merely react to local public sentiment, they actively sponsored it. A field officer of the New South Wales Department of Aboriginal Welfare noted the council's pro-active rôle while simultaneously observing "the council has as its images of Aborigines, age old stereotypes such as lazyness [sic], drunkedness [sic], immorality, lack of self and community pride . . . [T]he greatest amount of opposition toward the project stems from the aldermen themselves" (Trotman, 26 March 1973, in NSW Office of Aboriginal Affairs, file F107). By March 1973, the South Sydney Residents' Protection Movement had formed to fight, in its words, the "festering sore" at Louis Street. A petition to the Prime Minister traded boldly in the historically established repertoire of European stereotypes about an Aboriginal "race" that were circulating in Australian culture in the 1970s. These it appropriated to support the movement's position as follows:

> We the undersigned [226] residents of South Sydney vociferously protest, object and condemn the establishment of the ghetto in Louis and Caroline Streets by the Aboriginals who have squatted in these properties. . . . We want the Aboriginal ghetto stopped now – for if allowed to continue it will spread like the plague throughout the entire South Sydney area (South Sydney Residents' Protection Movement to Gough Whitlam, 10 March 1973, in Bryant papers).

If the non-Aboriginal ratepayers of South Sydney were the Labor aldermen's hold on local power, a mutually strategic arrangement was certainly being struck in these negative portrayals of Aboriginality. One group of residents assured Mayor Hartup in April, 1973: "We fully support you, sir, and the South Sydney Municipal Council that a . . . human zoo should not be allowed in this area" (Mann to Hartup, in Murphy papers). Yet, as we have seen, Aboriginal Redfern was being constructed out of federally empowered discourses as well as locally activated ones. Minister Bryant simply deflected criticism about the project from South Sydney with appeals to his government's self-determination platform, an agenda which took as one of its cues "the re-awakening in Redfern of Aboriginal confidence" (Bryant to Hunter, 30 May 1973, in DAA 73/1103). A bureaucrat in Bryant's office went further and informed Mayor Hartup that the federal government was committed to the project "whether Council liked it or not" (Hall to Bryant, cited in "Chronology of Aboriginal commune", in Murphy papers).

Not that local opinion was without effect. When South Sydney councillors learned that the owner–developer of the Louis Street holdings had held negotiations with Commonwealth officials over their sale, council recommended that "the situation in the Louis and Caroline Street area be referred to the Commissioner of Police with a recommendation that the area be regularly and frequently patrolled to ensure that the local ratepayers are free from molestation and the impact of anti-social behaviour" (City of Sydney Archives, South Sydney Council, item 17 Health Committee agenda, 4 April 1973). Police scrutiny of the occupied terraces was intense from late 1972 into 1973, with many violent confrontations and arrests (Kaye and Bob Bellear, Dick Blair, Colin James, Dick Hall, personal communication, June 1991).

Council also used its powers to full extent by refusing building applications for further renovations to houses in the area – a move designed to prohibit the occupation and upgrading by Aborigines of extra terraces in Louis Street. It also spoke out against the spectre of Commonwealth intervention in local affairs, as did branches of the Australian Labor Party in constituencies close to Redfern. Pat Hills, state representative for Redfern in the New South Wales parliament, also condemned the exercise of federal muscle in the area. So, too, did the federal member for Redfern, Jim Cope, who appealed to the doctrine of assimilation that had prevailed as an official management strategy between the Second World War and the referendum of 1967 (but which enjoyed popular support long afterwards). "I believe", said Cope, "it is entirely wrong for any government to imagine that they can benefit the Aboriginal cause by creating ghettoes which would, in my opinion, defeat the ultimate goal of true assimilation between Aboriginals and White people" (Cope to Bryant, 23 March 1973, in Bryant papers). The assimilationist ideal of incorporating the "survivors of a dying race" into European society did not extend to finding a place for people of Aboriginal origin in areas sought after by White people (voters).

At locations farther removed from Redfern, where few Aborigines lived, party concerns about Commonwealth intervention were apparently less pressing. The federal member for Banks, for example, found the scheme "admirable", while the Hornsby state electorate council for the Australian Labor Party told Minister Bryant it found the project "constructive and enterprising" (Martin to Bryant, 3 July 1973, Dyer to Bryant, 26 July 1973, in DAA 73/1103). The utopian projections cast upon the Aboriginal commune project continued to acquire support in circles with the ultimate authority to empower them until, eventually, on 14 April 1973, Minister Bryant triumphantly announced that he would approve a Commonwealth grant for the purchase of 41 houses in Louis and Caroline Streets. "The project will become a showplace of racial harmony", stated the new president of the AHC, Dick Blair (*Daily Mirror*, 29 March 1973), while Bryant, in a press release long on polemic, asserted: "It [the scheme] will be a model for inner city communities who wish to preserve their homes and the identity of their area . . . Small groups like this give strength to one another without developing a totally separate existence" (*Sydney Morning Herald*, 16 April 1973). Strength in numbers was certainly what the new residents of Sydney's Redfern needed in the months following the Commonwealth decision. Between March and May 1973, there were some 410 arrests in the Louis Street area, most being Aborigines on minor charges (O'Grady to Mayor, 7 May 1973, in Murphy papers). Relations with the media grew equally sour with many invocations to the ghetto idea appearing in the press[4] about a district that continues to this day to attract much negative publicity and harassment by authorities (see Cunneen 1990).

Conclusion

Australia's indigenous peoples have been defined within a racialized universe that for two hundred years has facilitated their dispossession and legitimated their specialized treatment by the state and its agents. The nature of relations has differed considerably by region, just as they have prompted variable modes of accommodation, adaptation and resistance on the part of Aborigines. This unevenness of Aboriginal oppression and resistance points to the need for further place-specific studies in the historical geography of colonialism and postcolonialism, studies which would get past reiterating a universal Black/White alterity and seek to contribute to a more regionally sensitive fund of knowledge. The account in this chapter of one of Australia's Aboriginal settlements – and the multiplicity of constructions of it – is such a contribution to the scholarship on Aboriginal Australia (see also Trigger 1992).

The story of the origins of Aboriginal Redfern does, however, speak of issues that range beyond the contours of a few tiny streets. In this chapter I have attempted to bring to the foreground the political stakes in the range of dialogues about Redfern that grew out of the struggle for Black housing in inner Sydney in the early 1970s. Specifically, I have sought to demonstrate the capacity of Black activists and their European sympathizers to appropriate select constructs of Aboriginal identity and place, just as I have done for those who vehemently opposed Black settlement in Redfern. Both parties worked with distinctive versions of "race" and place that owed a debt to impulses in Australian culture and politics that were manifest in the early 1970s.

Such a framework for analysis averts the moralizing tone that characterizes much revisionist history about Aborigines, including that essentialist tradition of work in the 1970s which sought to condemn White prejudice (Rowley 1970, Stevens 1972), and more recent research that characterizes (and reifies) contemporary Aboriginality as something which is heroically oppositional (see, for example, Cowlishaw, 1988). The perspective developed in this chapter reveals how the widely contrasting truth-claims about the Aboriginal settlement in Redfern gained their cultural and political efficacy through distinctive, historically specific modes of representation. Such a balancing of voices is not to impute an equivalence to the utopian and pejorative representations of Redfern – as if the violent history of cultural imperialism can by some relativist sleight of hand be so easily levelled and erased – because, of course, *both* constructs of identity and place grew out of the asymmetrical power relations of the colonial encounter. The objective here has rather been to historicize a local struggle, to deconstruct the constructions of the past, and so fill out the complexities of a relationship that, at this juncture in Australian cultural relations, saw Aboriginality effectively mobilized in resistance as well as imposed in dominance.

That the appeals to Aboriginality had not only ideological but also material impacts is borne out by the process of place-making this chapter has charted. Constructions of reality inform the making and transformation of real-world geographies. This, at least, is one of the lessons of contemporary cultural geography (see, for example, Jackson 1989, 1991, Anderson & Gale 1992). More specifically, in this case study, we have seen that versions of Aboriginality structured the practices out of which emerged a nucleus of Aboriginal residence in a district of Australia that would otherwise have experienced a quite different development trajectory. That this claim to territory was simultaneously contested and empowered by European authorities at different scales and with contradictory agenda, serves to highlight the complex cultural politics that inhere in the urban landscapes we so often take as naturally occurring.

Notes

1. The Latin term "Aborigine" (meaning "from the beginning") is used by some indigenous Australians. Others discard it in favour of regional designations (Koorie, Nyunga, Anangu, etc.) and there is not yet an agreed term for the collectivity, although there is a flag. Regarding the social construction of Aboriginality, see Beckett (1988) and Attwood (1989).
2. For a discussion of this strategy as it relates to "Black British", see Gilroy (1987).
3. The author is grateful to the many people and organizations that supplied the primary data for this research. Thanks are due to the Aboriginal and Torres Strait Islander Commission for granting me special access to view Commonwealth records on Redfern (1970–90), to the NSW Office of Aboriginal Affairs, to Terry Murphy who supplied official documents of the Council of the City of South Sydney for the period covered in this chapter, and to Australian Archives Victoria Branch for allowing me to view the papers of the late Gordon Bryant. I am also grateful to the people I interviewed and whose story forms the basis for this chapter, including Kaye and Bob Bellear, Dick Blair, Dr H. C. Coombs, Jim Cope, Barry Dexter, Dick Hall, Colin James, Ted Kennedy, Ian Kiernan and Kevin Martin.
4. See the news reports headlined "Sydney's Black ghetto" (*The Sun Herald*, 22 March 1973), "Whites leave as Blacks move to city block" (*Daily Mirror*, 23 March 1973), "'Imaginative' Aboriginal housing block for Aboriginals" (*Sydney Morning Herald*, 16 April 1973).

Acknowledgements

In addition to the people and organizations cited in note 3 (above), the author would like to acknowledge the assistance of Julie Kesby who proof-read and formatted the chapter, and the University of New South Wales which funded the research.

References

Abrams, P. 1982. *Historical sociology*. Shepton Mallet, Somerset: Open Books.

Alcoff, L. 1988. Cultural feminism versus poststructuralism: the identity crisis in feminist theory. *Signs* 13, 405–36.

Anderson, K. 1991. *Vancouver's Chinatown: racial discourse in Canada 1875–1980*. Montreal: McGill-Queens University Press.

Anderson, K. 1993. Place narratives and the origins of the Aboriginal settlement in inner Sydney, 1972–73. *Journal of Historical Geography*, in press.

Anderson, K. & F. Gale (eds) 1992. *Inventing places: studies in cultural geography*. Melbourne: Longman Cheshire.

Attwood, B. 1989. *The making of the Aborigines*. Sydney: Allen & Unwin.

Australian Archives (Victoria) Hon Gordon Bryant papers, Commonwealth Record Series M350 and M474.

Bagguley, P., J. Mark-Lawson, D. Shapiro, J. Urry, S. Walby, A. Warde 1990. *Restructuring: place, class and gender*. London: Sage.

Beckett, J. (ed.) 1988. *Past and present: the construction of Aboriginality*. Canberra: Aboriginal Studies Press.

Bellear, R. 1976. *The Black housing book*. Sydney: Amber Press.

City of Sydney Archives, Council of the City of South Sydney, correspondence files, 1973.

Cooke, P. 1989. *Localities: the changing face of urban Britain*. London: Unwin Hyman.

Coombs, H. C. 1978. *Kulinma: listening to Aboriginal Australians*. Canberra: Australian National University Press.

Cowlishaw, G. 1988. *Black, White or brindle: race in rural Australia*. Cambridge: Cambridge University Press.

Cunneen, C. 1990. *Aboriginal–police relations in Redfern: with special reference to the "police raid" of 8 February 1990*. Sydney: Human Rights and Equal Opportunity Commission.

Dear, M. 1988. The postmodern challenge: reconstructing human geography. *Institute of British Geographers, Transactions* 13, 262–72.

Department of Aboriginal Affairs (DAA), miscellaneous Redfern files, 1972–73.

Docker J. 1988. Those halcyon days: the moment of the new left. In *Intellectual movements and Australian society*, B. Head & J. Walter, 289–307. Melbourne: Oxford University Press.

Gilroy, P. 1987. *There ain't no black in the Union Jack: the cultural politics of race and nation*. London: Hutchinson.

Hall, S. 1988. New ethnicities. In *Black film, British cinema*. ICA Documents 7, 27–30. London: Institute of Contemporary Arts.

Head, B. & J. Walter 1988. *Intellectual movements and Australian society*. Melbourne: Oxford University Press.

Jackson, P. (ed.) 1987. *Race and racism: essays in social geography*. London: Allen & Unwin.

Jackson, P. 1989. *Maps of meaning*. London: Unwin Hyman.

Jackson, P. 1991. Mapping meanings: a cultural critique of locality studies. *Environment and Planning A* **23**(2), 215–28.

Lipmann, L. 1970. *To achieve our country: Australia and the Aborigines*. Melbourne: Cheshire.

Massey, D. 1984. *Spatial divisions of labour*. London: Macmillan.

Munro-Clark, M. 1986. *Communes in rural Australia: the movement since 1970*. Sydney: Hale & Iremonger in association with the Ian Buchan Fell Research Centre.

Murphy, T. Personal papers and Redfern records of Council of the City of South Sydney, 1970–75.

NSW Office of Aboriginal Affairs, miscellaneous Redfern files, 1972–73.

Paasi, A. 1991. Deconstructing regions: notes on the scales of social life. *Environment and Planning A* **23**(2), 239–56.

Parbury, N. 1986. *Survival: a history of Aboriginal life in New South Wales*. Sydney: Ministry of Aboriginal Affairs New South Wales.

Pettman, J. 1992. *Living in the margins*. Sydney: Allen & Unwin.

Pratt, A. 1991. Discourses on locality. *Environment and Planning A* **23**(2), 257–66.

Relph, E. 1987. *The modern urban landscape*. London: Croom Helm.

Rowley, C. 1970. *Outcasts in White society*. Canberra: Australian University Press.

Rowse, T. 1988. Tolerance, fortitude and patience: frontier pasts to live with? *Meanjin* **47**(1), 21–9.

Scott, W. D. 1973. *Problems and needs of the Aboriginals of Sydney*. Report of the NSW Minister of Youth and Community Services.

Smith, D. 1992. *Land and labor: worker resistance and the production of landscape in agricultural California before World War II*. PhD thesis, Department of Geography, Rutgers University.

South Sydney Community Aid, submission to Commonwealth Office of Aboriginal Affairs, 30 September 1970, unpublished document, in Murphy papers.

Stevens, F. (ed.) 1972. *Racism: the Australian experience*. Sydney: Australian and New Zealand Book Company.

Tanaka, H. 1984. Landscape expression of the evolution of Buddhism in Japan. *Canadian Geographer* **28**, 240–57.

Treffery, V. 1972. St Vincent's Church, Redfern Street, Redfern, unpublished report, 3 November 1972, in Murphy papers.

Trigger, D. 1992. *Whitefella coming: Aboriginal responses to colonialism in northern Australia*. Cambridge: Cambridge University Press.

Trotman, P. 1973. Circumstances in Louis/Caroline Street, Redfern, unpublished report, 23 March 1973, in NSW Office of Aboriginal Affairs F107.

Western, J. 1981. *Outcast Capetown*. Minneapolis: University of Minnesota Press.

Young, E. 1992. Aboriginal land rights in Australia: expectations, achievements and implications. *Applied Geography* **12**, 146–61.

CHAPTER FOUR
"Shake 'im this country":
the mapping of the Aboriginal sacred in Australia
– the case of Coronation Hill[1]

JANE M. JACOBS

Nargorkun made the features of the earth, and the people. He made the ground crack, made fire come out and pushed rocks and ridges up to their present elevations . . . Nargorkun . . . put his laws for the people on many rock faces in the form of paintings . . . Nargorkun was bitten on the knee by Palmura, the mud-dauber hornet, which caused him to swell up into all manner of monstrous shapes. He became very sick and thirsty and was so badly crippled that he had to crawl on his hands and knees to move about. After drinking at Eegoiloomor, the Sickness Waterhole, he crawled up and over a ridge to Yeleamukmoo, the Sickness Cave or Home for Sick People, leaving a well-defined path known as Kordabalbal, the Sickness Road. He left his story and shades on the walls of the Sickness Cave . . . before entering the ground peacefully. He will remain there harmless and peaceful unless disturbed by excessive noise. If disturbed he will wake up and by rising he will split the world and destroy it.

(The Jawoyn people's Bula Dreaming, according to Arndt 1962: 304).

Geography has long been seen as a discipline complicit with imperial intent. The map is a symbolic and technical language of space. Yet often implicit in the map is the construction of certain social categories. Within the colonial project, the making of maps constructed a possessable "other" place (and people) and provided a practical guide for dispossessing "others" of their place. The colonial history of nation-states such as Australia testifies to the symbolic and practical possession enacted through the map. Anticolonial nationalisms and minority insurgencies have challenged the surety of colonial possession, pushing colonial states to a point at which traditional strategies of authority, like the map, are disrupted.

The descriptive and explanatory authority of geographers is no longer dependent upon the cartographic exercise, and geographers and others have begun investigating the political implications of spatial representation at the discursive and cartographic levels. This chapter explores the relationship between spatial representation and power. It takes an example from contemporary Australia, where there has been an on-going struggle between the Jawoyn people's concern to care for the Bula Dreaming country and other interests wanting to establish a major mineral extraction venture at Coronation Hill in northern Australia.

The land rights process in Australia is an attempt by the government to acknowledge Aboriginal interests in land and to return to Aboriginal Australians lands over which they have a sense of affiliation and responsibility. In indigenous land claims, the mapping of Aboriginal land interests, particularly the sacred site and the tribal boundary, has proved a contentious procedure. The mapping of "traditional" or "culturally specific" Aboriginal land interests has become one of the mechanisms by which non-Aboriginal Australia arbitrates rights to land and the legitimacy of claims made. In granting land rights, Australia may be edging towards a statehood tenuously identifiable as "postcolonial". Yet the desire to fix spatially an "authentically" Aboriginal land interest as part of this procedure is an important site of contest. Clifford's (1988) rendition of the Mashpee land claim has demonstrated that the struggle of indigenous rights in settler states is often a struggle around the idea of "authentic" identity. As such, the rôle of land rights in the dissolution of colonial intent is far from clear.

Imperialism and the map

Harley (1988, 1992) provides an explicit critique of the relationship between the cartographic project, the acquisition of knowledge and the wielding of power. The quest to map may well have been undertaken as an "innocent" cartographic science, but it replicates not only the environment but also the "territorial imperatives of a particular political system". (Harley 1988: 278) Harley provides ample evidence of the link between cartography and the political project of European imperialism. He notes:

> There are innumerable contexts in which maps became the currency of political "bargains", leases, partitions, sales, and treaties struck over colonial territory and, once made permanent in the image, these maps more than often acquired the force of law in the landscape (1988: 283).

The spatial logic of the map provides a totalizing, panoptic gaze which homogenizes and flattens the "other" (Ferrier 1990: 38). As Huggan (1991) suggests, the cartographic exercise of colonialism depended upon a technique (and a hope) of representing a stable reality. Noyes (1992), using the

101

example of German colonialism in South West Africa, demonstrates clearly the links between "stabilizing" spatial discourses of the map and the colonialist processes of possession. The cartographic possession of Australia was premised on the conceptual emptying of the continent. There is of course an important discrepancy between the coherence of the conceptually emptied Australian continent and the reality of Aboriginal occupation. Declaring the continent *terra nullius* (land unoccupied) prepared the blank page upon which the Australian colony could be not only linguistically and cartographically inscribed but also enacted in everyday practices of genocide and dispossession (Carter 1987).

Land rights policy in Australia does not presume the blank canvas of early imperialism but adopts an alternative imperialist strategy of dividing and allocating space between Aboriginal and non-Aboriginal interests (Fabian 1983: 29–30). My own work on the rôle of mapping in contemporary land rights procedures demonstrates the continuing vitality of the cartographic project in processes of political domination (Jacobs 1988a, 1988b). Referring to the land rights process in Australia in the 1980s, I argue that the mapping of tribal boundaries and sacred sites has become a procedural prerequisite for Aboriginal groups seeking to prove their legitimate and distinctive interest in the land. In particular, the legislative and policy framework of early land rights options in Australia placed an over-emphasis on the sacred site – the "authentic" Aboriginal site – which testified to the unique spiritual affiliation between Aborigines and the land. Aboriginal communities who were unable or unwilling to disclose their sacred sites were disadvantaged in having their interests in land recognized by the granting of land rights.

Coronation Hill: one story

The land rights controversy associated with the proposed mining of Coronation Hill in the Northern Territory of Australia provides an example of an uncertain postcolonial geography. Coronation Hill is a not very imposing hill in remote northern Australia, in the southern reaches of the South Alligator River. This is *Crocodile Dundee* country. It is a place multiply mapped. It lies in the midst of Stage III of Kakadu National Park, which has World Heritage listing for its unique natural and cultural qualities. The part of the Park encompassing Coronation Hill was reclaimed from pastoral use by the government in 1987. At that time, the Hill and its immediate surrounds were excised and proclaimed a Conservation Zone, a status which recognizes the ecological value of the area, but also permits alternative activity, such as mining, albeit under strict environmental controls.

There have been mining claims and operations on and around Coronation Hill since the early 1950s, and since 1984 Coronation Hill Joint Venture have undertaken exploration activity with a view to establishing a large-scale gold, palladium and platinum extraction operation. For the mining lobby in Australia and some state interests, Coronation Hill represents the richest single source of these minerals ever located in Australia and, according to some, the only one of its kind in the world (Resource Assessment Commission 1991b: 127).

For the Jawoyn (or Djauan) people, Coronation Hill (Guratba) is part of an area which has a complex of interconnected sites associated with the Bula religious cult. Guratba is a place where Bula made wild rope. Coronation Hill is part of the "Sickness Country", and the Jawoyn argue that, if disturbed, Bula will "shake up the country", causing the ground to split open, earthquakes, widespread destruction. The many sites associated with Bula, of which Coronation Hill is one, have been recorded by anthropologists (Arndt 1962, 1966, Keen & Merlan 1990, Levitus 1990, Maddock 1987, Merlan & Rumsey 1982). More recently the complex of sites has been registered by government authorities established for the purposes of recording and protecting sacred sites and facilitating land claims.

The controversy of Coronation Hill has been fuelled by these many, but at times contradictory, recordings of the Bula mythology and its associated sites. The most recent "official" recording was not made until 1985, contentiously after mining exploration by Coronation Hill Joint Venture had commenced. The registration included not just one site but a complex of interconnected sacred sites covering a large area. Equally contentious has been the alleged vagaries in Jawoyn attitudes to the mining venture, with dissension between older and younger Jawoyn (some of whom work for the Joint Venture) and even, at times, between the three prime custodians for the site.

Maddock (1988) has noted the "volatile mix" that this multiple inscription produces. In an effort to appease the seemingly intractable interests interlocked at Coronation Hill, the Federal Government passed the issue on to a newly formed government inquiry body, the Resource Assessment Commission. The Commission reported that there was considerable Aboriginal opposition to the mining venture and that mining would pose a threat to sites associated with the Bula Dreaming. In a controversial decision (which overrode a Ministerial vote) the then Prime Minister, Bob Hawke, disallowed mining at Coronation Hill. It may have been a politically hard decision to make but, as Gelder (1991: 15) argues, it was viewed by the media and industry as "soft", a sentimental decision which responded to a poorly understood and little known religious cult, rather than the economic imperatives of a nation in recession.

"Postcolonialism" and the map

Said (1990: 77) argues that, because the imperial project is an act of geo-graphical violence, the imagination of anti-imperialism is distinguished by the primacy of the geographical. For the colonized, loss of local place is a consequence of imperialism and part of the insurgent act of reclaiming rights is the search for and restoration of place lost. Said (1990: 78–9) cites the example of insurgent nationalisms in which the decolonization process turns to a place-based, myth-making. He argues that this creative process of reclamation presents a "new territory" of the reflexive and fluid realm of the politics of difference. It is not the panoptic, flattening space of imperialist visions, nor is it pristine or prehistorical. Bhabha (1990: 312) describes this as an "interstitial space", a "third space", which is "undecidably at the frontiers of cultural hybridity" and which is hewn from a politics of difference.

For Bhabha (1992: 57), the writing of cultural difference must proceed from an understanding of a contingent culture "caught . . . in-between a plurality of practices that are different yet must occupy the same space of adjudication and articulation". Giroux describes an emphasis on the politics of difference as a shift to understanding how:

> power is inscribed differently in and between zones of culture; how
> cultural border-lands raise important questions regarding relations of
> inequality, struggle and history; and how differences are expressed in
> multiple and contradictory ways within individuals and groups. (1992:
> 204)

It is the very presence of cultural differences, brought into local conflict through globally linked imperatives of mining development, that leads to the (re-)narration of the place Coronation Hill.

Postcolonial theorists are persistent in depicting this politics as spatialized. It is one thing for the postcolonial critic to turn to spatial metaphors in conceptualizing a politics of difference. It is another thing to demonstrate how a politics of difference has, in an everyday sense, a geography. The case of Coronation Hill demonstrates clearly that the politics of difference oper-ates through and in place. This is not to propose an uncritical concept of place-based essentialism, but rather to invest it with a strategic sensibility. Furthermore, identities of difference may be fracturing into more localized and flexible formations, but they are at the same moment inextricably linked with global spatialities, such as multinationalism or global conservationism.

When Baudrillard (1983) outlined his concept of the simulacrum, he began with a reference to Borges' tale of the "cartographers of the Empire". In this allegory of simulation, the decline of the Empire sees the comprehensive map of possession becoming frayed, with only a "few shreds" discernible in the remote and, one presumes, unpeopled desert. Baudrillard argues that this allegory can no longer be sustained, for it presumes that the cartographic is representing a reality which both precedes and survives the act of mapping. For Baudrillard (1983: 2), "the territory no longer precedes the map . . . it is the map that precedes the territory" and it is "the territory whose shreds are slowly rotting across the map". In this inversion of the original allegory Baudrillard points to the demise of the authentically real and towards a "liquidation of referentials".

Such theorizing is both appealing and troubling in the context of indigenous rights in contemporary Australia. Coronation Hill demonstrates that there is a "problem" of referentials, as much of the debate hinges upon the unfixability of authenticity. Those wishing to obliterate or contain the Aboriginal claim to Coronation Hill question the authenticity of the Bula mythology. At the same time, the case of the Aboriginal claimants depends upon a wider acceptance of the authenticity of their claim to land. The discourses generated about Coronation Hill cannot be understood simply as antithetical, culturally exclusive positions. Rather, the Coronation Hill controversy is an exemplar of a place which is being (re)produced through a process of "transcultural negotiation" (Bhabha 1990: 312).

The concern of this chapter, then, is not with the truth or the validity of one claim over another, but with the context of enunciation and "processes of displacement and realignment" which may be traced through such encounters (Bhabha 1992: 58). This accords with Mani's (1992: 393) prescription of the tensions and disjunctions of the politics of difference providing the key point of analysis for a contemporary critique of power. This is a space which is neither exclusively of the margins nor of the centre, where such binary oppositions no longer exist with any security. Pursuing this third space does not divest this chapter, or my interpretation of events and discourses, from my position within a fraying colonialist state. As Clifford (1992: 97) suggests, "every focus excludes; there is no politically innocent methodology for intercultural interpretation". This is then, a writing of *relations* of domination and subordination manifest in the various practices of representation of the "in-between space" of Coronation Hill.

The picture show begins

From the outset of non-Aboriginal recordings of Bula, there has been an unusual level of concern about authenticity. At one level, this may be linked to the "professional paranoia" of the original non-Aboriginal recordist. The Bula Dreaming was first recorded in the early 1950s by Walter Arndt, a government Agricultural Research Officer who lived at the northern Australian town of Katherine. By Arndt's own account, the investigations were made "as a hobby", and in his published accounts much is made of the procedures of recording and verifying information (Arndt 1962, 1966).

Arndt was alerted to what he called the Nargorkun–Narlinji cult when a near-fatal epidemic of hookworm anaemia broke out in the Aboriginal labour camp he was supervising. An Aboriginal spokesperson in the camp explained to Arndt that the outbreak was due to the disturbances by dynamite being used in uranium mining operations at a site some distance away, known to the Jawoyn as the "Sickness Dreaming Place". The Aboriginal spokesperson warned Arndt that, if the mining operations did not stop, there would be cataclysmic results: everyone, including Europeans, would die.

Arndt's response to the passion of this warning was to presume not that the cataclysm would occur but that he had stumbled upon a vibrant and bizarre local belief system in need of recording (Arndt 1962: 299). The Aboriginal warning spurred Arndt into a frenzy of amateur ethnographic activity. Arndt decided the best way to verify the claims about the "Sickness Country" was to visit the site located near to the mining operations and take a "complete colour slide coverage" to be shown to local Aborigines at "free picture shows" where "spontaneous remarks of the audience" could be recorded (Arndt 1962: 299).

Arndt visited the site one weekend late in 1955. He does not mention going with an Aboriginal guide. He was shown to the site by personnel at the mining camp. Some 80 colour slides were taken in "a hectic 48 hours". These slides were then shown to Aboriginal audiences at several places and, according to Arndt, the Sickness Dreaming Place was recognized and the Aboriginal viewers were satisfied that mining operations had not caused any damage. Six years later, in order to check information for publishing purposes, Arndt returned to his hobby of the Bula Dreaming. The verification occurred at a bush camp some 25 km from the nearest town. A makeshift electricity supply sets the slide projector flickering. The show begins. Arndt's slides of the Sickness Place flash upon a flimsy screen, perhaps a wall. The Aboriginal informants discussed the slides in "Djauan" language and a younger Jawoyn man translated in pidgin English. Arndt is most satisfied with his verification procedure. His hobby enters into the public domain in two articles for a professional anthropological journal (Arndt 1962, 1966). Arndt was a firm believer in the "truth" of the Bula mythology. He argues in his first article: "Numerous informants . . . confirmed the existence of this important cultural centre before and after it became known to Europeans. This seems to preclude the possibility of a hoax" (Arndt 1962: 300).

Arndt's account of the way in which the Bula Dreaming first came to print is an account of dispossession and non-Aboriginal re-inscription of the site. I do not want to imply that if Arndt had followed more conventional ethnographic procedures that the Bula would today be standing on more believable ground. But the early translation of this Dreaming is certainly marked by a complexity of representation and distancing. The authenticating of the original account occurs with the site "present" in the visual imagery of photography. There is no enacting of associated ceremonial activity (ceremonial activity associated with Bula had ceased), and no mention of a site visit with local custodians (although one may have been made). Bula is made known to non-Jawoyn by a mirror box of imagery.

Arndt's early accounts of Bula raise questions which have remained vital components of the continuing Bula controversy. First, about the location of Bula. The Bula sites that Arndt recorded and published are located at Sleisbeck, not at Coronation Hill which lies further to the north. Arndt did, however, specify an extensive area associated with the Sickness Place, and described as the Sickness Country. The second source of controversy raised in Arndt's original accounts, was that of authorization. Some of the sites Arndt recorded as part of the Bula Dreaming were different from those known to have been recorded by another anthropologist working with another linguistically similar group. This raised the issue of which local Aboriginal groups had primary responsibility for the site. Thirdly, and linked to the issue of rightful authorization, ceremonial activity associated with Bula had been abandoned, although the story of Bula remained vital within Jawoyn belief systems and site visitation restrictions were observed. Much of the debate about Coronation Hill remains linked to the issue of "where" Bula actually resides, whether it is truly a Jawoyn responsibility to speak about the site and to care for it and whether, in the absence of active ceremonial activity, Bula is a "vital" component of Jawoyn cosmology and not "archaic".

The un-mapping of Coronation Hill

The Jawoyn have made various claims for land under the provisions of the Aboriginal Land Rights (Northern Territory) Act 1976. Under the provisions of the Act, only unalienated Crown land can be claimed. In their Jawoyn (Katherine Area) Land Claim, several areas of land were sought: most in Katherine Gorge, well south of Coronation Hill, and two smaller tracts of land, north of Coronation Hill.

The Jawoyn were assisted in their claim by the Northern Lands Council (a statutory body established for this purpose) and its consultant anthropologists. This land claim generated an extensive body of recorded material on Jawoyn religious and cultural life and associated land interests. The Jawoyn were prepared to expose this material to selected officials for the arbitration of their claim, in a form of exchange transaction in which secret sacred information was given over to ensure legal control of land. But in more public or open arenas of the claim procedure more care was taken in terms of what traditional knowledge was disclosed. In the land claim procedure, the Bula Dreaming was raised in a general summary of the protective responsibilities held by the Jawoyn towards their land. The specific intensity of the Jawoyn's sense of responsibility to their land was linked to the "highly apocalyptic" nature of Jawoyn cosmology. In the public land claim report, this was said of the Bula Dreaming:

> The most powerful Jawoyn Dreaming is Bula . . . Because most of the details of Bula mythology and ritual are not appropriately discussed in public, none will be disclosed here. These topics will instead be treated in a separate, restricted submission . . . The most pertinent belief about Bula for the present discussion is one which the Jawoyn people *have* chosen to publicize as a matter of great urgency: that if Bula sites are disturbed, widespread destruction will follow (Merlan & Rumsey 1982: 53).

The documentation of Bula, and its significance to the Jawoyn in the official land claim document, traced a difficult line between apocalyptic warnings and limited public non-disclosure of its details. Merlan and Rumsey argue that the non-disclosure of site information is not simply about internal rules of secrecy. It is, they imply, consciously strategic: "Jawoyn people know very well that many Europeans scoff at the specific content of Aboriginal mythology. This is one reason that they are often unwilling to discuss it" (Merlan & Rumsey 1982: 69).

Merlan & Rumsey's evidence to the Land Claim resulted in a public reiteration of the cataclysmic potential of a disturbed Bula, as first outlined by Arndt. But it also became an arena in which the unknowability of Bula for some was asserted. This occurred in two ways. First, the growing number of ethnographies were revealing the geographical complexity of Bula. The Resource Assessment Commission noted that by the early 1980s:

> Bula's presence and influence is recorded as extending beyond focal sites by a network of sensory links, or underground wires, connecting all Bula sites to each other and to the ocean, and by broad zones or spheres of influence extending up to ten kilometres around important Bula sites. (1991a: 171)

Secondly, the land claim procedure brought to public attention Jawoyn strategies of non-disclosure. Their strategy accorded with more general policies of non-disclosure of culturally specific knowledge being adopted by many Aboriginal communities. Such strategies ensure that Aborigines are not disempowered by culturally specific knowledge coming under the control and arbitration of state institutions and non-Aboriginal "experts". Non-disclosure cannot operate in a nation-state where decision-making still presumes the blank canvas of its original mapping. This strategy presumes that decisions over land-use and access are premised by an acceptance, albeit notional, of Aboriginal interests in land. Non-disclosure is an attempt by Aborigines to gain control of this premise; not only to ensure they may abide by customary rules of secrecy, but also to protect Aboriginal knowledges from a continuing process of interrogation and appropriation.

The Jawoyn (Katherine Gorge) Land Claim was only partially successful. Justice Kearney, Land Commissioner for the claim, found in favour of the Jawoyn claims for the southern Katherine Gorge area. With respect to the two small parcels of land to the north of Coronation Hill, Kearney found against the Jawoyn. In bringing down his findings, Kearney said "[i]t was clear on the evidence that the spiritual affiliations of the Jawoyn diminish the further north one goes", although he made an important exception with regard to Bula sites (Kearney 1988: 34).

Re-mapping the excesses of Bula

In 1978 the Northern Territory government passed legislation to provide for the establishment of an authority with the specific task of mapping and recording Aboriginal sacred sites: the Aboriginal Sacred Sites Protection Authority. Under the Aboriginal Sacred Sites legislation, sites so recorded are given limited protection. Before works on sacred sites can occur, the Authority must issue a permit which can be granted only after consultation with the relevant Aboriginal custodians and when the Authority is satisfied that work can proceed without risk of damage or with their custodial approval (Ritchie 1990: 5).

Soon after the introduction of legislation, two sites which were known to be places where Bula entered the ground were registered and at later dates other sites associated with the Bula complex went onto the official sacred sites register (Merlan & Rumsey 1982: 54; Resource Assessment Commission 1991a: 173). In 1985, after the Coronation Hill Joint Venture had begun exploration and local consultation, the Jawoyn asked the Sacred Sites Authority to gather a complete registration of the Bula Dreaming sites. In consultation with the Jawoyn, the Authority registered the "Upper South Alligator Bula Complex", which incorporated Coronation Hill. The 1985 registration of Bula became an important point at which the previous unmapping of Bula was transformed into an official representation. The "site" recorded covered some 250 km². The registered site was in fact a complex of interconnected sites and the surrounding country covered by Bula's "sphere of influence" (Merlan, quoted in Cooper 1985: 17). The recording of the Bula complex had to incorporate the known complexity of the Bula sites, the underground connectedness and the soft "edges" of discrete sites. The registration also dealt with that part of the Bula Dreaming referring to Ngan-mol, an essence found in human bodily fluids and a term also used to refer to mineral deposits in the Earth (Merlan & Rumsey 1986, cited in Ritchie 1990: 27). The gold discovered at Coronation Hill was seen by the Jawoyn to be the bodily substance of Bula or his wives. According to Keen & Merlan (1990), the discovery of gold at Coronation Hill provided for the elaboration of existing Jawoyn knowledge that this was a place where Bula had a presence and influence. At the time of site registration the Jawoyn reiterated their concern that only certain types of activities could safely proceed within the bounds of Bula's sphere of influence. Mining was not an accepted activity.

The registration process uncovered a Bula which was flexible in influence and spatial extent. The question of geography was raised specifically:

> The geographical extent of these prohibitions [on use], that is, the location of the site complex boundaries, calls for comment . . . [T]he concept . . . of a zone of influence around focal sites is not consistently incorporated in the designation of site limits . . . [but] ideas of zones of influence, underground inter-site linkages and ngan-mol were applied in the registration of the Upper South Alligator River Bula Complex (Levitus, cited in Ritchie 1990: 31).

Anthropologists familiar with Jawoyn cosmology also commented on the difficulty of mapping Bula:

> . . . the cult or cycle is not only attached to places which can be pinpointed on the map . . . it has a more general significance, in the sense that meddling with Bula could unleash destructive forces of a nature likely to be felt beyond those points on the map (Maddock 1987: 133).

Maddock (1987: 135) goes on to argue that the sacred site, whatever its spatial extent and location, cannot be simply protected by a perimeter fence (as one commentator suggested) for "the significance of sites radiates out from them", they are more like "smudges" on a map than "pinpoints". The official mapping of as large a tract of land as a Bula complex was intended to accommodate these qualities of the Bula Dreaming.

The "proper" mapping of Bula

The Sacred Sites Authority's official registration was seen as so potentially threatening, to not only the Coronation Hill mining venture but also others in the future, that the local Minister for Mines and Energy instigated an inquiry into the registration of the Upper South Alligator Bula Complex. The verification of the official recording of Bula was undertaken by a consultant, Steve Davis, who describes himself as a "political geographer". Davis had long been involved with Aborigines in northern Australia, acting as a consultant on their behalf, but also for the government and private bodies, including the Coronation Hill Joint Venture. Davis consulted with the traditional custodians of the Bula Dreaming and reported that Coronation Hill was not a main Bula site and that the pre-eminent Bula site was further south at Sleisbeck, as originally recorded by Arndt (Davis 1986, cited in Ritchie 1990: 28).

Davis approached Jawoyn claims over Coronation Hill as a (theoretically unrevised) political geography problem. In a recent publication (Davis & Prescott 1992), which draws on his evidence for mining company consultancy reports, the issue of mapping is central. But for Davis & Prescott it is not the unmappability of Bula sites which takes their attention, but the problem of Jawoyn territoriality. Davis & Prescott's account begins with the presumption that traditionally Aboriginal territories were "marked by precise boundaries in most cases and by frontiers in the others" (1992: 2), where a boundary is a line and a frontier is a zone. Largely ignoring an on-going anthropological debate about the difficulty of defining Aboriginal territoriality, Davis & Prescott are perplexed at the failure of government authorities to produce accurate maps of traditional Aboriginal boundaries and frontiers. They argue that it is "curious", "odd" and "strange" that experts on Aboriginal culture believe that Aborigines do not know the "exact limits of the territory in which they had primary rights" (1992: 3). Davis & Prescott suggest the failure to undertake an official mapping of Aboriginal territoriality has allowed claims to be negotiated without "self-imposed limits".

Davis & Prescott (1992: 60–61) consider the Jawoyn "do not appear to have the normal proofs [of rights to land] within Aboriginal tradition". They argue that the area containing Coronation Hill and incorporated into the official registration was originally occupied by the 'Wulwulam. This land was emptied of the 'Wulwulam during early years of contact. Davis & Prescott assert that the Jawoyn have not lived in the South Alligator region, visit it infrequently, and do not enact any rituals associated with the Bula Dreaming. All claims currently being made by the Jawoyn are then, by their reasoning, successionary claims over the "deceased estate" of the adjoining 'Wulwulam group. By using an "incremental approach" the Jawoyn are extending their territoriality "over vacant territory", and the land claim and site recording procedure is considered to be a "a tool" in this invasion (Davis & Prescott 1992: 76). The Jawoyn are depicted as strategic expansionists, who have exploited state-instituted land rights procedures to pursue Jawoyn identity and land ownership ambitions in country emptied of its traditional Aboriginal custodians.

The Davis & Prescott account demonstrates the way in which previous arbitrations and representations of Jawoyn territorial interest can be mobilized to discredit Aboriginal claims of interests in land. Citing the findings of Mr Justice Kearney, Land Commissioner in the Jawoyn (Katherine Area) Land Claim, Davis & Prescott evoke the authority of the judicial spatial narration:

> In an attempt to delimit the area over which the Jawoyn currently have spiritual affiliations, [Mr Justice Kearney] produced a description . . . which delimits the "country within the sphere of influence of the sites to which the Jawoyn have established common spiritual affiliations". The northern extremity of the area so described is found to lie approximately along a line of latitude 14 degrees 10 minutes south . . . and clearly does not include the South Alligator Valley or Coronation Hill which lies a further 65 kilometres north. (1992: 72–3)

They go on to assert that this line is consistent with the boundary for the Jawoyn appearing on the map of Aboriginal tribal boundaries produced by the anthropologist Tindale (1974). They conclude that this "excludes the Jawoyn from the entire South Alligator River Valley and the headwaters of the Katherine River". These official arbitrations are corroborated by evidence Davis collected "in the field" directly from Jawoyn custodians.

To identify such a process of the "elaboration of tradition" is not inconsistent with interpretations of indigenous groups within colonial states. Indeed, it resonates uncomfortably with Said's (1990) notion of "place-based myth-making". It is also a view held by some "right-wing" commentators such as the anthropologist Brunton (1991: 11) who has claimed the Bula "tradition" is "no more than a decade old". The distinctive dimension of Davis's political geography of the Jawoyn (as with the commentary of Brunton) is the fixed grid of authenticity upon which it is mapped. The complaint is not so much that there is change and adjustment within an Aboriginal group, which is apparently acceptable, but only if it is within the bounds of "tradition". The problem for Davis & Prescott seems to be that at least some agents of the state are complicit in this process and that this is overweighted in favour of the Jawoyn. They are emphatic in their account of what is and is not legitimate territorial expansion for Aboriginal groups:

> The territory of a deceased group cannot be conceptually filled in the
> short term by the use of a piece of legislation to aid, accelerate and
> validate the process of succession that might otherwise occur within
> Aboriginal tradition (Davis & Prescott 1992: 77)

Davis & Prescott are lost amid the mirror box of representations of Jawoyn
territoriality and cosmology. On the one hand, they uncritically evoke the
bounding authority of the "Kearney Line", as they call it, and the map of
tribal boundaries produced by Tindale. On the other hand, they assert the
unacceptability of the Sacred Site Authority's registration. Davis & Prescott
struggle to re-assert a surer colonial fixity to this unsettled terrain; to impose
a mapping of Aboriginal territoriality which confines and controls. As with
all "authentic" geographical texts, the final word in the Davis–Prescott
account comes by way of a map which marks out Jawoyn territory well south
of Coronation Hill, but with a threatening zone of northward succession.

The Davis thesis of territorial succession was placed by the mining lobby
as evidence with the Resource Assessment Commission into the Coronation
Hill area. His views were outweighed by evidence presented by other "experts", and by the testimonies of Aboriginal witnesses, and were eventually
rejected by the Commission. The anthropologist Merlan (1991) specifically
criticizes the "less refined" succession thesis of Davis. Referring to Davis's
Kakadu Commission evidence, Merlan tackles the map-making impulse of
Davis's version of political geography:

> The consultant [Davis] predicted that there would be further "expan-
> sion" northwards . . . and he produced maps showing how far he
> thought that expansion would go. These maps, confusingly enough,
> showed the Jawoyn expanding into country which is currently recog-
> nised by the Jawoyn and other Aborigines of the region as belonging
> to other Aboriginal groups . . . his maps and statement were shot
> through with inadequacies and inconsistencies. (1991: 346)

Merlan (1991) argues that in the Coronation Hill controversy "traditional
Aboriginal culture" bears the full weight of the arbitration of whether the
Jawoyn claims are legitimate or not. Yet this pursuit of "tradition" is deeply
problematic. It sets a pre-contact "truth" of an "innocent" and unstrategic
Dreaming against the post-contact "invented tradition" of Aboriginal strate-
gists. But the "true", possibly unstrategic, Bula is unknowable. As Merlan
(1991: 345) explains, most of what is known about Bula (by both Aborigines
and non-Aborigines) "has been learned precisely in relation to intrusions . .
. in the context of specific historical relations of White–Black interaction"
spanning some 120 years. The power of the Davis thesis rests on a contradictory position in relation to "tradition". It presumes that an Aboriginal

tradition deserving of land rights acknowledgement exists, but it does not exist in this place, with these people, or in this time. Rather, the Jawoyn are made to be less Aboriginal and "naturally political . . . just like the rest of us" (Davis, cited in Merlan 1991: 346).

The "proper" mapping of Jawoyn territoriality became a procedure to discredit the Jawoyn and to fix them spatially in a territory some safe distance from Coronation Hill. Containing the Jawoyn well south of Coronation Hill re-enacts the imperialist project of conceptually emptying land to make it available for possession, in the present moment, by one of the most promising mining ventures recently proposed in Australia.

Shaking up the country

Bula may have been appeased by the government's decision to disallow mining at Coronation Hill, but he has certainly "shaken up" the discursive formation of both Jawoyn-ness and the nation. Maddock (1988: 306) argues that "[w]ithout Bula, Coronation Hill may never have hit the headlines", for Bula added "an explosive and unpredictable element".

The Jawoyn have long been warning against the wrath of Bula, but in the recent history of Bula the Jawoyn have drawn on different discourses of cataclysm. Maddock (1987), for example, recorded the Jawoyn warning not only of the Earth erupting but likening the Bula cataclysm to "an atomic explosion". Gelder (1991: 16) suggests that while Bula is not necessarily strategic, the discourse the Jawoyn use to describe his effect certainly may be, invoking as it does "wider public fears about nuclear proliferation" and uranium mining (for there is uranium too at Coronation Hill), thereby connecting it with the global-ness of contemporary environmentalism. Similarly, Jawoyn specifications that the effect of a disturbed Bula will extend to "Sydney, Melbourne, overseas", as Merlan (1991: 348) describes it "the known limits of the world", explicitly target the geography of a globally linked Australian capitalism. Whether these recent expressions of the effect of Bula are strategic or not, the contemporary narration of Bula remains linked to a global spatiality.

Foucault (1986: 23) argues that some of the inviolable spatial oppositions of contemporary society are nurtured by the "hidden presence of the sacred". In the discourses produced by Coronation Hill, the distinctive feature is not the "hidden" sacred, but an excessive or unbound sacred (Gelder & Jacobs 1992). Bula jettisoned the sacred into the secular discourses of the nation and of the national sense of wellbeing. As Maddock (1988: 305) suggests, "the idea of the sacred has become part of the furniture of the

Australian mind".

The "excessive" effects of Bula can be easily detected in some of the recent mining industry discussions on the future of mining in Australia since the Prime Ministerial decision to disallow mining at Coronation Hill. The managing director of Western Mining, Hugh Morgan, likened the decision to another moment of catastrophic threat in Australia's history, the fall of Singapore to the Japanese and the pending invasion of northern Australia. Morgan continues:

> . . . the fate of the nation depends . . . on the common beliefs which unite the people and provide the foundation for national sovereignty. The decision on Coronation Hill . . . will grievously undermine the moral basis of our legitimacy as a nation." (1991)

Morgan sees the effect of the Coronation Hill decision as invading all proposed mining ventures in Australia: the mining industry is "beset on all sides with sacred sites". Morgan's defence of the nation is not simply made through a dichotomy of economy versus indigenous culture. It is the moral and religious nation which Morgan feels is most under threat from Bula: ". . . from the prime Minister's language we can deduce that any god will do. We can all have our own gods and we can put them wherever we want to have them" (Morgan 1984: 5). Morgan moves away from the secular, economistic constructions of the nation that are expected of the mining lobby and narrates the nation through a discourse of the sacred. This shift may well speak most clearly of the destabilizing effect of Bula on the modern nation of Australia, invading the very ways in which the nation is constructed and expressed.

Conclusion

Bula has indeed "shaken up the country". The Coronation Hill controversy challenged what constitutes the national interest. It has uncovered the complex positioning of authenticity in the politics of difference. It has disrupted the idea of the "nation-state" within a political context of internal difference and global imperative. It has "shaken up" the relationship between the secular and the sacred in the expression of the nation.

Jawoyn claims about the sacredness of Coronation Hill, and its cataclysmic effects, have evaded a fixity in space and time. In so doing they are deeply challenging to the continuing domination of non-Aboriginal interests in Australia. This controversy is not simply about the inappropriateness of the map for the task of representing the Dreaming, or even the political undesirability of the mapping process. The "excesses" of Bula live not only in Jawoyn cosmology but also in the continuing process of non-Aboriginal mappings, unmappings and remappings of Bula and Jawoyn-ness. Bula's links to a global spatiality of economic aspiration and environmental cataclysm suggest that seemingly parochial "postcolonial" political struggles are also entwined with global mappings of power and identity formation.

The Coronation Hill controversy provides an example of the way in which desires to map (and to de- or remap) Aboriginal sites and tribal boundaries are part of a power-laden politics of inscribing Aboriginality within the contemporary nation-state. The discourses produced by the Coronation Hill controversy hover around the notion of an authentic and "truly" traditional Aboriginal culture, existing somewhere, sometime. In the discursive terrain established by Coronation Hill, "myths of state" (Kapferer 1988) coalesce with legends of Bula. The evasiveness of "truth" in Coronation Hill presents the "unreal reality" of the politics of difference (Minh-ha 1989: 61). At Coronation Hill, the politics of national and insurgent identity worked through a mirror box of representations of place and people.

The act of mapping is both a spatial and social construction. Its technical form belies a political potential which is complicit in the continuing negotiation of power and identity in settler states such as Australia. Maps may be in one sense *mere* representations, but as the Coronation Hill controversy demonstrates, these mere representations have consequences for the material and political efficacy of indigenous groups in settler states. The map then is part of a political process. Uncovering the politics of production of the map excavates its complex rôle in the continuing practice of colonialism and hints at subversive spatialities of postcolonialism.

Acknowledgement

The author would like to thank Robert Levitus for his comments on an earlier draft of this chapter.

Note

1. The title is taken from a video of the same name produced by the Aboriginal Sacred Sites Protection Authority (1986) on behalf of Jawoyn custodians.

References

Aboriginal Sacred Sites Protection Authority 1986. *Shake 'im this country*. Video prepared for the Jawoyn community.

Arndt, W. 1962. The Nargorkun–Narlinji Cult. *Oceania* 32, 298–320.

Arndt, W. 1966. Seventy year old records and new information on the Nargorkun–Narlinji Cult. *Oceania* 36, 231–8.

Baudrillard, J. 1983. *Simulations* (translated by P. Foss, P. Patton, P. Beitchman). New York: Semiotext(e).

Bhabha, H. 1990. Introduction: narrating the nation. In *Nation and narration*, H. Bhabha (ed.), 1–7. London: Routledge.

Bhabha, H. 1992. Postcolonial authority and postmodern guilt. In *Cultural studies*, L. Grossberg, C. Nelson, P. Treichler (eds), 56–68. London: Routledge.

Brunton, R. 1991. Aborigines and environmental myths: apocalypse in Kakadu. *Environmental Backgrounder*, 4, April. Canberra: Institute of Public Affairs.

Carter, P. 1987. *The road to Botany Bay*. London: Faber & Faber.

Clifford, J. 1988. *The predicament of culture*. Cambridge, Massachusetts: Harvard University Press.

Clifford, J. 1992. Travelling cultures. In *Cultural studies*, L. Grossberg, C. Nelson, P. Treichler (eds), 96–116. London: Routledge.

Cooper, D. 1985. *Report for the registration of the Upper South Alligator Bula complex*. Darwin: Aboriginal Sacred Sites Protection Authority.

Davis, S. L. 1989b. *Expansion and succession among Aboriginal groups in the Upper Alligator River Area*. Resources Managers, Darwin, NT Attachment 2 to Coronation Hill Joint Venture Representation 4 to the Kakadu Inquiry (1990) under s. 10 (4) of the Aboriginal and Torres Strait Islander Heritage Protection Act 1984.

Davis, S. L. & J. R. V. Prescott 1992. *Aboriginal frontiers and boundaries in Australia*. Melbourne: Melbourne University Press.

Fabian, J. 1983. *Time and the other*. New York: Columbia University Press.

Ferrier, E. 1990. Mapping power: cartography and contemporary cultural theory. *Antithesis* 1, 35–48.

Fisher, W. J. 1991. Job hopes die on Coronation Hill. *The Australian*, August 23.

Foucault, M. 1986. Of other spaces. *Diacritics* 16, 22–7.

Gelder, K. 1991. Coronation Hill: contesting the sacred. *Arena* 96, 14–17.

Gelder, K. & J. M. Jacobs 1992. "Talking out of place": contesting the sacred in postcolonial Australia. Unpublished paper, University of Melbourne.

Giroux, H. 1992. Resisting difference: cultural studies and the discourse of critical pedagogy. In *Cultural studies*, L. Grossberg, C. Nelson, P. Treichler (eds), 199–212. London: Routledge.

Harley, J. B. 1988. Maps, knowledge and power. In *The iconography of landscape*, D. Cosgrove & S. Daniels (eds), 277–312. Cambridge: Cambridge University Press.

Harley, J. B. 1992. Deconstructing the map. In *Writing worlds: discourse, text and metaphor in the representation of landscape*. T. J. Barnes & J. S. Duncan (eds), 193–230. London: Routledge.

Huggan, G. 1991. Decolonising the map: postcolonialism, poststructuralism and the cartographic connection. In *Past the last post: theorizing postcolonialism and postmodernism*, I. Adam & H. Tiffin (eds). London: Harvester Wheatsheaf.

Jacobs, J. M. 1988a. Politics and the cultural landscape: the case of Aboriginal land rights. *Australian Geographical Studies* 26, 249–63.

Jacobs, J. M. 1988b. The construction of identity. In *Past and present: the construction of Aboriginality*, J. R. Beckett (ed.), 31–44. Canberra: Aboriginal Studies Press.

Kapferer, B. 1988 *Legends of people, myths of state: violence, intolerance and political culture in Sri Lanka and Australia*. Washington: Smithsonian Institution Press.

Kearney, W. J. 1988. *Jawoyn (Katherine Area) land claim*. A report by the Aboriginal Land Commissioner, Mr Justice Kearney, to the Minister for Aboriginal Affairs and to the Administrator of the Northern Territory.

Keen, I. & F. Merlan 1990. *The significance of the conservation zone to Aboriginal people*. Resource Assessment Commission Kakadu Conservation Zone Inquiry Consultancy Series. Canberra: Australian Government Printing Service.

Levitus, R. 1990. *Historical perspective*. In AAPA Submission 77 to the Kakadu Conservation Zone Inquiry, Canberra: Resource Assessment Commission.

Maddock, K. 1987. Yet another "sacred site": the Bula controversy. In *Contemporary issues in Aboriginal studies: proceedings of the first Nepean conference on Aboriginal studies*, B. Wright, G. Fry, L. Petchkovsky (eds), 119–40. Sydney: Firebird Press.

Maddock, K. 1988. God, Caesar and Mammon at Coronation Hill *Oceania* **58**, 305–10.

Mani, L. 1992. Cultural theory, colonial texts: reading eye witness accounts of widow burning. In *Cultural studies*, L. Grossberg, C. Nelson, P. Treichler (eds), 392–408. London: Routledge.

Merlan, F. 1991. The limits of cultural constructionism: the case of Coronation Hill. *Oceania*, **61**. 341–52.

Merlan, F. & A. Rumsey 1982. *The Jawoyn (Katherine Area) land claim*. Darwin: Northern Lands Council.

Minh-ha, T. 1989. *Woman, native, other: writing postcoloniality and feminism*. Bloomington: Indiana University Press.

Morgan, H. 1991. *Reflections on Coronation Hill*. Speech presented at the Adam Smith Club, Melbourne, July 1991.

Noyes, J. K. 1992. *Colonial space: spatiality in the discourse of German South West Africa, 1884–1915*. Chur, Switzerland: Harwood Academic Publishers.

Pickles, J. 1992. Texts, hermeneutics and propaganda maps. In *Writing worlds: discourse, text and metaphor in the representation of landscape*. T. J. Barnes & J. S. Duncan (eds) 231–47. London: Routledge.

Resource Assessment Commission 1991a. *Kakadu Conservation Zone inquiry, final report, Volume 1*. Canberra: Australian Government Publishing Service.

Resource Assessment Commission 1991b. *Kakadu Conservation Zone inquiry, final report, Volume 2*. Canberra: Australian Government Publishing Service.

Ritchie, D. 1990. *Submission to the Kakadu inquiry*. Report by the Aboriginal Areas Protection Authority to the Resource Assessment Commission, Canberra.

Said, E. 1990. Yeats and decolonization. In *Nationalism, colonialism and literature*, T. Eagleton, F. Jameson, E. Said, 69–95. Minneapolis: University of Minnesota Press.

Tindale, N. B. 1974. *The Aboriginal tribes of Australia*. Berkeley: University of California Press.

PART III
PLACES OF RESISTANCE

The previous chapters emphasized various forms of identity as a locus for reproducing and resisting hegemonic ideas about "race", place and nation. The chapters in Part III focus on everyday places, such as the home and the school, as contexts in which the various dimensions of social relations intersect and are contested. The school and the home provide key contexts for the reproduction of imagined national communities, but they also serve as potential sites of resistance to such hegemonic views.

In her chapter, **Heléne Clark** suggests that social constructions can have an emancipatory potential to alter existing social relations. Drawing on Habermas's distinction between *system* and *lifeworld*, Clark shows that this potential is related to people's ability to understand how those constructions incorporate myths which reify the status quo and hence how they can appropriate their meaning. Clark illustrates this process through an examination of the ways in which low-income tenants in New York City have made emancipatory use of socially constructed categories and attitudes. She shows how tenant groups have used ideas about places that have value, about notions of "race" and gender, as well as conceptions of their own marginalized identities, to organize collectively and appropriate space. By employing prevailing constructions of their non-threatening social position, Clark's tenants have used conceptual space to construct new social definitions and to translate these into action, securing practical space for themselves and their new identities. Even though this process of redefinition and appropriation is rarely smooth and must be accomplished in negotiation with hegemonic structures, social constructions can be used to reinscribe place and to empower the gender- and "race"-based identities with which they are associated.

Like Clark, **Claire Dwyer** examines the social construction of identity in specific places, looking in this case at the school. As a key site in the construction of national culture, the school serves a dual rôle in the production of hegemony and in its resistance. Like all the chapters in this collection, Dwyer's chapter highlights the invisibility of dominant discourses until they are challenged. Such challenges set in train a whole series of contradictory responses, generating unexpected alliances among those who see an opportunity to realize various political ends.

Through an examination of the debate about state-funded Muslim schools in the UK, Dwyer shows how different constructions are mobilized to circumvent legislation that was designed to guarantee people's religious freedom. The fact that Catholics and Jews have long received state support for separate schools, while Muslims have so far been refused such support, demonstrates how groups receive differential treatment according to the perceived threat that they pose to the hegemonic culture. By defining citizenship in terms of loyalty to shared British values, and allegiance to Islam as "fundamentalism", Muslims are asked to abandon part of their cultural identity and civic rights in order to demonstrate a fealty that is seldom required of other British subjects. Similarly, Dwyer shows how different conceptions of "multiculturalism" squeeze Muslims into competing political discourses, leaving little room for self-definition or internal divergencies. As these chapters show, everyday spaces provide a vital ideological forum in the production and reproduction of unstable and competing social identities.

CHAPTER FIVE

Sites of resistance:
place, "race" and gender as sources of empowerment

HELÉNE CLARK

Introduction

As social movements become characterized more frequently as struggles over culture and identity rather than distribution, the small-scale, localized fights for rights to space seem to be less visible than their broader-based counterparts that focus on issues such as environmental degradation, equality (of gender, lifestyle, ethnicity) and oppression. In some cases, however, experiences of discrimination and lack of power combine with material threats to survival. This is often the situation faced by residents of the poorer neighbourhoods of most cities, who are confronted with the threat of displacement from their housing for a myriad of reasons. The tenuousness of the right to occupy space may result from deteriorated conditions, landlord abandonment, high crime rates, gentrification or eviction.

This chapter presents a social-theoretical framework for understanding possibilities and opportunities for social change based on the connection between specific forms of action and place. The empirical base is in limited-equity tenant co-operatives in New York City. It is an analysis of the actions of residents, who were often elderly, low-income, Black women, and the processes by which they reclaimed their homes and empowered themselves and their neighbours. Their efforts were drawn from their life experience of poverty, of raising their families and interacting with neighbours in particular neighbourhoods. To engage in a battle for control of their homes, these residents also drew on the effects of past experiences of racism and sexism,

121

as well as prevalent ideologies about places, homes and ownership. The result was the collective accomplishment of saving their homes from abandonment by landlords, deteriorating services and ultimately total loss.

To understand the formation of housing co-operatives in New York City as places of social change, it is necessary to understand their history, their geographic locations within the city, and the specific actions and action contexts of residents. Here, I use a social theoretical perspective of *system* and *lifeworld*, derived in part from Jürgen Habermas, to place these actions within a broader perspective. In addition, I contend that residents took advantage of many social constructions, about what places have value in society, about "race" and gender, about the rôle of domestic responsibilities, and about their own identities, to organize collectively and appropriate space.

The chapter ends with a discussion of the relevance that this local example may have for other efforts to effect social change. This focuses on how emancipatory use can be made out of socially constructed attitudes towards "race", ethnicity, gender, age and locales, such that social definitions are reconstructed at the same time as a safe space can be secured in which to nurture them.

The history of housing co-operatives in New York City

Housing co-operatives have a long but largely hidden history in New York. The reasons that so little is commonly known about this history provide another interesting look at the power of social constructions (see Leavitt 1993). Until the current movement of low income housing co-operatives, which began in the 1970s, most active periods in New York co-operative history provided housing for the middle and working classes. The almost 800 limited-equity co-ops in existence today have a genesis very different from those middle-income co-ops of earlier periods or the market-rate co-operatives that proliferate today. They began as a direct response by tenants to displacement from their homes. In New York, the 1970s were a time when several factors combined to create a crisis in thousands of buildings across the city. Recession, ageing infrastructure, rising costs and proportionally lower incomes of tenants often resulted in the decreasing profitability of rental apartment buildings for owners. In some cases, landlords did not collect enough rent to cover repairs; in many other cases, basic maintenance and payment of taxes was deferred in favour of reaping income from buildings. Overwhelmingly, landlords lived far away from the buildings they owned. Low-income tenants in the city's poorest neighbourhoods were little threat to landlords, as racism and lack of money prevented them from moving out or from forcing their landlords to change.

Eventually, hundreds of landlords stopped paying taxes and just ignored their buildings. In the mid–1970s, New York changed its housing law to allow the City to foreclose on any property that was not paying real estate tax. By reducing the default period from three years to one year, the City sought to reduce the number of buildings in arrears. The result was surprisingly unanticipated by City officials. Almost overnight, the City found itself owning thousands of apartment buildings that had been abandoned by their landlords. Tenant organizations and rent strikes had a long history in New York and, in some City-owned buildings, tenants followed this earlier practice and began to run their own buildings. Although it was illegal, it removed the burden from the City, and tenant groups gradually gained some support from housing advocates. In the late 1970s, the City of New York created a programme so that these "homesteaders" could manage, and then buy their buildings from the City at nominal cost. The City's goal was to get rid of a management nightmare and to return housing to the private market. Residents' priorities were a little different. They wanted to improve their buildings which were often uninhabitable after years of neglect, avoid displacement, and ensure long-term affordability. They also wanted to maintain the networks of social support they had developed over a period of years and which were vital to their survival.

The residents and co-operatives of this study

The analysis presented in this chapter has a variety of empirical bases. The main one is a study of 122 residents of fourteen limited-equity co-operatives which were established between five and ten years before the study. It was a direct follow-up to a study done by Leavitt & Saegert in the early 1980s in which they interviewed tenants in City-owned buildings to gain an understanding of what made some of them move to co-operative ownership while others did not, and what processes and resources were involved. In our follow-up study (the detailed results are presented in Clark et al. 1990b), we were interested in what problems co-operatives faced after the initial crisis, organizing and transfer of title occurred. We were also concerned with the type of strategies that were employed to solve problems and maintain buildings.

The research was done as part of a larger effort in partnership with a non-profit organization that provides training, technical assistance and information to limited-equity co-operatives city-wide. Our approach was an action research model, where we were participants in problem-solving and revealing little-known experiences, such as the commonality of certain problems among co-operatives. Following the completion of a final report on our findings, we participated with co-operative residents, technical assistance providers, housing advocates and policy-makers in a "professional exchange" which was convened to tackle some of the issues residents had expressed during the interview and meeting process. For example, one issue that concerned many residents and leaders in co-operatives was the lack of clarity on rules governing resale of apartments. Even sophisticated technical assistance providers could not get a clear policy from the agency responsible. Everyone agreed that the intent of the policy was to make sure that apartments remained affordable to low-income families. The original purchase price when tenants buy their apartment from the City is a nominal $250 per apartment. However, after five or ten years, many co-operatives faced original tenants moving, and each established their own policy. Most residents felt that this put a burden on individual buildings and residents to be altruistic and sell apartments for very small amounts, when legally they could sell them at market value. In some neighbourhoods, considering the excellent condition of the buildings themselves, and the end of the 1970s recession, apartments could have a market value of $100,000. Compounding the rising market value of apartments, buildings are often in need of funds to replace boilers, roofs, plumbing and other building systems due to their age. Co-op boards debated the value of using the sale of apartments to raise money for needed repairs against the importance of keeping prices very low. Amazingly, reviewing resale records for co-operatives all over the city since co-oping began in the late 1970s, we found that almost none chose to sell apartments at anywhere near market value, although they could have done so. Although committed to maintaining affordable housing for low-income families, guidelines for how to set consistent prices that fit the income levels of local residents were considered crucial. Residents were not asking for yet another rule or limit to be put on them by a City agency, but for assistance in figuring out an equitable policy that preserved affordability and removed the burden of constantly having to re-decide to forego profit.

Finally, the action research effort moved to the community level. Residents had expressed a great desire to know of other co-operatives, or City-owned buildings, that they could assist in moving to co-operative ownership. Even though City-owned buildings and co-operatives are very densely clustered geographically, following the patterns of both racism and disinvestment, few residents knew their neighbours. Even leaders were frustrated that they had accomplished so much in their buildings, but did not know how to move beyond that.

The formation of neighbourhood networks is now under way. Networks are being established through the efforts of residents, the technical assistance provider, and the researchers. My colleagues and I are actively engaged in assisting residents in the networking process, but are also responsible for evaluating the process and providing residents and technical assistants with an analysis of where co-operatives, residents and networks fit into the larger context of grass-roots organizing, political legitimation, low-income housing provision and empowerment. The ideas that follow come from all of the activities described above, and are evolving as residents move in other directions, hopefully expanding their space as they challenge the legitimacy of their oppression.

A system and lifeworld perspective

Co-operative housing is attracting increasing interest as a housing alternative for low income as well as higher-income groups. In Europe, co-operative housing has long been a major form of housing. However, little theoretical work exists explicating the rôle that co-operatives play in the national economy or the functioning of advanced capitalism. Even less theoretical attention has been directed to the people who actually live in and, in the case of New York City, also create co-operative housing.

The critical theoretical concepts of *system* and *lifeworld* provide useful starting points in understanding the struggle between residents of disinvested neighbourhoods who want to keep their homes, and economically motivated actors and institutions whose actions have resulted in landlord abandonment. These concepts can help to illuminate the processes and problems of co-operative building under different conditions, because they allow us to differentiate between the need for housing – for homes – from the perspective of residents, and the needs of bureaucrats, politicians and developers in the provision of housing. Because this theoretical framework does not hide the daily life and actions of residents from analysis, I believe it to be an ideal approach to understanding how people interact with bureaucracy, economic forces and political realities, as well as the significance that social constructions of gender, class, age and place play in forming their actions.

The term *system* in this framework means the sphere of economic, political and bureaucratic structures through which a society is organized. The *lifeworld* is the sphere of daily life in which the symbolic structures of a society are reproduced. Symbolic structures are the language, images, meaning and culture through which members of the society communicate and reach understanding about the nature of the world and their actions in it. These symbols form the background of daily life and experience, and allow for the reproduction of society (Habermas 1987). The *lifeworld* contains the norms and values of individuals and groups. It is in the *lifeworld* that social constructions, such as beliefs about racial differences, gender rôles or personal identity are reproduced and guide actions, and where challenges to their legitimacy can first arise.

System and *lifeworld* are mutually reinforcing and interdependent. However, the goals and values of each are different and they often clash. In Habermas's theory of society, it is the encroachment of the more powerful sphere, the *system*, on the areas of life more appropriately not decided by *system*-logic which results in both oppression and the undermining of the legitimacy of the *system* (Habermas 1975).

The most important point made by Habermas about *system* and *lifeworld* for understanding the struggles of residents to save their homes is that the *system* and *lifeworld* have different goals and are guided by different logics. The goals of the bureaucratic economic sphere are technical, geared to achieving the best, most cost-effective solution for the maintenance of the *system*. The goals of the *lifeworld* are primarily orientated toward understanding and actions that are based on mutual understanding and which sustain daily life and relationships. The difference between goals leads to a difference in the decision-making process between those made to sustain daily life in all of its social and cultural aspects and those made to achieve a technical goal. As residents, we all operate primarily with a *lifeworld* orientation to sustain our living environment, while bureaucracies operate primarily to achieve a technical goal of cost-efficient housing provision. Each type of decision is necessary and informs the other, but they are reached through different processes and they serve fundamentally different aims. While decisions made as some sort of social contract require intersubjective understanding, decisions made to meet technical needs require efficiency, cost-effectiveness, appropriate tools, and often power.

Habermas has suggested that different forms of rational action guide *system* and *lifeworld* to attempt to meet disparate goals. Habermas was the first to suggest that rationality may have more than the one meaning ascribed to it. This constitutes a significant departure from those, such as Weber, Horkheimer and Adorno, who viewed rationality as synonymous with technical mastery over both things and individuals, and therefore incompatible with emancipatory goals (Horkheimer & Adorno 1935). Instrumental rationality derives from *system* imperatives and therefore can only serve to maintain the existing *system*, never to transcend or transform it. Hence it is unable to bring about liberation. Habermas identified a second rational process in society which, unlike the seemingly ubiquitous instrumental rationality, contains emancipatory potential. This is the rationality of intersubjective communication which arises from *lifeworld* concerns.

The form of rationality usually engaged to provide housing in a private market is technical, in that it is directed towards the goal of constructing marketable housing units with maximum profit. However, non-profit housing, which also must be cost-conscious, is directed primarily towards other goals, such as creating more housing, providing access to housing for those who cannot afford the private market, affordability for residents, or meeting special needs. Housing that is controlled directly by the residents who live there has yet another set of primary goals, which arises from the need to make housing decisions compatible with the logic, norms and values of daily life. Unlike the technical rationality underlying most housing provision, residents rely primarily on the rationality that they use to construct their norms, values and social interactions.

This second rationality has been referred to by different theorists in differing ways. Gilligan (1982) describes moral reasoning in women as being based in communication and relationship to others, and contrasts this with moral reasoning in men which tends to focus on ethics and obligations. Habermas ties this second rationality to the *lifeworld*, rather than to gender. However, it is women's situatedness in the *lifeworld* that can account for Gilligan's findings, providing a social instead of biological basis to gender differences in forms of reasoning. For Habermas, communicative rationality reproduces symbolic structures, and instrumental rationality reproduces material structures. Gilligan does not distinguish between symbolic and material reproduction. My usage of the concepts of communicative rationality and action draws on Habermas's distinction and integration of *system* and *lifeworld*, and the association of communicative action with the *lifeworld*. However, in recognizing the identity of gender with spheres of action, and the interrelationship of symbolic and material reproduction, I depart from Habermas. My interpretation suggests that it is the social construction of gender, rather than an innate perspective, which locates women in the spheres guided by actions orientated towards understanding.

Social constructions of gender and "race" in the formation of action

The categories of *system* and *lifeworld* provide a starting point for understanding the actions of tenants in creating limited-equity co-operatives, but they are not sufficient without examining how specific social constructions create possibilities and barriers for the reclamation of space. In the case of tenant leaders forming co-operatives in the wake of landlord abandonment, "race", gender, age and income are more than incidental demographic descriptors. They are socially powerful constructions which combine to establish position in the hierarchy of social relations, self-identity and material need. They also give rise to an orientation that derives from the (enforced) experience of being on the periphery of the *system*. It is this non-*system* orientation that provides the potential for resistance.

In the mid–1980s, Leavitt & Saegert described the methods and activities of women who organized and saved their buildings. They identified a unique style that these women had evolved from their experiences of social and domestic organization. They termed this method of organizing the "community household" (Leavitt & Saegert 1988). It identifies a leadership style and organizing technique that builds on experiences of gender, "race" and class, and which has resulted in strong resident-managed co-operatives.

As Leavitt & Saegert described in their book *From abandonment to hope: community households in Harlem* (1988), the process of organizing collectively was in itself an empowering experience. It was neither gender-neutral nor "race"-neutral. Rather it arose directly from social relationships and shared values. Organizing the building was linked to how they had organized their domestic life. It was the skills and experiences of older, Black women who had lived in Harlem for many years that shaped leadership style.

The women who Leavitt & Saegert interviewed had always relied on social ties to maintain their households. When building survival was at stake, they used the longstanding social ties (previously applied to family survival) to organize actions at the building level. The networks grew larger to include all tenants, but the same acts of housekeeping and socializing were employed, as were strategies for social control, such as yelling at drug dealers on the stoop to make them go away.

Socially constructed gender differences in styles of action organization lead to a consideration of the connection between gender and forms of rationality, where action organization is theoretically linked to conceptions of rationality. Gilligan (1982) and Young (1990) identify women with a form of moral reasoning that is based in collectivity and communicative practices, rather than autonomy and abstract ideals. Whether one uses Habermas's or feminist concepts of an "other" rationality, examinations of its contextual use reveal that women often use a style that fits the sphere and location of their activity, and this "fit" derives from socially constructed beliefs about what constitutes public, private, domestic, and home.

Okin (1990) has pointed out that the categories of public and private, which underlie all traditional political theory, are rarely defined. Rather, an assumption that they are unproblematic and separate categories is a myth upon which traditional theory, political institutions and the gender division of labour rest. Benhabib (1992) explains gender differences in forms of reasoning as arising from women's locations in the home and personal relationships. In these spaces, women are seen as relating to others as "concrete" others, whereas men tend to form moral judgements based on an idea of an "abstract" other, which in turn comes from their relatively looser connection with home and with the maintenance of relationships.

Colonization and oppression

Habermas has conceptualized oppression as arising from the inappropriate dominance of the *system* and the instrumental rationality that guides it. Where *system* imperatives control aspects of life that should be directed by action rooted in normatively based consensus, the result is what Habermas calls "colonization of the *lifeworld*" (Habermas 1987). An example of colonization is the establishment of a client relationship between households and the state. As a client, households have to make personal decisions, such as whether or not to have a child, based on state rules that control their income, status or rights. The rôle of the household as a buffer or mediating zone between what has been characterized as the outside world and the individual – the public and the private, the *system* and *lifeworld* – has not been explored as a sphere of competing needs, existing as a key element of the *lifeworld* that must also meet the needs of the *system* for socialization. However, Wallerstein (1984) has characterized the household as a site of resistance.

For low-income residents, choices about the location, quality, permanency and daily management of their homes is severely circumscribed. When they are renters, they have little control over the economic decay or growth of their neighbourhoods, the profit available to their landlords, and the buying and selling of the properties in which they live. Publicly owned and administered housing eliminates some of these uncertainties in return for a set of rules under which the tenant must live. However, publicly owned housing is not itself isolated from *system* imperatives. Historically, the state and the economy have often reinforced mutually useful priorities. While during reform eras the state may buffer the demands of the economy, the current period of flexible capital accumulation has more often placed constraints on the amount that can be spent on welfare goals. As the state aligns itself with economic forces, tenants may be subject to decreased services, increased charges, or a lack of publicly owned housing. In both cases, the relationship of the resident to her/his housing can be disempowering, as the organization of daily life, which is intimately integrated with one's home, is guided by forces outside the logic of its residents.

The picture of increasingly economically *system*-dominated lives (that is, of ever-increasing colonization), would be bleak were it not for attempts occurring throughout society to prevent further encroachment and to regain control of the co-ordination of social action through normatively validated consensus. Co-operative housing, organized through the understanding of collective norms, can reverse this process, at least temporarily. Some of the material resources dominated by the *system* must be commanded for the physical maintenance of life.

Areas of resistance described in most of the critical theory literature are represented as organized around needs for identity, or sometimes ideological social movements. However, resistance can be place-based and the possibilities for empowerment may be different in struggles over specific places. In the case being discussed here, that struggle is over specific territory, but not just land. It is a place-based struggle to regain control of one's own home.

Emancipatory potential

If the concept of different rationalities is to be useful as a critical theoretical tool, the question that remains to be explored involves their implications for social change and individual or collective empowerment. Answering the question requires more than theoretical clarification. It also requires empirical evidence derived from the details of day-to-day decision making. Moreover, in addition to demonstrating that different rationalities exist, it must show that some significant transformation, which is emancipatory, takes place.

What constitutes a significant transformation is not an easy question. However, if we identify sets of social relationships which are oppressive, *in part* because of unchallenged meanings attributed to social categories, then one criterion for transformation may be the delegitimizing of those meanings. Low-income co-operative housing in New York seems to have successfully challenged the limits of the traditional meanings of domesticity, home ownership and self-help by relying on the accepted meanings of these terms to make the residents' actions politically acceptable before challenging them. For example, home ownership is an ideologically laden goal in American life. It is associated with having a stake in society, economic status and security, and individuation. Co-operatives were presented as a form of home ownership that would make low-income people more middle class, give them a stake in society and so on. That made them politically feasible. However, co-operative residents ascribe completely different meanings to their ownership. In interviews and meetings with hundreds of co-operative residents, they expressed the following values: freedom from fear of displacement, control over their homes, collective decision-making, maintenance of social relationships, a permanent place for low-income housing, and legal rights to their space. Most did not place any importance on their home as having exchange value, and viewed it as a collective, not individual, entity.

A second, more common, criterion is the reallocation of resources. In co-operatives the resources are rights to space and control over specific places. An interesting aspect of understanding co-operatives as social transformation is how the two criteria are interrelated. Further exploration is required into the ways in which the appropriation of specific places, and the economic and symbolic value they hold in society, alters their original value and thereby changes accepted meanings of other social categories, such as gender, "race" and age.

The significance of place

Critical theory lacks an analysis of the relationship of people to built form, of the material aspects of the *lifeworld*, and of the meaning of places in social movements and social resistance. Housing co-operatives are, quite obviously, physical places. What is less obvious, and remains to be worked out, is the significance of the location of co-operatives, the rôle of the physical form of one's home in the creation and maintenance of self-identity, and the very material, place-based nature of resistance which may occur in co-operatives. As John Forester has said:

> Habermas's reformulation of relations of power in terms of *lifeworld* colonization or penetration suggests a far wider range of sites of resistance . . . including homes, the public sphere, schools . . . Resistance to illegitimate power is itself social action, itself interpretive and contingent, itself an offering to others to act together, to learn together, to make possible life in a community. (1985: xv)

The community household model discussed above also recognizes the integral importance of the specific experience of place in tenants' organizing. The meaning of the community and the home to co-operative residents, and the connection between organizing and the sentiment and experiences of the neighbourhood and buildings they lived in have also been explored (Clark & Saegert 1989).

The daily social practices that occur in this particular form of resistance exemplify the many concrete acts and physicalities that constitute co-ordination of action based on shared meaning. Daily communicative acts that, taken together, maintain the social fabric of the co-operatives and lead to decisions that keep buildings running, represent a philosophical shift in action co-ordination. This shift undermines the legitimacy of actions taken by the *system*, when those actions violate intersubjectively agreed-upon norms.

Residents who lived together in declining neighbourhoods and who have experienced landlord abandonment share common and overlapping *life-worlds*. The actions they took to save their homes and gain control over them arose from intersubjective communication and were rich in the value orientations of the actors. As such, they provide a vivid example of the intersection of the *system* and *lifeworld*, colonization and ultimately resistance.

Limited-equity co-operatives as places of resistance

My own research on co-operatives, my colleagues' experiences and the earlier work of Leavitt & Saegert all made apparent the difference between co-operatives as a housing programme and the daily experiences of residents attempting to remake their environment. We later came to characterize this as a *system/lifeworld* difference. Without this distinction (regardless of the terminology used) housing types or programmes are discussed and evaluated only from the point of view of policy, efficiency and economics. The daily lives, experiences and place-making activities of residents are hidden from view by the constituted sphere of dialogue which operates as if only the *system* mattered. The term "abandonment" provides a useful example of how *system*-orientated our discussions usually are. The economic crisis that precipitated landlords' disinvestment in buildings is usually called abandonment. Marcuse (1986) has said that abandonment could be defined as occurring when public or private parties act on the assumption that long-term investment is not warranted. Displacement of residents from buildings and neighbourhoods in which disinvestment occurs is assumed to be inevitable.

"Abandonment" as commonly used, refers to the capital-investment status of a building or neighbourhood, rather than whether or not residents continue to live there. The irrelevance of residents' activities in this process is demonstrated by the supposed inevitability of displacement. The logic of this course assumes that there is no alternative. Limited-equity ownership opens up a space in which another logic comes into play, preventing displacement through the use of collective, communicative practices. These practices would not be transformative, however, if they did not lead to a reclamation of some power and control. For co-operatives, leaders were able to appropriate meanings and understand the myths upon which the *system* functioned, transferring the rights to reproduce those meanings in ways that suited their intersubjective norms.

A full understanding of the context and possibilities of any form of housing requires breaking loose *system*-dominated discussion and recognizing the legitimacy of everyday experiences as a sphere where meanings are constructed, given value, and acted upon. Just as women have been invisible in traditional research settings, poor and minority residents have been invisible in housing policy, except as powerless groups that government legislates for without asking about the values and valued activities of their *lifeworld*.

It is the "unmasking" nature of a critical theoretical perspective that provides a possibility for the emancipation of residents from housing decisions made as if *only* the *system* forces were operative or important. Without a critical intent, we may see only dilapidated buildings in devastated neighbourhoods – tangible remains of the movement of capital out of inner cities, of the inefficiency of housing provision and the disempowerment of the poor. Reconstructed critically, we may see a stage for acts that are played out on a daily basis. These acts are gradually redefining the rôle of purposive action in modern society, and liberating the actors as they follow their own scripts.

It would, however, be simplistic to ignore the interdependency of *system* and *lifeworld* or to suppose that any residents engaged in communicative action have freed themselves from *system domination*. It is the combination of empowering, collective, norm-based actions and particular institutional circumstances that creates an opening for transformation. To make use of that opening, meanings must be negotiated and appropriated.

Huber (1980) has described areas within society which can be characterized as "liberated" because they function as counter-institutions which are based on action co-ordinated through understanding and they lie outside the steering of action through money and power. Co-operatives seem to be such "liberated" areas and the distinction of action co-ordination appears analogous to communicative and instrumental rationality. However, Huber's assumption that such counter-institutions arise within the *lifeworld* and will divert an informal, non-profit sector out of the main economic *system* underestimates the interrelationship between *lifeworld* and *system*, and the situatedness of such counter-institutions.

The co-operatives began outside the main economic system which had devalued them and have actually re-entered it now that they are back on the tax rolls, in good physical condition and again have exchange value (although this is not acknowledged as important by residents, except insofar as it indicates the improved condition of their homes). Housing co-operatives, like all social institutions, maintain themselves through a combination of instrumental action and communicative action. Homes and households have been theorized as buffer zones in which the needs of both the *system* and the *lifeworld* are met. Individuals are socialized in such a way that they will be able to function both in the *system* and develop their personal identity and values.

The dual function of the household under conditions of landlord abandonment helps reveal the problem of equating the material dimension of life with the *system*. Habermas has identified the *system* with outer nature and the *lifeworld* with inner nature. For the older Black women who led the tenant organizations that were included in my research, perceptions of the material and social aspects of their home were continuous. This is because, within the household, people are physically produced as well as socialized. The household organizes and distributes the goods it gains from the economy according to its own rationality. This mode of organization responds first to the imperatives of producing and maintaining the lives of household members. Only incidentally does it accept *system* imperatives. However, it is itself guided by *system* imperatives to produce members of society that will function and be socialized appropriately for that system. When *system* and *lifeworld* imperatives conflict, the household can serve as a point of resistance to the system. Of course, this resistance is limited by the power and resources the household can command.

Problems in maintaining communicative processes

The general theoretical framework I use comes from a composite picture of buildings and people with unique stories and personalities. However, in a small sample of fourteen co-operatives at different stages of development, a discernible pattern of similarities and differences emerged (see Clark et al. 1990b). Co-ops that were most successful several years after their creation all had a high level of social integration and communication among tenants. This is consistent with Leavitt & Saegert's (1990) findings in newly established co-operatives. Here, it became apparent that buildings were most likely to move successfully to co-operative ownership when the social life of tenants and the co-oping process were integrated.

An important similarity in successful co-operatives was the longstanding ties which residents had with their neighbourhood. On average, residents of the co-operatives had lived in the immediate neighbourhood for seventeen years. This included years spent in buildings which were deteriorating as landlords reduced and eliminated services. Many of the Black women who led their tenant organizations had lived in the building or neighbourhood for thirty or forty years, particularly in Harlem (Saegert 1989). Their mutual knowledge and support systems were strong and long-term. Residents shared perceptions about their neighbourhoods that were based on its history, even though to an outsider these perceptions seemed hard to conceptualize under current conditions of deterioration. Patterns of conflict and dislike were so familiar that most people were comfortable with them.

Common experience of community was also linked to common experiences of "racial" oppression. The culture of older Harlem residents, for example, integrated experiences of racism with African–American traditions of resistance (Saegert 1989). Similarly, the predominantly Latino co-ops usually housed expatriates of a particular Latin American country who shared a culture of origin, the economic and social conditions of that country which prompted migration and the experiences of immigration.

Discourse between residents cannot always be free of *system* constraints and technical imperatives. Consequently, a tenant organization may reach consensus based on shared norms, but lack the legal authority or material resources to act. The success of co-operatives depended on those who were active at the beginning of the movement recognizing the need to interact with the *system* in a way that would lead to political and legal change. They had a point of entry for change, which was not of their own making, in the space opened up by disinvestment. The fact that their buildings had no economic value according to the *system* allowed them a degree of control which they could not otherwise have had. It was also the absence of economic value that allowed women to take charge. The traditional association of men with the economic sphere and women with the domestic, worked in favour of the women leaders, who were not challenged by either male residents, or by the bureaucrats who tended to see the buildings as having no value as real estate, only as homes. The traditional structure of Black family life also supported the rôle that women took on to provide for the survival of the building. For the most part, men in the buildings approved of what the women leaders did, and felt it was consistent with their jobs in the household.

Leaders with access to outside resources, and leaders able to talk in the language of the *system* to bureaucrats, were also important elements in the success of co-ops. Technical assistance, training and access to professionals were all utilized by successful buildings. The layer of technical assistance providers and the social organization of the building were both intermediate zones between the *system* and *lifeworld* that served as a buffer for competing needs, a base for reaching in both directions and a site of integration for the *system* and *lifeworld*. Buffer areas are similar to what Kunneman (1989) has termed "zones of interference". Within zones of interference, the goals of both the *system* and the *lifeworld* are met. As noted before, this is precisely the rôle of the household in promoting the growth of the individual, but one which adapts the rules and values of the larger society.

These buffers between the *system* and the *lifeworld* are necessarily filled with tensions. One of the processes Kunneman identifies, that of systematically distorted communication, exemplifies the difficulty of retaining truly communicative rationality when material existence and legal rights depend on *system* forces. The cases of distorted communication that Kunneman presents occur when the "client" of an institution, charged with mediating between the *system* and the *lifeworld*, encounters an employee of that *system*; for example, a school counsellor and a troublesome student, or a resident in a co-op and a manager hired by the housing association (van Wezel, 1990). However, the same sort of distortion can occur within co-ops by the various members involved in decision-making.

Successful co-ops were able to sustain participation among members after the initial purchasing phase was over. Those with the most democratic organization and the greatest levels of communication and shared understandings had the best participation. A more common experience was the emergence of conflicts and a falling off of participation after the period of crisis was over and something like normal management began.

Durkheim's (1933) work on the transitory nature of participation based on interest offers insight into this tendency which has been confirmed by more recent studies of participation (Ungar & Wandersman 1985, Gittell 1980). Durkheim believed that a lack of unity may be concealed by having a common interest. When the "moment of interest" passes, nothing remains to unite the individuals. Therefore the total harmony of interests really conceals a latent conflict, which may surface after the initial convergence of interests ends (Durkheim 1933). This may have some explanatory value as we identify the life-cycles of tenant organizations. The co-operatives experienced similar problems and stages after initial purchase of the building from the City. Although the histories and residents of the co-operatives were unique, and even though the details of problems differed, the succession and range of difficulties encountered both during and after the formative years were remarkably alike (Saegert et al. 1990).

Originally, the common interest was to avoid displacement and the common enemy was the City. After the crisis was over, those co-operatives that made a successful transition to continuing participation without crisis were those whose actions were based on common understanding to begin with. The greatest level of satisfaction with management and resident involvement was reported in buildings that had the clearest consensus and norms. In buildings where the communication process was thwarted or distorted, participation declined, often dramatically.

In his study of tenant management in the Netherlands, van Wezel (1990) describes the frustration that arose from what he called quasi-communication. This occurred as residents interacted with representatives of the Dutch housing system. The state representatives managed a large budget and followed national regulations for efficiency, repairs and cost–benefits. Residents tried to talk to representatives about how to maintain their homes. For example, residents chose different paint colours for doors, but this was not allowed as it increased the paint cost, which was lower if only one colour was bought in bulk. Residents were willing to paint their own doors, but this was not allowed. Discussion led to frustration on both sides. However, the representatives of the state housing system held more power; therefore, in this example, communication was distorted and coerced. Its primary aim was not towards reaching understanding, but towards reaching compliance.

Every building- and resident organization we worked with experienced some level of social conflict, and almost all considered it a personal failing. In some buildings, there were minor personality clashes, in others conflict debilitated the decision-making process. The strong feelings that residents held about conflicts may be related to their assumptions about how decisions and actions should be reached. A normative, communicative process that aims at consensus depends on shared meanings and an understanding among participants that others will listen to you, and that when you listen to them they are interested in being fair and truthful. In theoretical terms, Habermas (1984) uses the term "validity claims" to describe the criteria we all assume will be met if we enter into communication orientated towards understanding with others.[1]

If individuals question the good intentions of others, then the norms of the process are seen to be violated. A violation of the normative assumptions attendant upon communicative action means a breakdown in the process of decision-making. In such circumstances, not only do social relationships suffer but decisions to maintain the housing co-operative are adversely affected as well. In one building, we found a stalemate in decision-making based on mutual distrust, which prevented a new boiler from being installed for two winters.

A very complex source of difficulty or conflict in a co-operative is the need for leaders to move constantly between communicative rationality and instrumental rationality. Leaders must interact regularly with professional building managers, loan providers, lawyers, the courts, tax collectors and suppliers, all of whom perform their functions technically, and are guided by instrumental rationality. However, as leaders of the residents' decision-making process, the representatives of co-operatives must not subordinate the decision-making process to technical demands. Rather, decisions about how to use money or regarding repairs, sales or even evictions, must arise out of the shared normative values of the *lifeworld* to be seen as legitimate.

Of course, no leader can perform this balancing act perfectly, and errors appear to residents as violations of norms and good faith. They then blame leaders for bad decisions, and maintenance and repair problems can become personalized. How much a communicative breakdown affected building operations seemed to depend on how consciously residents and leaders attempted to separate technical decisions about the building from personal feelings towards leaders, and whether the leaders felt incapacitated by hostilities. In either case, the democratic process of the co-operative was compromised and participation declined. Conversely, the most successful co-operatives are those where this balance is most well maintained. Leaders who developed the knack of using technical assistance and outside resources to fulfil the communicatively arrived at needs of residents, rather than vice versa, were best able to keep the empowering element of the subordination of *system* imperatives intact.

In general, policy-makers and even technical assistance providers have been insensitive to the importance of a viable communicative process. As a result, they have tended to focus all of their efforts on technical training, such as book-keeping, and on the technical expertise of residents. One of the goals of our research (after we learned of its importance ourselves) was to legitimate social and communicative skills and to promote technical assist-ance for conflict resolution, participatory processes, and social cohesion in addition to the technical training. Given that most of the useful solutions were those which some co-ops were already using, training had to be developed by meeting with residents. It was not assumed that the technical assistance provider or the researchers had any superior knowledge in these areas. Nevertheless, it was recognized that these people could legitimize and disseminate solutions found by residents. This effort has been reasonably successful. For example, new workshops have been offered at co-operative conferences, often led by leaders or residents from buildings that used a particularly effective technique. Broadening technical assistance meant much more than adding new training categories. It meant a change in ideas about what constitutes training and skills, and a reconstruction of beliefs about things that people (residents as well as technical assistants or bureaucrats) previously considered to be personality issues.

The tendency for technical assistance providers and bureaucrats to privilege technical knowledge, while residents privilege group cohesion and understanding, derives in part from their socially constructed location within society. Habermas (1987) draws a conceptual line of conflict separating the productive core of society from those outside of it. Poor, older, Black resi-dents of disinvested neighbourhoods are located in the outside "peripheral amalgam". While this does not make them less subject to *system* constraints, it does mean that they are less tied to reproducing their norms according to *system* needs.

Space and resistance

To claim any real possibilities for social transformation stemming from transformations in rationality, we must be able to show that co-operatives support resident struggles to sustain their *lifeworld*, both in its normative content and its material substance. Much feminist writing begins with calling for a need to "locate" the female subject. Such location has provided much insight into social relations. However, it is also important to locate the female subject in a more physical sense. Geographical segregation of poor women and female-headed households is a reality in urban areas. Women and low-income residents lack access and opportunity to appropriate physical spaces to pursue personal projects.

The significance of these dimensions of "situatedness" means that the emergence of women leaders and the organizing style that they developed is directly related to the physical space of their particular *lifeworld*. The importance of home and of the actual sites of social reproduction are often neglected by critical theorists. Habermas has moved the location conceptually to the social processes that reproduce culture and society, but has not recognized the importance of the physical and spatial reality of that domain.

Urban theorists have also tended to separate the social processes of urban life from their spatial dimensions. In the more recent analyses of gentrification, however, there have been attempts to conceptualize the expansion and contraction of the housing market as spatial expressions of social processes (Smith & Williams 1986). Landlord and institutional abandonment of the living spaces of the urban poor, and the subsequent reclamation of that space by its residents, is also an inextricably place-based and spatial representation of both the processes of capital and the resistance to it.

Castells believes that such place-based movements are "organized according to a logic of power which is distinct from, and at odds with, the global logic which increasingly penetrates and determines the lives of local populations" (1987: 17). To illustrate the polarity of daily life and the global economic *system* Castells has coined the phrases "placeless power" (the global economy) and "powerless places" (communities). He uses these terms to juxtapose the growth of communication technologies that allow the transfer of capital without the need for face-to-face or place contact with the local social relations of lived experience. The different logics of which he speaks could easily be thought of as parallels to instrumental and communicative action. In fact, Castells says that while internationalization relies on the flow of communication, communities are organized around "their own communi- cation codes on the basis of an historically specific territory" (1987: 7). Is this the communicative rationality of the shared *lifeworld*? If we draw this parallel, we can begin to spatialize the effects of the two means of co-ordinating action. Considering a "dominant logic based on flows" to be a form of colonization, we can then concretize its abstract nature by identifying a spatial manifestation. One possibility is that the very form of conflict and defence has become increasingly localized as Castells maintains. In this way it is seen as physically reduced to common territory and to shared, physically dependent, communication means.

The importance of place and of the appropriation of space for housing co- operatives suggests that the distinction between symbolic reproduction and material reproduction made by Habermas, and that between struggles over identity instead of distribution, made by many urban theorists (see, for example, Castells 1983), is not as clear-cut as recent discussions indicate. Struggles for identity may, as in co-operatives, be struggles simultaneously over rights to space. For example, gay and lesbian oppression has included a lack of public (or even private) spaces to meet and this has made the development of an individual, let alone group, identity difficult and invisible (Wolfe 1990). The home, as a site for both material and symbolic reproduc- tion, is an important place in which women achieve identity and empower- ment. The increased sense of self-confidence and empowerment that resulted from the saving of the home would not have occurred without achieving control of the space.

Conclusion

Housing co-operatives have the potential to be empowering, not only in a psychological sense but also as a source of real political legitimation of previously ignored members of society. However, it is important to under- stand the conditions in which this occurs. As a new form of social and spatial practice existing within a *system* of advanced global capitalism, low- income co-operatives have more than just local significance.

In this chapter I have presented a theoretical framework that challenges the traditional dominance of housing provision over housing experience, and of the *system* over the residents. By giving voice to the experiences and actions of residents, a new perspective emerges which legitimizes communi- cative action and recognizes its emancipatory potential. Opening up space in discussion for everyday practice also reveals the social construction of the *lifeworld* and the association of its rationality with gender. Moreover, in understanding some of the conditions for the success of co-ops, I have also tried to stress how important it is that leaders are able to understand existing social myths and constructions so that they can gain entry into the *system* and appropriate resources necessary to challenge those myths in practice. I believe that other social movements can learn important lessons from the continuing history of limited-equity co-operatives in New York. In particular, they may recognize the power of combining an environmental, place-based change with the development of democratic practices that delegitimize social relations of domination, thereby giving empowerment a place to take root.

Acknowledgement

Special thanks to Dr Susan Saegert in the Environmental Psychology Program at the Graduate Center of the City University of New York for her advice and insight in our many discussions of these ideas.

Note

1. See Habermas's (1984) discussion of validity claims and the ideal speech situation, which identifies conditions under which communicative action is "rationally motivated". The ideal speech situation assumes equality of power and no external constraints on participants, and is posited as a counterfactual. As such, it provides a means to understand how far from "rational" a consensus is, and requires explication of power relationships to evaluate any discourse.

References

Benhabib, S. 1992. *Situating the self.* New York: Routledge.

Castells, M. 1983. *The city and the grassroots.* Berkeley: University of California Press.

Castells, M. & J. Henderson 1987. Techno-economic restructuring, socio-political processes and spatial transformation: a global perspective. In *Global restructuring and territorial development,* J. Henderson & M. Castells (eds), 1–17. Beverly Hills,: Sage.

Clark, H., S. Saegert, E. K. Glunt 1990a. Emerging issues in New York City low-income co-operative housing. Paper presented at CILOG–Plan Urbain Conference: Les Enjeux Urbains de l'Habitat, Paris.

Clark, H., S. Saegert, E. K. Glunt, W. Roane 1990b. *The future of limited-equity housing in New York City: residents struggle for stability.* New York: Center for Human Environments.

Durkheim, E. 1933. *The division of labor in society* (translated by G. Simpson). New York: The Free Press.

Forester, J. 1985. Introduction: the applied turn in contemporary critical theory. In

Critical theory and public life, J. Forester (ed.), ix–xix. Cambridge, Mass.: MIT Press.

Gilligan, C. 1982. *In a different voice: psychological theory and women's development.* Cambridge, Mass.: Harvard University Press.

Gittell, M. 1980. *Limits to citizen participation: the decline of community organization.* Beverly Hills: Sage.

Habermas, J. 1975. *Legitimation crisis.* Boston: Beacon Press.

Habermas, J. 1984. *The theory of communicative action,* Volume 1. Boston: Beacon Press.

Habermas, J. 1987. *The theory of communicative action,* Volume 2. Boston: Beacon Press.

Horkheimer, M. & T. Adorno 1972. *Dialectic of enlightenment.* New York: Continuum.

Huber, J. 1980. *Wer soll das alles Andern?* Berlin (as cited in Habermas 1987).

Kunneman, H. 1989. Therapeutisation of the teacher–pupil relation as an instance of the interference between system and lifeworld. Unpublished paper, University of Amsterdam.

Leavitt, J. 1993. The interrelated history of alternative housing tenure: cooperatives and public housing from the thirties to the fifties. Unpublished paper.

Leavitt, J. & S. Saegert 1988. The community household: Responding to housing abandonment in New York City. *American Planning Association, Journal,* **54,** 489–500.

Leavitt, J. & S. Saegert 1990. *From abandonment to hope: community-households in Harlem.* New York: Columbia University Press.

Marcuse, P. 1986. Abandonment, gentrification and displacement: the linkages in New York City. In *Gentrification of the city,* N. Smith & P. Williams (eds), 153–77. Winchester, Mass.: Allen & Unwin.

Okin, S. M. 1991. Gender, the public and the private. In *Political theory today,* D. Held (ed.), 67–90. Stanford, California: Stanford University Press.

Saegert, S. 1989. Unlikely leaders, extreme circumstances: older Black women building community households. *American Journal of Community Psychology* **17**(3), 295–316.

Saegert, S. & H. Clark 1989. *The meaning of home in low-income cooperative housing in New York City.* New York: Center for Human Environments.

Saegert, S., H. Clark, E. K. Glunt 1990. Life-cycle development in low-income housing cooperatives. Paper presented at combined American and British Applied Anthropology Conference, York, England.

Smith, N. & P. Williams 1986. Alternatives to orthodoxy: invitation to a debate. In *Gentrification of the city,* N. Smith & P. Williams (eds), 1–12. Winchester, Mass.: Allen & Unwin.

Ungar, D. & A. Wandersman 1985. The importance of neighbors: the social, cognitive and affective components of neighboring. *American Journal of Community Psychology,* **13**(2), 139–69.

van Wezel, R. 1990. Tenant management vs management by tenants: a contribution from the perspective of communicative action theory. Paper presented at CILOG-Plan Urbain Conference: Les Enjeux Urbains de L'Habitat, Paris, France.

Wolfe, M. 1990. Whose culture? Whose space? Whose history?: learning from lesbian bars. Keynote address, 11th Biennial Conference of the International Association for the Study of People and Their Surroundings (IAPS), Ankara, Turkey, July, 1990.

Young, I. M. 1990. *Justice and the politics of difference.* New Jersey: Princeton University Press.

CHAPTER SIX

Constructions of Muslim identity and the contesting of power:
the debate over Muslim schools in the United Kingdom

CLAIRE DWYER

Introduction

Contemporary cultural geography has employed a dynamic notion of culture as "a domain in which economic and political contradictions are contested and resolved . . . meanings are negotiated and relations of dominance and subordination are defined and contested" (Jackson 1989: 1). This conception of culture has enabled geographers to focus on the extent to which land- *school* scapes can be subject to different readings (Cosgrove & Jackson 1987, Duncan 1990) and how different groups may compete in space to produce expressions of culture (Jackson 1989, Anderson & Gale 1992). Such struggles over meaning are also struggles over different modes of being or different identities (Minh-ha 1989). What such studies suggest is that the social construction of space plays an important rôle in the production of culture and in struggles over different cultural identities. Culture is not simply contested within particular territories but is spatially as well as socially *spatially + socially* constituted.

 Several theorists have argued that the school is a key site of the production of culture, where cultural meanings are contested and struggled over (Giroux 1981, Willis 1977). The school becomes the site where the dominant culture is to be transmitted, but is also the site where cultural meanings can be resisted or contested. In this chapter I examine how a contestation over *School* culture and the desire to protect particular constructions of meaning and identity intersects with a struggle over space at the site of the school.

The chapter considers the recent and continuing efforts by some groups of Muslims in the UK to gain state funding for existing private Muslim schools. While in British law there is a right to establish state-funded religious schools, Muslim attempts to do so have so far been unsuccessful. This struggle can be seen as a symbolic issue which represents a challenge to the hegemonic culture. State funding for Muslim schools is sought because it constitutes one way of obtaining control over the construction of space and its capacity to produce cultural meaning.[1]

This challenge revolves around the construction of competing discourses about "race", religion and nationalism. In my discussion of these discourses I illustrate some of the constructions of "race" and place employed by the main parties involved in the debate about state-funded Muslim schools. My argument here is three-fold. First, I want to illustrate the significance of particular places in the constructions employed in debates about Muslim schools. As the discussion below illustrates, particular places became racialized in the debates about multicultural education in the 1980s and some of these places emerged as key sites in the struggle to secure state funding for Muslim schools. Secondly, in a discussion of the range of constructions employed in the debate about Muslim schools, the cross-cutting of some previous alliances is drawn out to demonstrate the fluidity of cultural identities. This evidence of the instability of categories is identified as an important insight into the emerging politics of difference (Hall 1992). Finally, the implications of emerging constructions of a distinctive Muslim identity and its relation to the social construction of "race" and place are considered.

Multicultural education: a context

In reading the debate about state-funded Muslim schools as symbolic of the contestation of culture at the locus of the school, it is important to situate the discussion within the history of debates about the nature of education in the UK. In particular, the debate about Muslim schools has to be seen in the context of discussions about multicultural education since the late 1960s. These debates about the cultural meaning of education have often been focused in particular places.

In the 1960s, the school was seen as the primary site where the "integration" of "ethnic minority" populations was to be achieved. Multicultural education emerged in the late 1970s, specifically in response to concerns about the perceived academic "underachievement" of "ethnic minority"

children, which was seen as linked to a monocultural experience of education. The aim of multicultural education was to provide a curriculum which
broadened the range of resources and activities offered, so that they reflected
the diverse cultural backgrounds of the pupils. For example, a multi-faith
approach could be offered in religious education, or books from a broader
geographical and cultural background could be studied in English literature.
Under the auspices of the Swann Committee, which produced its report in
1985, the agenda of multicultural education was expanded to include the
education of all children as members of an increasingly "plural society". Thus
multicultural education was not simply focused on the minority status of
"ethnic" children, but it emphasized instead a policy of Education for all
(HMSO 1985).

By the end of the 1980s the efficacy of multicultural education was being
challenged from both sides. There was an argument for a "stronger" version
of multicultural education – "anti-racist education" – which went beyond the
symbolic level of "saris, samosas and steel bands" (Troyna 1990: 404) to the
roots of racism by examining the operation of unequal power relations. Within this curriculum, pupils were encouraged to understand the historical
processes of colonialism and immigration as a means of understanding the
existence of the contemporary British "multicultural" society. Anti-racist
policies were developed by many urban local education authorities (LEAs)
including the Inner London Education Authority (ILEA). Such policies were
implemented against a backcloth of a progressive diminution of local authority power, culminating in the abolition of the Greater London Council by
central government in 1986.

The control of the political and fiscal power of local government coincided
with the emergence of a doctrine of "anti-anti-racism" articulated both by
members of central government and in the press, but also fuelled by disquiet
from parents expressed in different ways in different places (see below).
Reflecting these trends, in 1988, the incumbent Conservative Government
passed the Education Reform Act (ERA) which introduced significant changes
in education in Britain. Education was identified as the primary means by
which British economic competitiveness could be restored by the "raising of
educational standards". In part, this improvement was to be achieved by the
implementation of a national curriculum, a curriculum which can be interpreted as a rejection of many multicultural initiatives in favour of an
implicitly monocultural agenda. For example, ERA reiterated the centrality of
Christianity in school assemblies, which suggested a rejection of previous
pluralistic interpretations of the rôle of religion in education. Thus, a
reactionary educational policy was introduced at precisely the time when a
new progressive doctrine was taking shape, but when local powers to

implement such policies were being undermined.

In summary, it is possible to identify three alternative positions with regard to multicultural education in the preceding discussion. The first is a "liberal" position which is supportive of a "many cultures" approach which encourages children to celebrate diversity and plurality. The second is a more radical approach which seeks to challenge the status quo and to examine why some cultures are dominant. The third is a more reactionary stance which would adopt a "neutral" position, arguing that all children should accept a "British" culture. In the debate about Muslim schools, both sides draw upon a variety of constructions of multicultural education, appealing to both radical and reactionary strands of the argument, as the following discussion demonstrates. Reaction to the demand for Muslim schools was strongly influenced by the history of multicultural education and I want to focus on two places which became politicized around issues of multicultural education and where the question of Muslim schools emerged in the context of a racialized debate about education.

The first example is the northwest London borough of Brent, which has been a significant site in the politics of multicultural education. Brent was one of the earliest boroughs to adopt an anti-racist education policy, reflecting a commitment to its ethnically diverse population which includes people of Caribbean, Asian and Irish origin. In 1985, Brent received critical media coverage of its suspension of Ms McGoldrick (later reinstated), a head teacher accused of making a racist remark. In 1986, the setting up of a "Development Programme for Racial Equality" in the borough was the subject of a government inquiry, headed by David Lane, former head of the Commission for Racial Equality. The report (Lane 1988) was broadly supportive of the programme, but warned of the rôle of negative press coverage of anti-racism policies in Brent in contributing to "widespread uneasiness" about education in the borough. It was against this background of a highly politicized discussion of multicultural education that the attempts by Muslims to open a state-funded school in the borough were rejected (see below).

A second significant site in the politics of multicultural education has been the city of Bradford in West Yorkshire. In 1982, calls for Muslim schools in Bradford prompted the establishment of guidelines for multicultural education, which included the provision of Islamic teaching and halal meat as well as the safeguarding of places in single-sex schools. This constituted a successful consensus between the education authorities and Muslim parents. Events in 1984, the so-called "Honeyford Affair", were to result in increased polarization between the Muslim population and the education authorities. The "Honeyford Affair" describes a campaign launched against Ray Honeyford, the head teacher of Drummond Middle School in Bradford which contained a large percentage of children of Asian descent, following his publication in early 1984 of articles critical of multicultural education policy. After a two-year dispute, Honeyford accepted an early retirement offer. The case became a *cause célèbre* for debate about issues of "race" and education both nationally and in Bradford itself (see Halstead 1988) and it provoked the media-driven articulation of discourses of "anti-anti-racism" (Murray 1986).

These events in Bradford not only increased support for Muslim schools among a wider sector of the Muslim population but also marked the increasing radicalization of young Muslim men in particular, and a resulting deterioration in "race relations". This helps to explain the prominence of the rôle played by Bradford Muslims in the "Rushdie Affair" (Samad 1992). The "Rushdie Affair" refers to events provoked by the publishing of *The Satanic Verses* by Salman Rushdie, a book considered blasphemous by many Muslims.[2] While the "Rushdie Affair", and the anti-Muslim sentiments it inspired, unquestionably resulted in a widespread feeling of hurt and bitterness in the Muslim community (Alibhai 1989, Akhtar 1989), it also politicized issues of identity for Muslims in Britain (Eade 1992) and is thus an important context for the debate about Muslim schools.

In the preceding discussion I have sought to place the campaign for Muslim schools within the context of evolving debates about multicultural education in the UK and to suggest that the places where the debate about Muslim schools has emerged are places where the politics of education have become racialized. However, the constructions of multiculturalism employed in both places vary. While the call for Muslim schools in Bradford may have emerged in reaction to the anti-multiculturalism sentiments of Ray Honeyford, the campaign for a Muslim school in Brent reflects a dissatisfaction with the secularism of existing multicultural education. Hence, as I discuss below, different constructions of multiculturalism are employed in different situations.

Having outlined the general context in which the campaign for state-aided Muslim schools occurred, the remainder of this chapter focuses primarily on one particular campaign to gain a state-funded Muslim school. It examines the range of constructions of "race", religion, education and nationalism which the schools campaign prompted. The discussion is based mainly upon "public discourse" in the media and political debate, although this is also supplemented by interviews carried out with some of the individuals involved.[3]

British Muslims and education

Education has been an important concern for the Muslim population in the UK, and educational campaigns have provided a unifying call for some Muslim leaders. Concern about education has focused on both the need to provide for dietary and religious observances and on the importance of religious and language teaching as a means of retaining cultural and ethnic identity (see Anwar 1986, Ashraf 1988). The provision of single-sex education has also been a focus of concern. At the same time there is widespread recognition of the value of academic achievement for success in British society (Joly 1986, Afshar 1989). Educational needs have been met in a variety of different ways, via supplementary schools, the establishment of private Muslim schools, campaigns to incorporate Muslim needs into state schools and, finally, by attempts to establish state-aided Muslim schools.[4]

In theory, Muslim schools can be established according to existing legislation which allows the formation of denominational voluntary-aided schools.[5] Department of Education and Science (DES) figures (January 1988) state that 32 per cent of schools in England and Wales are voluntary-aided. It is estimated that pupils at such schools account for 23 per cent of all pupils being educated in state schools. The majority of these are Church of England schools, but there are also 2,284 Roman Catholic schools and 23 Jewish schools (CRE 1990: 4).

There have been several attempts by different Muslim groups to establish state-aided Muslim schools. These have included efforts by the Muslim Parents' Association in Bradford in 1982 (see Khan-Cheema 1984) efforts to gain state funding for the Zakaria Girls' school in Batley, West Yorkshire, in 1989, and, most notably, attempts by the Islamia Schools Trust to obtain voluntary-aided status for the Islamia primary school in Brent. Islamia School was founded in 1982 under the patronage of Yusuf Islam,[6] to provide nursery and primary education. Islamia first applied to the DES for state funding in 1986, an application which was backed by Brent Council. The DES rejected the application on the grounds that the school, housed in a two-storey Victorian mansion, was too small to be viable. Subsequent attempts to expand the school, were blocked by the Brent Planning Subcommittee. A further appeal to the DES in 1988 was rejected because of the existence of surplus places in neighbouring schools. Significant in this second rejection was the lack of backing from the now Labour-controlled Brent Council which argued that the establishment of a Muslim school was contrary to their policy of "multicultural" education. The Secretary of State for Education formally rejected the application in May 1990. The trustees of Islamia School subsequently applied for a judicial review and, in May 1992, the High Court ruled that there was "manifest unfairness" in the DES decision. Thus the case has been referred back once again to the DES.

The rejection of Muslim schools, and the processes through which rejection has been achieved, reveal some of the complexities of hegemonic power in action. To campaigners for Muslim schools, the over-riding objective has been to retain a distinctive culture and identity; specifically a religious identity. Their position also reflects an awareness of the capacity for places to reinforce and protect constructions of culture and identity – an awareness which is fortified by the demonstrated importance of schools to the survival of other religious minority groups such as Jews and Catholics. Yet, where these other groups have been supported by the wider society, Muslims have come up against resistance.[7]

As the following discussion demonstrates, this situation has arisen because Muslim schools are seen to offer a particular threat to the hegemonic culture and to notions of identity. Through an examination of the debate about Muslim schools, particularly the reasons for their rejection, it is possible to identify varying constructions of "race" and place and to explore differences in the ways in which they have been employed. In the process, it will become apparent that both the Muslim and the "British Authority" positions reveal an awareness of the capacity for social constructions to be activated in contests over power.

The rôle of social constructions in the contesting of power

As I have suggested above, Muslim schools offer a challenge to the existing discourses about issues of "race", religion and nationalism in the UK. To explore these challenges, I have chosen to focus on the constructions employed in discourses of citizenship, multicultural education, fundamentalism and gender.

Constructions of citizenship

Discourses of citizenship have been central in the discussion of "race relations" in the UK, usually narrowly defined as legal rights of settlement. In recent years, however, discourses of "race" and nationalism have grappled with an expanded understanding of the concept of citizenship, often linking it with a notion of "Britishness" (see Gilroy 1987: 46). While Britain contemplates closer links with Europe, citizenship has become a much-discussed issue as rights of national versus European citizenship and the protection of minorities are questioned. Thus, in the late 1980s and early 1990s, the political discourse of both the Right and the Left has evoked a new emphasis on citizenship, although the rhetoric is configured in different ways (see Held 1989, Smith 1989). The debate about Muslim schools is an important intervention into current discussions, since it raises crucial issues of how citizenship is defined and contested. In the ensuing debate, various constructions of citizenship are employed by the supporters of Muslim schools and their opponents.

From the beginning, the campaigners for state-funded Muslim schools argued that they were entitled, as citizens, to enjoy the same rights as other religious groups. Thus the construction of citizenship employed was one of equality for all under the law. As one Muslim parent puts it:

What I don't understand is when people say, why should Muslims be given their own schools? Well, why not? Catholic and Jewish people have their own schools, so why not Muslims? We are taxpayers and ratepayers, too. And we're peaceful citizens (Mohammed Ismail cited in *The Times Educational Supplement*, 9 November 1990: 22).

This construction of citizenship was also evident in the ambivalent support given by political parties to the notion of Muslim schools. The Labour Party, divided on the issue of Muslim schools, acknowledged that: "The right to such status already exists in law and it has been exercised and enjoyed in practice by Anglicans, and Roman Catholics. In equity, that right cannot be denied to others" (Labour Party Education Policy Review 1990: 49).

The same arguments were used by the Conservative peer, Baroness Cox, when she introduced her attempted amendment to the Education Bill which would have extended state school status to Muslim schools. Cox admitted: "I believe that, as Christians, we should have enough confidence in our faith to give our fellow citizens the democratic rights which we have given ourselves" (Hansard 1991: 1249). This construction of citizenship rests on a universalistic notion of equality which suggests that all individuals in a society have the "right" to be treated equally and it depends on the rhetoric of "fairness", "equity" and "justice".

The campaigners for Muslim schools also gained support from the pressure group Parents Alliance for Choice in Education (PACE). This group used the rhetoric of the Prime Minister, John Major, who established a Citizens' Charter giving increased rights to the individual, including the "right" of parents to choose schools for their children. Thus an expanded construction of the citizen as an individual was employed.

In contrast, government ministers opposed to Muslim schools relied on a conception of citizenship which stressed not the rights of citizenship, but its responsibilities. This construction emerged during the "Rushdie Affair" when various Home Office ministers visited the Muslim community.

In February 1989, the Home Secretary, Douglas Hurd, addressed Muslim leaders reminding them of their responsibilities, as citizens, to obey the laws of the land (*The Guardian*, 25 February 1989). In July 1989, John Patten MP wrote to Muslim community leaders addressing the question of "what it means to be a British Muslim". Patten explained:

> . . . there cannot be room for separation or segregation. It is to the benefit of all, including the minorities themselves, that they should be part of the mainstream of British life . . . Of course, British Muslim children should be brought up faithful in the religion of Islam and well versed in the Koran according to the wishes of their parents . . . But if they are also to make the most of their lives and opportunities as British citizens, then they must also have a clear understanding of British democratic processes, of its laws, the system of Government and the history that lies behind them, and indeed of their own rights and responsibilities (*The Times*, 5 July 1989).

Such rhetoric seems to mark a re-definition of citizenship for "ethnic minority" groups. Citizenship was defined beyond legal incorporation to include the adoption of shared "British" cultural values. This was represented in the press with headlines such as "How to be a true blue Briton" (*The Daily Mail*, 19 July 1989) and "Groundrules for the British way of life" (*The Sunday Times*, 23 July 1989) which stressed the incommensurability of being British and Muslim. Thus in the opposition to Muslim schools, British authorities depended upon the construction of a "cultural" definition of citizenship. This construction relied upon existing discourses of nationalism, where a static, supposedly homogeneous "British culture" is both "White" and implicitly "Christian".

Such constructions of nationalism were effectively challenged by both the "Rushdie Affair" and the campaign for Muslim schools which revealed the difficulties of defining citizenship in a plural society. As Stuart Hall & David Held argue, there is an inherent tension with the "universalizing" thrust of the idea of citizenship, such that:

> Differences of all kinds will continue to create special and particular needs, over and above those which can be addressed within a universalistic conception of citizenship. As the Rushdie affair demonstrates, it is not always possible to keep universal political claims and particularly cultural ones in separate compartments (Hall & Held 1989: 24).

This inherent tension in the notion of citizenship reflects the differential incorporation that different groups may have within a state. As Yuval-Davis (1991) argues, the concept of citizenship depends on a notion of shared community but fails to take account of the way in which such a collectivity is constructed. This question is complex in the case of Muslim schools. While Muslim schools offer a forum for contesting the terms of citizenship for

British Muslims, doubts have also been raised about whether or not the supporters of such schools represent the interests of all Muslim citizens, particularly women (see Sahgal & Yuval-Davis 1992).

Constructions of multiculturalism

I suggested in the introductory section of this chapter that the case of Muslim schools must be considered within the context of the history of debates about multicultural education in the UK. This context is important for explaining why particular places have emerged as significant sites for the contestation of Muslim schools. It is also necessary for understanding the different constructions of multicultural education employed by those who support Muslim schools and by those who oppose them. As an overview of these two general positions reveals, such understanding is complicated by the cross-cutting of alliances. Beginning with supporters of Muslim schools, it soon becomes clear that a variety of constructions of multicultural education have been employed and that not all of them have been progressive.

The original attempts to establish state-aided Muslim schools have their roots in dissatisfaction among Muslim parents about the capacity for state schools to accommodate their cultural and religious needs. In both Brent and Bradford, demands for Muslim schools prompted the local councils to produce multicultural education policies which attempted to provide increased facilities for the specific needs of Muslim children. However, the continuing experience of racism led some Muslim parents to argue that these policies had not gone far enough and that multicultural education had failed to address their needs. Thus, a campaigner for Muslim schools in Bradford argues that multicultural education policies are tokenistic, "a pretence, a device for supporting the dominant culture" (Mustaqim Bleher, leader of the Zakaria parents, cited in *The Guardian*, 31 January 1989).

This was also a view accepted by the Commission for Racial Equality in their publication *Schools of faith* (1990), which gave cautious support for Muslim schools, while arguing for a more wide-ranging discussion about the future of all voluntary-aided schools. The report argued:

> We would estimate . . . that the demand for voluntary status would substantially diminish if existing state provision offered and delivered . . . schools with a genuine, active commitment to multi-cultural, anti-racist and non-discriminatory education, including facilities to meet needs for prayer, diet and dress requirements, as well as curricular and organizational matters, and especially with regard to procedures for dealing with racial harassment (1990: 20).

Thus, demands for Muslim schools are presented as necessary because the existing forms of multicultural education have been inadequate in either enabling Muslim children to retain and develop their distinctive religious identity or in preventing them from being victims of racial harassment. The response to such failure is thus the development of separate institutions where a Muslim identity can be protected, and discrimination can be combated from a position of "cultural strength". This argument draws parallels with the experiences of the British Jewish population, who established separate schools in the 1930s as a refuge from anti-semitism, and also with predominantly Afro-Caribbean schools such as the John Loughborough School in Tottenham which is a Seventh-Day Adventist foundation.

However, by highlighting the failures of multicultural education, campaigners for Muslim schools have also been able to arouse support from groups who have always been opposed to multicultural education. Thus, campaigners for Muslim schools have been supported in their campaign by Parents Alliance for Choice in Education (PACE). PACE is opposed to multicultural education as both secular and liberal, and sees the establishment of Muslim schools as a return to the "traditional" values which they support. The irony of this "alliance against multiculturalism", is that PACE had also supported White parents in Dewsbury, West Yorkshire, in 1987 in their campaign to remove their children from a school where the majority of the children were of Asian descent. The parents had argued that the "cultural identity" of the White children was threatened by the practices of "multicultural education" in the school. This alliance represents a different construction of multicultural education. Instead of being seen as an enabling structure for "ethnic minority" children, multicultural education is seen as antithetical to the needs of Muslims because of its secular foundations.[8]

Thus, campaigners for Muslim schools have drawn upon a variety of constructions of multiculturalism. In challenging the efficacy of multiculturalism to redress racism, they reject attempts to forge a new stronger version of "anti-racism", particularly in places such as Brent, which had been leading exponents of this form of education. In alliance with groups which favour monocultural education, such as PACE, they reject any notion of multiculturalism.

Opposition to demands for Muslim schools has also employed a variety of social constructions of multiculturalism. The "establishment" position has been to employ a weak construction of multicultural education which postulates that existing "accommodations" of Muslim needs are sufficient and that "separate" schools will prevent Muslim children from gaining the skills and values they require to participate in "mainstream" society. Hence, multicultural education is constructed as a means to assimilation.

However, there has also been strong opposition to Muslim schools from those who promote a convincing construction of multicultural education as an anti-racist education. This was the view expressed by Brent Council in its opposition to Islamia School. Anti-racist education depends upon a consensus of the value of a shared "Black" identity as a means of solidarity from which to resist racism. Campaigners for Muslim schools rely upon a distinctively "Muslim" identity. Thus the school becomes a site where this distinctive Muslim identity can be produced and reproduced. The argument here is over the most effective way of combating discrimination.

The recent writing of Tariq Modood (1988, 1990) has explored these issues. Modood suggests the irrelevance of the identity term "Black" for Asian communities and argues:

We need a concept of race that helps us to understand that any oppressed group feels its oppression most according to those dimensions of its being which it (not the oppressor) values the most; moreover, it will resist its oppression from those dimensions of its being from which it derives its greatest collective psychological strength. . . .

Authentic anti-racism for Muslims, therefore, will inevitably have a religious dimension and take a form in which it is integrated to the rest of Muslim concerns. (1990: 92)

Modood's assertions for the need to recognize new categories of identity for a "mature anti-racism" have attracted criticism from the proponents of anti-racist education. The denial of a "Black" consensus is seen as a fragmentation of the minority population, which can be exploited by those who oppose any form of anti-racism. The "Black" consensus is united around the common experience of racism according to ascribed racial characteristics. As Hannana Siddiqui (1991: 83) argues:

The failures of the antiracist left, and of progressive movements generally, have allowed the space for a new identity based along religious line to be created, an identity which threatens the radical secular notion of uniting as Black or even as Asians against racism. Instead a religious identity divides us, demanding segregation into religious schools and forcing minority groups to compete for power and resources instead of uniting in the face of common enemies.

Siddiqui writes as a member of the campaigning group, Women Against Fundamentalism, concerned with the implications of Muslim schools for women.

This debate exposes the failure of previous initiatives to address the needs of a plural society through education. The call for Muslim schools is a rejection of both radical and liberal constructions of multicultural education as being inadequate and unsuccessful in addressing Muslim needs.

Constructions of fundamentalism

As I suggested in the introduction, debate about Muslim schools has been undertaken against a background of the politicization of particular events involving the Muslim community – most notably the "Rushdie Affair". Such events have allowed the construction of one particular Muslim identity which has framed most coverage of issues relating to Muslims in the press. This construction depends not only on a notion of the "Muslim community" as a homogeneous whole, but also employs the notion of "fundamentalism".

The term fundamentalism has been widely used in the discussion of Muslims within the UK and yet there have been few attempts to define or explain the term. As Bhikhu Parekh, then deputy Director of the Commission for Racial Equality, writes about the "Rushdie Affair":

The widely used and never clearly defined term "fundamentalism" became a popularly accepted disguise under which racism masqueraded itself. Catholic, Jewish and Anglican fundamentalism were acceptable, but not Muslim. Every Muslim parent who disapproved of sexual permissiveness, mixed sports or girls wearing shorts was dismissed as a fundamentalist. (Parekh 1989: 72)

Thus, "fundamentalism" becomes a widely and indiscriminately employed construction, which is an explanatory paradigm for all forms of Muslim behaviour. Its assumed opposition to "the British way of life" makes "fundamentalism" an implicitly derogatory term which can be used to dismiss any alternative attitudes as irrational and primitive.

In the construction of fundamentalism, writers in Britain are drawing upon on a long legacy of Orientalist discourse which relies upon the oppositions of West and East, rationality versus irrationality, modernity and liberal tolerance versus fundamentalism (see Said 1978). In constructing Muslims in Britain as "fundamentalist", direct parallels are drawn with previous constructions of fundamentalist Others in the Middle East. Thus in an article in *The Sunday Times*, 28 May 1989, Cal McCrystal draws a parallel between the protest of British Muslims about Salman Rushdie's *The Satanic Verses* and the familiar discourses about the militancy of Islamic fundamentalism elsewhere:

For several decades Islamic militancy existed for Britons only as indignantly reported outbreaks in far-off countries of which we knew nothing. The past few months have shown that it is now a potent, living organism in the body of Britain itself, impossible to wish away or assimilate or suppress. (p. 24)

This comparison is important in the construction of British Muslims as "outsiders" who owe allegiance to Islam and thus threaten to destabilize the British state. Muslim schools are seen, therefore, as places where pupils will be encased in "pockets of pure Islamic culture sealed off from the influence of the majority culture of Western Europe" (*The Times*, editorial, 18 May 1989) and diverted "into some isolated and possibly militant tributary" (de Candole 1991).

This construction of fundamentalism is effective because it mobilizes existing constructions about Islam and the threat it allegedly poses to the West. It is also effective, particularly in the events of the "Rushdie Affair", because it could be constructed from the mouths of Muslims themselves. The British press was able to polarize the debate by selecting particular individuals as the "authentic" voices of the Muslim community (Parekh 1990, Alibhai 1991). However, the category of fundamentalism was inherently unstable since it was never defined. In many cases, as in the McCrystal article cited above, anyone who professed a belief in Islam could be defined as "fundamentalist". On other occasions the campaign for Muslim schools was conceived as particularly dangerous because it was not the belief of "Muslim fundamentalists, but of the ordinary Muslim leadership in Britain" (*The Times*, editorial, 18 May 1989).

The construction of fundamentalism was also gendered. The greatest concern expressed about Muslim schools has been the impact such schools may have on women. While Islamia, the test-case school, is co-educational, many existing private Muslim schools are for girls only, and concern is expressed about the lack of opportunities for girls in such schools. Again, this aspect of the construction of fundamentalism relies upon the Orientalist legacy which constructs Islam as specifically and peculiarly repressive to women, instead of acknowledging the rôle of patriarchy, inherent in most religions, in the construction of the position of women within contemporary forms of Islam (see Ahmed 1992, Kabbani 1986).

In an attempt to counter such anti-Muslim constructions of fundamentalism, the organization Women Against Fundamentalism (WAF) has explored definitions of fundamentalism in a feminist critique which argues that all religious schools seek to control women (Sahgal & Yuval-Davis 1992). Such critiques expand the definition of fundamentalism to include other religious groups in the UK, some of which have been granted state-aided schools. Yet this attempt to expand the margins of the debate about Muslim schools to include the status of all religious schools has met with resistance from the existing religious foundations, some of whom have supported the campaign for Muslim schools.[9]

Conclusion

This chapter has explored some of the ways in which attempts to gain state-aided Muslim schools may challenge the hegemonic culture. In considering this challenge and some of the responses to it I have focused on the constructions employed in the debate. I have also illustrated the extent to which the debate has been concentrated in particular places which have been politicized and often polarized around issues of education.

While the campaign for Muslim schools has offered important challenges to dominant discourses about "race", religion, nationalism and, in particular, has challenged existing understandings of a "plural" society, the debate has been narrowly confined. Opposition to Muslim schools has relied upon existing constructions of citizenship and the rôle of "ethnic minorities" within nation-states and has fallen back upon notions of "fundamentalism" to dismiss the case for Muslim schools. At the same time, the campaigners themselves have forged links with groups such as PACE, which do not have a progressive agenda and have been active against anti-racism. This narrowing of the debate has prevented the development of a much more wide-ranging discussion in the public arena about the nature of a plural society. Instead, the refusal to grant Muslim schools and the anti-Muslim rhetoric evident in much of the media coverage of the debate has served only to alienate further the British Muslim population.

Notes

1. The struggle over the construction of space and its capacity to produce meaning can also be seen in disputes over the construction of mosques and community centres (see Eade 1993).
2. For a full account of the "Rushdie Affair", see Appignanesi & Maitland (1989).
3. The fieldwork for this chapter, which was the focus of my Master's thesis, was carried out between May and July 1991 and was funded by a scholarship from Syracuse University.
4. I am not suggesting that state-funded Muslim schools are perceived by all Muslim parents as the best way of educating their children. First, I would reject the notion of a homogeneous Muslim population. Secondly, there is conflicting evidence about the support from parents for Muslim schools ranging from 80% (Muslim Educational Trust, private communication) to 50% (Kelly & Shaikh 1989, CRE 1990) to "little" (Derek Fatchett, MP, private communication) depending on whose argument is being supported. However, I would argue that the issue of state-funded Muslim schools has a symbolic significance for a wider spectrum of the Muslim population beyond those Muslim parents who would choose to have their children educated in such schools.
5. Voluntary-aided schools were established by the 1944 Education Act. The Act provided for the existence of religious schools, which are funded largely by the

Local Education Authority but require some funding from the religious or charitable organization of foundation. These schools retain greater control than ordinary state schools over admissions policy, staff appointments and the curriculum. Voluntary-aided schools can be seen as reflecting a compromise between the state, the churches and Jewish and other private foundations, which had been for a long time the major providers of education (Nielsen 1992: 53). Since the Education Reform Act (1988), another option for state-funded Muslim schools has emerged via "opting-out". If a majority of parents are in favour, a school can remove itself from Local Authority control and be run by the school governors. In an area where Muslim parents who favour an explicitly Muslim school are in the majority, this could prove to be an easier route to gain state funding.

6. Yusuf Islam, the former pop singer Cat Stevens, is a convert to Islam and now a major contributor to the funding and development of Muslim social services.
7. A new Jewish voluntary-aided school was granted permission to open in Redbridge in January 1990 (*Times Educational Supplement*, 12 January 1990: 3).
8. See the response of the Council of Mosques to the Swann Report: *The Muslims and "Swann"* (1986).
9. See *The Times Educational Supplement*, 4 January 1991, p. 3.

References

Afshar, H. 1989. Education: hopes, expectations and achievements of Muslim women in West Yorkshire. *Gender and Education* 1(3), 261–72.

Ahmed, L. 1992. *Women and gender in Islam*. New Haven, Connecticut: Yale University Press.

Akhtar, S. 1989. *Be careful with Mohammed*. London: Bellew.

Alibhai, Y. 1989. A member no more. *Marxism Today*, December 1989, 46–7.

Alibhai, Y. 1991. Beyond belief. *New Statesman & Society*, 15 February, 17–18.

Anderson, K. & F. Gale (eds) 1992. *Inventing places: studies in cultural geography*. Melbourne: Longman Cheshire.

Anwar, M. 1986. *Young Muslims in a multi-cultural society. Their educational needs and policy implications: the British case*. Leicester: The Islamic Foundation.

Appignanesi, L. & S. Maitland (eds) 1989. *The Rushdie file*. London: Fourth Estate.

Ashraf, A. 1988. Education of the Muslim community in Great Britain. *Muslim Education Quarterly* 5(1), 82–6.

Brah, A. 1992. Difference, diversity and differentiation. In *"Race", culture and difference*, J. Donald & A. Rattansi (eds), 126–45. London: Sage.

Commission for Racial Equality 1990. *Schools of faith*. London: Commission for Racial Equality.

Cosgrove, D. & P. Jackson 1987. New directions in cultural geography. *Area* 19, 95–105.

Council of Mosques of UK and Eire. 1986. *The Muslims and "Swann"*. Bradford: Council of Mosques.

Cumper, P. 1990. Muslim schools: the implications of the Education Reform Act. *New Community* 16(3), 379–89.

de Candole, J. 1991. The politics of Muslim schooling. *The Salisbury Review*, March 1991, 23–5.

Duncan, J. 1990. *The city as text: the politics of landscape interpretation in the Kandayan Kingdom*. Cambridge: Cambridge University Press.

Eade, J. 1992. Quests for belonging. In *Where you belong: government and Black culture*, A. Cambridge & S. Feuchtwang (eds), 33–49. Aldershot, England: Avebury.

Eade, J. forthcoming. The political articulation of community and the Islamisation of space in London. In *Religion, minorities and social change*, R. Barot (ed.). A. C. Kampen: Kok Pharos.

Gilroy, P. 1987. *There ain't no black in the Union Jack*. London: Hutchinson.

Giroux, H. 1983. *Theory, resistance and education*. South Hadley, Mass.: Bergin & Garvey.

Hall, S. 1992. New ethnicities. In *"Race", culture and difference*, J. Donald & A. Rattansi (eds), 252–9. London: Sage.

Hall, S. & D. Held 1989. Left and rights. *Marxism Today* (June), 16–22.

Halstead, M. 1988. *Education, justice and cultural diversity*. London: Falmer Press.

Held, D. 1989. *Political theory and the modern state: essays on state, power and democracy*. London: Polity Press.

Jackson, P. 1989. *Maps of meaning*. London: Unwin Hyman.

Joly, D. 1986. *The opinions of Mirpuri parents in Saltley, Birmingham about their children's education*. CRER Research Papers in Ethnic Relations 2, University of Warwick.

Kabbani, R. 1986. *Europe's myths of Orient*. Bloomington: Indiana University Press.

Khan-Cheema, A. 1984. Islamic education and the maintained-school system. *Muslim Education Quarterly* 2(1), 5–15.

Kelly, A. & S. Shaikh 1989. To mix or not to mix: Pakistani girls in British schools. *Educational Research* 31(1), 10–19.

Lane, D. 1988. *Brent's development for racial equality in schools: a report*. London: London Borough of Brent.

McCrystal, C. 1989. Is Rushdie just the beginning? *The Sunday Times Magazine*, 28 May 1989, 22–9.

Minh-ha, T. 1989. *Women, native, other*. Bloomington: Indiana University Press.

Modood, T. 1988. "Black", racial identity and Asian identity. *New Community* 14(3), 397–404.

Modood, T. 1990. Catching up with Jesse Jackson: being oppressed and being somebody. *New Community* 17(1), 85–6.

Murray, N. 1986. Anti-racists and other demons: the press and ideology in Thatcher's Britain. *Race and Class* 17(3), 1–19.

Nielsen, J. 1992. *Muslims in Western Europe*. Edinburgh: Edinburgh University Press.

Parekh, B. 1990. The Rushdie affair and the British press: some salutary lessons. *Free speech: report of a seminar*. CRE Discussion Paper 2, 58–77.

Parekh, B. 1989. Britain and the social logic of pluralism. *Britain: a plural society*. CRE Discussion Paper 3, 59–79

Sahgal, G. & N. Yuval-Davis 1992. *Refusing holy orders: women and fundamentalism in Britain*. London: Virago.

Said, E. 1978. *Orientalism*. New York: Pantheon Books.

Samad, Y. 1992. Book burning and ethnic relations: political mobilisation of Bradford Muslims. *New Community* 18(4), 507–19.

Siddiqui, H. 1991. Review essay: winning freedoms. *Feminist Review* 37, 78–93.

Smith, S. 1989. Society, space and citizenship: a human geography for the "New Times"? *Institute of British Geographers, Transactions* 14, 144–56.

Troyna, B. 1990. Reform or deform? The 1988 Education Act and racial equality in Britain. *New Community* 16(3), 403–16.

Willis, P. 1977. *Learning to labour*. Westmead, England: Saxon House.

Yuval-Davis, N. 1991. The citizenship debate: women, ethnic processes and the state. *Feminist Review* 39, 58–68.

PART IV
POLITICS AND POSITION

The next two chapters examine the increasingly complex "politics of position" that is emerging around questions of "race", place and nation, focusing here on teaching and the police. Both professions have conventionally been thought of as "neutral" positions of authority. Teachers were supposed to impart knowledge impartially to all students while the police were there to protect the rights of every citizen. Once it was realized that certain kinds of knowledge and certain people's rights were privileged above others, the rôles of teacher and police officer began to generate troubling questions about compliance and resistance.

In his chapter, **Alastair Bonnett** charts the development of a self-critical, reflexive attitude among anti-racist teachers in Britain. Defining reflexivity as "the social self-consciousness of social process", he shows how educators began to engage with the socially constructed nature of their own political ideas, facing up to the contradictions of being representatives of the status quo while simultaneously being charged with questioning received ideas. Bonnett argues that teachers resolve these contradictions by adopting "common-sense" constructions. For example, a belief in equality of opportunity generally triumphs over the idea that racism is an entrenched and systematic aspect of educational and wider social structures. In times of crisis, however, "common-sense" attitudes may be subverted, allowing a questioning of orthodox educational policies.

Bonnett highlights the interconnections between constructions of "race" and place, contrasting Britain's (racialized) inner cities with the "White highlands" of Devon in South West England. The experience of crisis over the implementation of explicitly anti-racist policies permits a critical evaluation of conventional social constructions and the emergence of a critically reflexive consciousness. Returning to the argument that Penrose introduced in the first chapter, Bonnett shows that it is only by making the mutability of social categories explicit that the rigidities of reification can be subverted.

In the final chapter, **Peter Jackson** also points to the rôle of crisis in creating new openings for critical debate. Here, a series of conflicts between Black people and the police in metropolitan Toronto are forcing a re-evaluation of Canadian multiculturalism. Despite an official commitment to equal treatment under the law, many Black people in Toronto are not convinced that they receive even-handed treatment by the police. Jackson explores these conflicts as events which open up a dominant culture's cherished idea of itself to critical scrutiny. His analysis shows how very different "definitions of the situation" exist among different groups, challenging the institutionalized demand for clear-cut dichotomies, unambiguous boundaries and unshifting identities.

Jackson focuses, in particular, on the way that different "definitions of the situation" embody different constructions of the relationship between "race" and crime. His concluding reflections on his own position as an "outsider", trying to make sense of competing constructions of reality, underline our troubled rôles as academics in contemporary debates about representation and the politics of difference, a point to which we return in the conclusion.

CHAPTER SEVEN
Contours of crisis:
anti-racism and reflexivity

ALASTAIR BONNETT

Introduction

"It is clear, perhaps, that I'm tied here, trying to be sort of radical and serve the existing educational service. Though it's taken an explosion in the Black community to push these issues open. But once open what can one do? You cannot ignore it but you've got to recognize the conflict as real, and at the same time confront it" (Teacher A, London, 1988).[1]

The teacher quoted above is articulating a somewhat unsettling point of view. He is admitting to being caught in a contradiction, to be grappling with a dilemma, a dilemma which needs to be openly discussed rather than glibly resolved. The gesture is an unsettling one because it calls into question the conventional image of the educator as an apolitical, socially detached, authority figure. The speaker's apparent willingness to confront the ambiguity of his social location dissipates the aura of intellectual self-confidence which surrounds this occupational rôle. The public professional's traditional hesitancy to discuss the uncertainties and multidimensionality of her or his own political consciousness is challenged.

This chapter seeks to chart the development of reflexivity among anti-racist school teachers (for a discussion of tertiary educators see Bonnett 1993a). It sketches a social geography of the emergence of critical self-aware-ness, a spatial and historical analysis of educators' engagement with the socially constructed nature of their own political ideals and assumptions. My account falls into four parts. In the first section I provide an overview of some of the ways reflexivity has usually been approached in the social research literature. Following this largely definitional discussion I outline the context for the emergence of reflexivity among teachers, a context delineated by reference to teachers' contradictory political experiences working both for and against contemporary capitalism. It is noted that this experience is usually resolved into unreflexive, or "common-sense", forms of consciousness. However, the latter process can be disrupted. In the third and fourth sections I will be looking at how, why and where anti-racist educators have come to develop a reflexive critique. Using material derived from interviews with teachers who are committed to the advancement of the "race" and education debate, I explain how the experience of crisis subverts common-sense attitudes and provokes a tendency towards a questioning of the orthodoxies of educational politics. This process is also shown to be geographically specific. By comparing the attitudes of interviewees in Devon and London I show that, in those localities where teachers have not experienced crisis, the tendency towards reflexivity is far less apparent.

The reflexive attitudes that will be introduced here represent a fragile phenomenon. They are a marginal tendency, existing outside any of the recognized currents of educational politics. This marginality may help to explain why the history and geography of reflexivity have never been written. However, this absence in the research literature should not lure us into imagining that reflexivity is a frivolous or uninteresting process. Indeed, as we shall see, reflexivity (or the absence of reflexivity) constitutes one of the most fascinating and important strands within political and educational debate. The explication of this "counter tradition" is particularly prescient for those engaged in anti-racist activity in Britain. The recent attacks on anti-racism by conservative political forces and the failure of anti-racism to attract broad-based community support have provoked a profound crisis of direction and "political inertia in what was once an anti-racist *movement*" (Gilroy 1990: 192; see also Nelson 1990). As the pitfalls and limits of anti-racist intervention in the public sector have become increasingly evident, the need for a socially self-conscious anti-racism, and educational radicalism, has become apparent. As the teacher quoted at the beginning of this essay noted, educators need "to recognize" and "confront" the conflicts within their own political consciousness. For, as another teacher argued, "it's vital to know where you're coming from if you're to be an effective agent of change" (B).

Reflexivity

Reflexivity is a famously difficult idea. In order to provide some background on the meaning of the term, and to avoid any confusion about my own usage, I have chosen to open this essay with a comparative account of some of the ways it can be defined.

The notion of reflexivity has a central but ambiguous position within contemporary social research. The affirmation and/or description of self-consciousness provides a common thread running through all of the commentaries that invoke the concept. However, this thread weaves its way through an extremely disparate body of strategies and theories. To add to the confusion, each of these approaches tends to claim reflexivity as its own unique praxis, rarely referring to the existence of other definitions. In sketching some of the ways the idea of reflexivity has been commonly understood I do not claim to be offering an exhaustive treatment of the subject. Each of the four currents isolated below (primary reflexivity, auto-critique, textual reflexivity and social self-consciousness) may be said merely to represent a widespread and influential perspective on the subject.

The phrase "primary reflexivity" refers to those forms of self-consciousness that are axiomatically implied in all acts of social interaction (see, for example, Garfinkel 1967) or personality development (see, for example, Mead 1962). Such reflexive acts are essential to any form of social being. As such, they differ from the other forms of self-consciousness that I address here, each of which involves a decision on the part of their practitioners to be more self-aware. The distinguishing characteristic of the tradition of auto-critique is the commitment its adherents demand to the revision and correction of errors and absences contained within past work. Perhaps not surprisingly, this tradition has been most vigorously advanced within those critical tendencies that have maintained a commitment to the possibility of supplying a comprehensive model of societal process, most notably Marxism (see, for example, Althusser 1976, Balibar 1973, Hindess & Hirst 1977). Thus, Hindess & Hirst (1977: 1), although in other ways trenchant critics of orthodox Marxism, introduce their auto-critique of *Pre-capitalist modes of production* as "working on the unevenness of the earlier text". In other words, Hindess & Hirst give their auto-critique the task of producing a more complete, smoother theorization of their subject matter.

Auto-critique can be highly effective in opening up one's past activities to critical scrutiny. However, this process is enacted without any necessary commitment to the analysis of the social context that surrounds a work's intellectual or material production. Thus, the social location of auto-critiquers is effaced even as they subject themselves to a seemingly rigorous exercise in self-criticism.

The effacement of social context is also apparent in the third of the approaches to reflexivity which I wish to isolate: "textual reflexivity". This phrase refers to those practices and theories that seek to make explicit an "author's" presence in a "text" and the traditions and techniques that are associated with her or his medium of communication. Examples of textual reflexivity may be found in films that call attention to their own conditions of production (for example, the films of Jean-Luc Godard) and paintings that seek to expose the boundaries and strategies of traditional forms of visual representation (for example, the work of *Art and Language*). However, the most widely debated version of textual reflexivity refers to the use of printed language. Within social research some of the most interesting examples of this approach have been developed by a group of British sociologists of scientific knowledge (for example, Woolgar 1988, Ashmore 1989). The two central strategies adopted by these researchers have been the use of so-called "new literary methods" to disrupt and problematize conventional modes of presentation (for example, entering into a literal dialogue with oneself in a written text), and the attempt to make explicit the construction and immediate context of a text's production. Self-consciously playful examples of both approaches can be found within Malcolm Ashmore's *The reflexive thesis* (1989). The subject of this published PhD is the sociology of the sociology of scientific knowledge. However, the book also reads as a commentary on its own development as a PhD, complete with a subversively hilarious, if apparently fictional, transcript of the author's oral exam.

Like auto-critique, textual reflexivity can offer revealing instances of, and insights into, self-awareness. However, this tradition also shares the lack of interest shown by the proponents of auto-critique in the wider political and social processes that structure and enable people's attitudes and activities. This characteristic distinguishes these examples of reflexivity from the form of self-consciousness that I will be exploring in the remainder of this essay: social self-consciousness. Commitment to this form of reflexivity is characterized by a willingness to consider one's own social location as an issue to be brought into debate. Needless to say, this broad definition conceals a diversity of ways such an ambition may be enacted. Two principal approaches can be abstracted; the social self-consciousness of fixed identity and the social self-consciousness of social process. The former phrase refers to the practice of speaking "as" a particular kind of person (for example, as a White person) and is usually communicated through a brief (often just a one or two word) biographical note appended to, or introducing, statements. The most widely used forms of these mini-biographies vary over time and by social grouping. The ubiquitous modern formulation of speaking "as a" class or "racial" or gendered subject (or all three; for example, "as a middle-class White male . . . ") is not a universal or immutable practice but represents a particular moment in the history of social self-awareness. However, although such formulations do not necessarily share a common content they all tend to be characterized by the presumption that the identities they refer to have a definite, fixed and comprehensible meaning. To speak "as a White person" implies that you and your audience share an understanding of what attributes a White person possesses and why they are relevant to the debate in which you are engaged. Thus, for example, among political liberals and radicals, someone who introduces her or himself "as a White person" is generally supposed to be implying that she/he is speaking from a position of "racial" privilege and political dominance, from a position of power that is shared by all White people.

This form of social self-consciousness may help to build solidarity and develop self-knowledge among the group who form the subject of such identifications. However, this reflexive praxis also reifies its creations, cementing a misleadingly static and narrow range of characteristics around certain weakly defined, or undefinable, categories, characteristics that seem to stand outside historical process or social interpretation. As this implies, if our view of social self-consciousness were limited to assertions of fixed identity, we would be left with a depressingly crude and impoverished portrait of the possibilities of social self-consciousness. Thankfully a second and more nuanced variety of this reflexive form can also be detailed, a form that may be termed the social self-consciousness of social process. This inelegant phrase denotes what I believe to be the most intellectually interesting and politically engaged of all the forms of self-awareness introduced here. It refers to people's ability to talk about their social interpretations *as* social interpretations, as socially constructed and mutable re-presentations rather than as common-sense facts.

It will be recalled that the reflexivity evinced by the teacher quoted at the beginning of this chapter was enacted by opening up a series of questions about the political contradictions of public education. Clearly, this teacher's statement can be classified as an example of the social self-consciousness of social process. However, in order to understand how this reflexive consciousness may have emerged, we need to understand the wider context of public educationalist politics. More specifically, we need to discuss why educators have traditionally sought to deny their contradictory experiences working both in support of, and in opposition to, modern capitalism. It is towards the experience and effacement of this contradiction that I now turn.

Common-sense constructions

Outlining the most pressing and pervasive contradictions faced by public professionals, Marshall (1971: 45) noted that they have to live with what he called the "dilemma or antithesis inherent in the principles and structure of the welfare state". Marshall summarized this dilemma as "the problem of establishing equal opportunity without abolishing social and economic inequality". This tension, which has been identified by many theorists of contemporary capitalism (Offe 1984, Gough 1979), is experienced by the public professional through concrete, practical conflicts within his or her day-to-day working life (see also London Edinburgh Weekend Return Group 1980). Thus, for example, on the one hand the public educationalist is under enormous and constant pressure to produce an endless stream of trained, disciplined and credentialized students and, on the other, constantly to strive to treat students as equally valuable and valued members of society. The educator must treat students as a group whose interests should be met on the bases of the principles of need and equality, and of their ability to compete in an hierarchical and anti-egalitarian economy and society. To be caught in such a moral bind, to be contributing to the reproduction of capitalism while being committed to values that come into conflict with capitalism, is, day-in, day-out, to experience contradiction.

This contradiction has been resolved by educators into a variety of common-sense constructions that combine a commitment to both egalitarian and anti-egalitarian political ambitions. An example of this tendency may be found in the rhetoric of individualism (for other examples see Bonnett 1990a, 1993a). As noted by several commentators, individualism has a central place within the attitudes and practices of teachers (Sharp & Green 1975, Lee 1988). Educational individualism has two main characteristics. It affirms the principle of egalitarianism and people's right to be treated as equivalently valuable members of society. It also supports the socially atomizing culture of the "free market" and the subordination of group rights. The ideology of individualism brings these two political projects together into an apparently unified rhetoric of prerogatives and responsibilities. The seemingly coherent rhetoric of individualism, which binds these antagonistic political tendencies together, thus forges a compromise between egalitarianism and competitive capitalism.

Individualism has not appeared as common sense through its own innate, objective rationality. It has come to make sense within a wider political and economic context. As an example of this process we may point to the strength of individualist ideology in periods of perceived economic well-being and high social mobility. Thus, for example, in the 1950s and 1960s in

Britain, the notion that equality and material progress could be and were being achieved through the provision of opportunities for individual better-ment appeared almost beyond doubt within most educational commentary (for example, Vaizey 1962). In an optimistic and economically expanding society the premise that the most serious barrier to social mobility was lack of personal confidence, skill or "opportunities" could easily be deemed an unremarkable, self-evident conclusion.

The resolution of the contradictory political experiences of public educa-tors has also structured the way issues of "racial" inequality have been approached. We may return to the example of individualism to see how. Individualist common sense pervades the education and "race" agenda. Indeed, two of the most characteristic aspects of the ideology of multi-culturalism are examples of individualism: self-image theory and the principle of equality of opportunity. The poor academic performance of minority children relative to majority children has often been linked by educators to their lack of respect for themselves and their own cultural heritage (Milner 1975, Verma & Bagley 1979). In a caricatural but usefully concise summary of self-image theory, Maureen Stone (1981: 26), argues that it hinges upon the notion that, "When dealing with Black children", teachers should work on the assumption that, "attitudes to the self must . . . be changed as Blacks hate and despise themselves and this causes them to fail at school". Self-image theory has also been rationalized through the principle of equality of opportunity. Within the "race" and education debate this principle has been expressed as a commitment to the right of students to compete with one another without fear of colour or cultural prejudice. Thus, equality of opportunity has been viewed as a way of providing minority students with the chance to prove they are as intelligent and skilled as White children. Multiculturalism's general philosophy, as Roberts (1973: 232) noted, "stresses the importance of the individual and of his freedom to cultivate his individual powers". One of the consequences of this emphasis is the efface-ment of the notion that racism could be entrenched within educational and wider social structures or that its eradication may require acts of explicitly political collective struggle rather than, or as well as, individual initiative.

I have suggested that unreflexive consciousness (common sense), is repro-duced through social experiences that affirm its plausibility. As this implies, common sense can be disrupted by social experiences that shed doubt on its assumptions and ideals. It is to how the latter process has been enacted in London, and its relationship to the development of reflexive consciousness, that I now turn.

Crisis and reflexivity: evidence from London

The experience of crisis is both historically and geographically variable. Those crises that have tended to undermine the plausibility of the kind of ideological resolutions outlined above have not been experienced in the same way same across Britain. They have tended to be most deeply felt within urban "multiracial" areas and least influential in "all-White" localities. In the remainder of this essay I will look at the development of reflexivity within one of each of these kinds of environment. The two examples are London and Devon. These case studies are not presented as ideal types, to be understood as representative of all "multi-racial" areas or all "all-White" areas. The history of anti-racism is far too diverse to be reduced to a pair of contrasting paradigms. Rather, these studies should be read as indicating (as opposed to detailing every strand within) the diversity of anti-racist debate.

Between January 1987 and November 1988 I conducted a series of semi-structured, mostly tape-recorded, interviews with twenty eight school teachers involved in "race"-equality work in London and Devon. These interviews, undertaken as part of my PhD research (Bonnett 1990b), resulted from letter or telephone approaches to a total of 63 educationalists (in both tertiary and pre-tertiary education) identified as sympathetic to anti-racism. This initial identification was made on the basis of an individual's membership of, or contribution to, anti-racist/multiculturalism groups or journals, or through the recommendation of another interviewee. In each encounter discussion focused on the national and local politics of racism and anti-racist education.

The majority of the London interviews were with educators working in the most "multiracial" parts of the city. These encounters took place in the wake of a series of crisis events that, since the mid–1970s, had radicalized the "race" debate in London and problematized established forms of common sense. None of the constituent elements of these events – which included neo-Nazi activity, minority economic disadvantage, police harassment and riots – was in itself new. However, their intensification in this period, and their conceptualization within sections of the Left and minority population as symptomatic of a deep-rooted and pervasive racism, made their impact on the educational debate both profound and catalytic.

These crisis experiences undermined optimistic views of individualist, reformist or consensus-seeking solutions to "racial" inequality. To many educators confronted with the everyday realities of White racism and minority resistance, these liberal ideals appeared increasingly naïve. I shall not attempt here to paint a panorama of the full landscape of crisis. I will, however, sketch two sets of events that, perhaps more than any others, acted to disrupt teachers' traditional vision of "race relations". The first turns on the issues of minority–police and teacher–police relations, the second on the riots of 1981 and 1985.

As Trevor Carter (1986) relates, throughout the 1960s and 1970s a disproportionate number of Afro-British people had been stopped and/or arrested under section four of the 1824 Vagrancy Act (often termed the "sus" law) for being suspected of "loitering with intent to commit an arrestable offence". In 1975 the inadequacy of the police response to racism, and the question of "racial" harassment by the police themselves, provided one of the spurs to the formation of the North London based Black Students' Movement and Black Parents' Movement. However, in the late 1970s and 1980s, police racism was drawn dramatically to the attention of educators by a series of violent confrontations between the police and minority youth. The high-profile policing of Afro-British communities and events, such as the Notting Hill Carnival, proved particularly incendiary. Violent confrontations between police and Afro-British youth at the 1976 Notting Hill Carnival and between the police and anti-fascist demonstrators at Lewisham in 1977 solidified an emergent cynicism towards the police within the anti-racist movement. The police, noted All London Teachers Against Racism and Fascism (founded 1978), are "a very powerful political force" (ALTARF 1982: 1). Anti-racists, ALTARF continued, must "convince our colleagues of [police] non-neutrality, and explain . . . their racism".

However, it was the killing, by a member of the police force's Special Patrol Group, of the London teacher Blair Peach, that became the central symbol of police brutality. An active member of an anti-racist group called Teachers Against the Nazis, Peach was killed by a truncheon blow to the head at an anti-fascist demonstration in Southall in 1979. In his honour a Blair Peach Teachers' Resource Centre was established in London to provide anti-racist material. Although the centre was short-lived, Peach's death had a considerable impact on other anti-racist teachers (see, for example, North 1979). It intensified their conviction that anti-racism could not plausibly be conceptualized as a polite professional campaign. Anti-racism was decreasingly viewed as a conventional reformist pedagogy and increasingly as a necessarily militant struggle.

However, the most powerfully unsettling influence on London educators were the riots of 1981 and 1985. Between 10–13 April 1981, one of London's largest Afro-British communities, in Brixton, saw three days of rioting. The following weekend police and youth fought in Finsbury Park and Ealing Common. The violence recurred in June and July. The Smith et al. (undated) summary of the events of 1981 lists 25 "riot areas" in London, most of which were situated in areas with large minority settlements. Rioting returned to London in 1985 in Brixton and Tottenham. Among anti-racists, the disturbances of 1981 and 1985 were widely interpreted as expressions of Black rebellion and as symbolic of the failure of traditional liberal solutions to issues of social injustice. They succeeded, as Richard Hatcher (1985: 9) noted in the wake of the 1985 events, in "undercutting, in education, the Liberal middle-ground on which the 'soft multiculturalists' stand, trying to hold together a consensus on race and 'education'". "The riots", commented one teacher in interview, "were the result of the anger of oppressed Blacks finally boiling over . . . show[ing] us . . . that bleeding heart liberalism isn't enough"(B).

Of course this process of radicalization represented a tendency, not a mass conversion. Liberal perspectives remained the majority view, while radicals continued to see themselves as a struggling minority. Nevertheless, a significant change had occurred within the debate, a change indicated by the fact that radical anti-racists were now able to position themselves at the forefront of "race" equality commentary, while portraying liberal attitudes (often represented as "multiculturalism") as dated and conservative. As one teacher expressed it: "the multicultural edge of the early years is no longer the edge "(C).

However, the radical anti-racist educator faces a dilemma. He or she is overtly committed to a militant critique of British society and its education system. Yet he or she is also still working within and contributing to that society and system. The process of radicalization may have altered the agenda of the "race" and education debate, but it did not change the realities of teachers' pedagogic, disciplinarian and credentializing duties. Thus the mutually subversive nature of teachers' political rôles was made explicit, the ambiguity of their commitments made visible. It is precisely this process of opening up, of making contradiction explicit, that creates a tendency towards the articulation of the social self-consciousness of social process.

The tendency towards reflexivity is, however, a fragile one. Crisis experiences do not *necessarily* lead to the abandonment of unreflexive consciousness. Indeed, elsewhere I have discussed in some detail the way anti-racists have developed forms of theory and practice that tie together liberal and radical political projects (Bonnett 1993a, 1993b; see also Troyna 1992). Nevertheless, the latter process, which may be described as the formation of anti-racist ideology, has not been able entirely to repress the consciousness of contradiction that crisis experiences enable. The nagging uncomfortable realization that one is part of the problem one is seeking to remedy cannot always be denied. Indeed, persistent incursions of reflexivity arose time and again in my interviews. Below I have transcribed four such reflexive moments:

– So as an educationalist, a professional, I'm caught out . . . on one [hand]

I'm a beacon of "all that is decent", on the other, though, I'm all that is subversive . . . and our politics, even our interpretations of what "the Black struggle" means are refracted through that glass. (D)

- I know I'm moving in two, if not more than two, [political] directions at . . . once here. But . . . that's the dilemma of being a teacher in a capitalist state and being a radical. It's not easily solvable. (C)
- The gradual path to equality . . . policy after policy and so on, is [the one] I'm committed to, but only at one level. It's an avenue leading nowhere. We know that by now, so, on another level I don't believe it for one moment. And so I'm caught out by myself . . . it's a real headache . . . Anti-racism is as radical or as conservative as you want to make it. The fight for Black equality . . . is something we come to with our own agenda and sets of assumptions. (E)
- The conflict is obvious to me, in as much as the fact that I advocate forms of change that I inevitably, as a teacher in this sort of society, run headlong into. That is, my rôle as an anti-racist takes me in all sorts of different directions at once . . . It's convenient to generalize about Black people's needs and imagine you can understand them but it isn't as easy as that. Just saying those things stops you thinking too hard about your own position . . . so it's vital to know where you're coming from if you're to be an effective agent of change. (B)

These remarks point to the development of the social self-consciousness of social process. Each of these educators is explicitly rejecting the common sense closure of contradiction. Respondent D notes that her political perspective is both "all that is decent" and "all that is subversive". Both C and B point out that they are moving in two or more political "directions . . . at once". Similarly both D and E contend that they are "caught out" between radicalism and liberalism.

It is interesting to note that these reflexive considerations are tied by respondents B, D and E to their own ability to speak for "the Black community". "Our interpretations of what 'the Black struggle' means", argues D, "are refracted through" educators' contradictory social location. B similarly problematizes generalizations about "Black people's needs" which stop "you from thinking too hard about your own position". "The fight", notes E, "for Black equality . . . is something we come to with our own agenda and sets of assumptions". It seems then that these educators' movement towards self-consciousness is encouraging them to question some of the orthodoxies of anti-racist and radical representation. The notion of a homogeneous "Black struggle" and the reification of minority groups as the resistant Other, to be defined in opposition to White racism, are subtly undermined by these interrogations (cf. Spivak 1988, also O'Hanlon 1988). The emergence of a common-sense anti-racist rhetoric is contested by an awareness of the social context and construction of political interpretation.

Reflexivity is not, of course, unique to London. Undoubtedly educators with similar ideas could be found in the remotest reaches of Britain. However, the tendency towards reflexivity has not been of the same intensity or taken the same form in every part of the country. There is a geography of reflexivity as well as a history. This geography may be mapped by looking at the spatial variability of educators' experience of crisis. In my second case-study the mutability of anti-racism's political identity will be explored further. We leave London and move to a very different context for the development of radical and/or anti-racist consciousness – the predominantly rural and overwhelmingly White county of Devon in South West England.

Anti-racist common sense in Devon

There is no part of Devon that cannot be categorized as a predominantly White area. Indicative of this reality is the fact that the number of residents whose "head of household" was born in the New Commonwealth or Pakistan was just 1.1 per cent in 1981 (Taylor 1990). The low percentage of minority residents was widely regarded by interviewees as in itself sufficient explanation of why Devon education has, as F noted, "been very slow to develop a consciousness of race issues". However, over the past decade, "race" equality and cultural pluralism have become the focus of local initiatives in the region (see *Perspectives* 1985, 1987, 1988, 1990), a trend Devon shares with many other "White" localities in England (Tomlinson 1990, Bonnett 1992, although see Taylor 1990). One of the earliest developments was the founding, in 1981, of a multicultural support group based at Exeter Teachers' Centre. Following an in-service course on multicultural education held in 1987, this organization was incorporated into a county-wide support network consisting of four groups (North, South, West and East Devon). Institutions of higher education (for example, the School of Education at Exeter University) have also developed and disseminated multicultural and anti-racist strategies and ideas, particularly through their rôle as centres for teacher training. Moreover in 1989 Devon County Council formally adopted its first multiculturalism policy.

Eleven teachers were interviewed in Devon, the majority coming from institutions in and around the county's two largest urban centres, Plymouth and Exeter. My respondents were part of the small community of educators in Devon interested in placing issues of "racial" equality on the local educational agenda. However, the social and political environment within which this tendency has emerged is very different from that experienced in London. Although pockets of radicalism do exist within the county (especially in higher education) the ideals and orthodoxies of conservatism and liberalism have remained a virtually unchallenged paradigm for the discussion of "racial" issues. The absence of the strong radical current identified in London can be related to the absence of the daily experience of crisis. Although issues of "racial" conflict, minority residence and disadvantage have been perceived as problems by concerned teachers, they have not generally been interpreted as undermining the plausibility of established forms of educational, multicultural and/or anti-racist common sense. Referring to "social breakdown" in "multiracial" cities, respondent G explained that:

Thank goodness nothing like that really goes on down here, we don't have riots, we don't have people pushing in windows, all that [sort of] thing . . . just doesn't occur. So it's a bit like "it's all on TV", everything's at a distance . . . we're just spectators.

Expressing a similar sense of the remoteness of "race crisis", H noted that "there is prejudice here. It's not like in London . . . where the situation is very tense, as far as I understand it". Respondent I opined that, unlike "Black cities", "we don't have burning cars on the streets".

The remoteness of crisis cannot simply be traced to the absence of overt "racial" antagonisms in Devon. As several studies have shown, racist attitudes are ingrained within the educational and wider culture of "White" areas (Tomlinson 1990, Troyna & Hatcher 1992). Moreover, although neo-Nazi activity seems to be at a relatively low level compared with London, it remains virulent (see Exeter Anti-Fascist Action 1992). Indeed, survey evidence from Plymouth suggests that visible minority groups feel "they would be safer in a multicultural city" (Harris et al. 1990).

Thus, when explaining the perceived lack of "race crisis" in Devon, we need to think beyond the deeply misleading and dangerous cliché that "White" areas do not have a "race problem". A more appropriate explanation is already implicit in the remarks of those Devon interviewees quoted above. For these respondents can be seen to be correlating crisis with certain stereotypes and assumptions about the nature of racist activity and minority resistance. G's suggestion that "we don't have riots" and I's reference to the lack of "burning cars on the streets" exemplify a tendency to equate "real" "race-related" events with images of violent disturbance in "multiracial" cities. As this implies, the absence of crisis experiences among anti-racist teachers in Devon is less a manifestation of a relatively low level of racism than of a particular interpretation of what constitutes an authentic "race" crisis.

For Devon teachers, crisis is experienced as a crisis "elsewhere", a displacement that dispels its threat to the reproduction of unreflexive common sense. As this might suggest, a comparison of the attitudes of interviewees in London and Devon reveals a characteristic resistance on the part of the latter group to the social self-consciousness of social process. The following dialogues each represent attempts to probe the boundaries of interviewees' reflexivity. In each case these boundaries appeared quickly and decisively, despatching reflexivity beyond the limits of legitimate debate.

AB: *What is the teacher's rôle in society?*

J: That rôle is simply to inform and sustain, by which I mean inform White children and sustain Black children, sustain their identity that is . . . [the teacher's rôle is] straightforward, agent for change, I think that obvious.

The individualist themes of self-image and equality of opportunity can both be discerned in J's emphasis on children's identity and need for information. The unreflexive assertion of these ideas also finds echoes in I's response to the following query:

AB: *What about your rôle, some of the problems of working for equality in this kind of institution?*

I: Well, this is an institution dedicated to equality. The problems they are facing are ones of esteem, aren't they really? It's the same with our ones here some of the time.

This teacher deflected my question by switching the focus of the "problems" she was asked about from the politics of education to pupils' self-image. The tendency to avoid engaging with questions about the contradictions of public professionalism is seen again in this response by K to the same query:

I don't have "problems", I don't have a "rôle" . . . I'm just here to teach; multiculturalism is part of being a good teacher isn't it?

For each of these respondents the teacher's rôle was "straightforward" and "obvious". Concepts such as "Black identity" and phrases such as "the problems they [i.e. Black students] are facing" are used without any indication that they might represent interpretations rather than statements of objective fact. The rigidity of these views may be contrasted with the reflexive, self-exploratory perspectives upon social representation developed by London interviewees. Although the latter group had begun to dispel common sense, their Devon peers were actively (although unwittingly) engaged in reproducing it.

Conclusion

This chapter has sought to introduce a theory and case study of the social geography of reflexivity. It has been suggested that the contours of crisis correspond to the contours of reflexive consciousness. This relationship, I have argued, is not coincidental. It indicates a social process, a process that has been described in terms of crisis experiences *enabling* the formation of reflexive consciousness. Thus I have sought to show that crisis provokes social self-consciousness, while the absence of crisis allows the maintenance of unreflexive or common-sense attitudes. It has also been noted that crisis is less a matter of objective fact than social interpretation. Dramatic breakdowns in "law-and-order" in "multiracial" areas have been perceived as crisis pressures, pressures that have threatened the plausibility of educators' established ideologies. In the absence of such clichés of disorder, the endemic racism found in Devon has had no comparably disruptive effect upon the reproduction of common sense.

I have not presented reflexivity as a clever methodological innovation or as resulting from the peculiarly sensitive or enlightened minds of intellectuals. Neither has it been wedded to the supposedly "reflexive, self-monitoring culture of critical discourse" generated, in the view of Alvin Gouldner (1979: 29), and many other sociologists of contemporary radicalism, within institutions of higher education. Rather, the development of reflexivity has been viewed within the context of a complex history and geography of social interpretation and experience. As this implies, reflexivity, defined as the social self-consciousness of social process, cannot be promoted merely as an interesting theoretical novelty capable of being cursorily tacked onto one's work. Indeed, the form of reflexivity I have traced is better understood as having been forced upon educators rather than as being freely chosen. It has occurred when it could no longer be avoided. Social self-consciousness is not, after all, an easy or comfortable form of consciousness to maintain. It presents particular challenges to educators more familiar with a self-image closer to aloof authority than vulnerable ambiguity. However, despite its attendant traumas (for example, self-doubt), an awareness of the contradictions of public professionalism and the social construction of anti-racism can enable a far more nuanced and critical engagement with the politics of "race" and equality. Such a position enables the mutability of social classifications to be made explicit. Moreover, it opens the ambiguities of teachers' social representations to critical discussion, a process which acts to subvert the rigidities of reification and the suffocating presence of professional authority.

This chapter has returned repeatedly to the theme of social interpretation, of representation. It has however been the effacement of the act of representation, its denial, that has been construed as objectionable not the fact of representation itself. Representation is not a "problem" to be "overcome". Anti-racist educators, along with everyone else, will always "speak for" or "speak about" certain subjects. Such acts require no apology. However, their interpretive status needs to be acknowledged. Reflexivity enables this to happen. It allows social representations to be understood as re-presentations. It disrupts the power and process of appropriation and enables political implications to come into focus.

However, I cannot conclude this chapter with a simple panegyric to reflexivity. The need for self-awareness is, after all, already one of the great clichés of our age, the subject of many superficial homilies by postmodern artists and writers. Yet, although the critical allure and potential of reflexivity are undeniable, it offers no simple answers or magic cures for the problems of contemporary anti-racism. Indeed, if its deconstructive power is allowed to destabilize every social construct, every attempt to "speak for" the needs and desires of others, it may offer a dangerously inadequate and enfeebling response to the unreflexive, and highly potent, forms of representation developed by less progressive political forces. As this implies, reflexivity needs to be treated critically. It needs to be placed in its historical and geographical context, opened up to questions that probe its formation, politics and implications. In summary, reflexivity needs to be understood, not merely as a new intellectual paradigm, but as a social process.

Note

1. To preserve anonymity and avoid imposing culturally loaded pseudonyms, interviewees are identified by an alphabetical letter.

References

ALTARF. 1982. Police in schools? *ALTARF Newsletter* 1, 1–3.

Althusser, L. 1976. *Essays in self-criticism*. London: New Left Books.

Ashmore, M. 1989. *The reflexive thesis: Wrighting sociology of scientific knowledge*. Chicago: University of Chicago Press.

Balibar, E. 1973. Self-criticism. *Theoretical Practice* 7/8, 56–72.

Bonnett, A. 1990a. Anti-racism as a radical educational ideology in London and Tyneside. *Oxford Review of Education* 16, 255–67.

Bonnett, A. 1990b. *The geography and politics of anti-racist ideology*. PhD dissertation, University of London.

Bonnett, A. 1992. Anti-racism in "White" areas: the example of Tyneside. *Antipode* 24, 1–15.

Bonnett, A. 1993a. *Radicalism, anti-racism and representation*. London: Routledge.

Bonnett, A. 1993b. The formation of public professional radical consciousness: the example of anti-racism. *Sociology*, in press.

Carter, T. 1986. *Shattering illusions*. London: Lawrence & Wishart.

Exeter Anti-Fascist Action. 1992. *The National Front in Devon: a catalogue of crime and terror*. Exeter: Exeter Anti-Fascist Action. [available from Exeter AFA, c/o *The Flying Post*, Post Office Box 185, Exeter, Devon, EX4 4EW].

Garfinkel, H. 1967. *Studies in ethnomethodology*. Englewood Cliffs, New Jersey: Prentice-Hall.

Gilroy, P. 1990. The end of anti-racism. In *Race and local politics*, W. Ball & J. Solomos (eds), 191–209. London: Macmillan.

Gough, I. 1979. *The political economy of the welfare state*. London: Macmillan.

Gouldner, A. 1979. *The future of intellectuals and the rise of the new class*. London: Macmillan.

Harris, D. et al. 1990. "There's no problem here": an examination of racism in a "monocultural" city. Paper presented to the British Sociological Association Annual Conference, April 1990, University of Surrey.

Hatcher, R. 1985. Handsworth 1985: what has changed since Brixton 1981? *Socialist Teacher* **30**, 9.

Hindess, B. & P. Hirst 1977. *Mode of production and social formation: an auto-critique of pre-capitalist modes of production*. London: Macmillan.

Lee, J. 1988. Pride and prejudice: teachers, class and an inner-city infants school. In *Teachers: the culture and politics of work*, M. Lawn & G. Grace (eds), 90–116. Lewes, Sussex: Falmer Press.

London Edinburgh Weekend Return Group. 1980. *In and against the state*. London: Pluto Press.

Marshall, T. H. 1971. Social selection in the welfare state. In *Readings in the theory of educational systems*, E. Hopper (ed.), 38–55. London: Hutchinson.

Mead, G. 1962. *Mind, self, and society*. Chicago: University of Chicago Press.

Milner, D. 1975. *Children and race*. Harmondsworth: Penguin.

Nelson, A. 1990. Equal opportunities: dilemmas, contradictions, White men and class. *Critical Social Policy* **10**, 25–42.

North, D. 1979. Blair Peach: a personal tribute. *Issues in Race and Education* **20**, 1.

Offe, C. 1984. *Contradictions of the welfare state*. London: Hutchinson.

O'Hanlon, R. 1988. Recovering the subject, "subaltern studies" and histories of 1 resistance in colonial South Asia. *Modern Asian Studies* **22**, 189–224.

Perspectives 1985. 22 [*Perspectives* is available from Media and Resources Centre, University of Exeter, School of Education, Saint Luke's, Exeter, Devon, EX1 2LU]

Perspectives 1987. 35.

Perspectives 1988. 39.

Perspectives 1990. 42.

Roberts, C. 1973. Education in a multi-cultural society. *New Community* **1**, 230–36.

Sharp, R. & A. Green 1975. *Education and social control: a study in progressive primary education*. London: Routledge & Kegan Paul.

Smith, W. et al. nd. *Like a summer with a thousand Julys*. London: B. M. Blob.

Spivak, G. 1988. Can the subaltern speak? In *Marxism and the interpretation of culture*, C. Nelson & L. Grossberg (eds), 271–313. Urbana: University of Illinois Press.

Stone, M. 1981. *The education of the Black child in Britain: the myth of multiracial education*. London: Fontana.

Taylor, W. 1990. Multicultural education in the "white highlands" after the 1988 Education Reform Act. *New Community* **16**, 369–78.

Tomlinson, S. 1990. *Multi-cultural education in White schools*. London: Batsford.

Troyna, B. 1992. Can you see the join? An historical analysis of multicultural and anti-racist education policies. In *Racism and education: structures and strategies*, D. Gill et al. (eds), 63–91. London: Sage.

Troyna, B. & R. Hatcher 1992. *Racism in children's lives: a study of mainly White primary schools*. London: Routledge.

Vaizey, J. 1962. *Education for tomorrow*. Harmondsworth: Penguin.

Verma, G. & C. Bagley (eds) 1979. *Race, education and identity*. London: Macmillan.

Woolgar, S. (ed.) 1988. *Knowledge and reflexivity: new frontiers in the sociology of knowledge*. London: Sage.

CHAPTER EIGHT
Policing difference:
"race" and crime in metropolitan Toronto

PETER JACKSON

Despite Canada's enviable record in the field of "race relations" and human rights, recent events in Toronto have highlighted the shortcomings and contradictions of Canadian multiculturalism. These events have included demonstrations outside the Into the Heart of Africa exhibition at the Royal Ontario Museum in 1990; protests in Queen's Park and looting in Yonge Street in May 1992 following the Rodney King verdict in Los Angeles; and, over a longer period, a series of sometimes deadly conflicts between police and Black people (including three fatalities in police shootings since 1988).[1] One indication of the limitations of official multiculturalism and equality rights legislation is the contradictory language in which it is written. For example, and despite their progressive aims, policies which aim to offer equal treatment "regardless of race" actively perpetuate the idea of natural "racial" difference from which racism and discrimination derive their moral and intellectual force (Kobayashi 1993). Accepting the premise that such differences are socially constructed rather than biologically given would generate a completely different policy agenda. Likewise, official multicultural policy (enshrined in the Multiculturalism Act of 1988 but with roots stretching back to the debate about bilingualism in the 1970s) can be criticized for its tendency to look *backwards* to minority cultures and "ethnic" heritages rather than *forwards* to the complete "multiculturalization" of society (Kelner & Kallen 1974).

Some observers have argued that the Metropolitan Toronto Police Force offers a model that other nations should follow in the field of community policing and "race relations" (Todd & Todd 1992). However, I will argue that

181

the events referred to in the previous paragraphs suggest that the policies and practices of this police force reflect deep conflicts over matters of principle and vision. Unless these contradictions are addressed, the current deterioration of police–community relations in Toronto is likely to continue.

The contradictions of Canadian multiculturalism have already been revealed in recent battles over the rights of Native Peoples, dramatized in the conflict at Oka outside Montreal in the summer of 1990 when Native Peoples engaged in armed confrontation with the police and the army over the proposed expansion of a golf-course on land whose ownership was disputed. But the contradictions of multiculturalism are also revealed in less starkly territorial form in recent confrontations between police and Black people in metropolitan Toronto.

The chapter draws on interviews conducted in Toronto over the summers of 1990–91 with police officers, members of the Toronto Police Services Board and the Black Action Defence Committee.[2] The interviews were tape-recorded and transcribed in full. They were then analyzed and presented for discussion around the twin concepts of "identity" and "difference". The analysis reveals the extent to which different people are working with quite different "definitions of the situation" and the potential for conflict and misunderstanding that can arise from such differences.[3] For example, ambiguity and plurality may be welcome aspects of contemporary human identity for members of various "visible minority" groups, while these same characteristics may pose a threat to institutionalized demands for neat dichotomies, fixed boundaries and unambiguous identities.[4] Legal discourse and official statistics require clear-cut distinctions; while blurred boundaries and multiple identities open the way for all kinds of dangerous uncertainties. As I hope to show, the discourse about "race" in contemporary Toronto is full of such tensions and ambiguities over potentially deadly questions of identity and difference.

Elsewhere (Jackson 1994) I have provided an account of the recent deterioration of police–community relations in metropolitan Toronto, reconstructed from press reports and a review of evidence submitted to the provincial Task Force on Race Relations and Policing (Ontario 1989). Here, I focus on a series of semi-structured interviews with key informants, conducted in Toronto in August 1991, which highlight some of the tensions and contradictions in the way that different people construct the relationship between "race" and crime. After a discussion of the interview material, I return to the debate about identity and difference before concluding with some remarks on the politics of fieldwork in such highly charged circumstances.

The business of policing

In comparison with other North American cities (and especially in relation to comparably sized US cities), Toronto remains a relatively safe city in which to live and work.[5] Although the annual number of violent deaths is low, the figure is rising and it is becoming the focus of increased public concern (*Toronto Life*, June 1991). Of particular concern, the number of Black people killed in violent confrontations with the police is out of proportion to their overall numbers within the metropolitan population. The person with overall responsibility for the policing of Toronto is Ms Susan Eng, a Chinese-Canadian tax lawyer who was appointed Chair of the Metropolitan Toronto Police Service Board (formerly the Police Commission) in 1991.

Ms Eng's appointment was not universally welcomed. She drew heated criticism from members of the rank-and-file Police Association for commenting that, in contrast to her predecessor Ms June Rowlands (who has since been elected mayor), she would act as a watch-dog not a lap-dog.[6] Following this remark, the Association's newsletter ran a feature which criticized "the ambitious Miss Eng" for bringing her "political activism to the chair's job" (*News and Views*, August 1991).[7] Recalling her previous 15 years in the business world, Ms Eng described her job as little different from managing any other large corporation:

> If you look upon this Board as the Board of any other large $530m corporation, what are its responsibilities? It includes a very strong management function, finance and management of the budget, accountability, insistence on having proper reporting. It means that there is a discipline problem in the policing context. There is also a quasi-judicial function, that is part of the discipline process. There's a quasi-legislative process which is the policy study process and of course there's the ceremonial function. (interview with Susan Eng, 28 August 1991)

This business model sometimes comes into conflict with a much more idealistic vision of policing whose roots go back to Sir Robert Peel and the foundations of the Metropolitan Police Force in London:

> . . . fundamentally the model that we've adopted in Canada has its roots in the British policing system . . . which many of the top brass proudly reiterate from time to time. And when they say that "the police are the public and the public are the police", in Peel's words I think, . . . "which part of the public?" is the question that many people are asking. (ibid.)

Policing in Canada, as in Britain, has been slow to adjust to the problems of an increasingly multicultural society (Sewell 1985). Although Canada has progressed beyond the "race relations" paradigm that is still prevalent in Britain, the implementation of multicultural policy and equality rights legislation still leaves much to be desired. In Toronto, important developments in police–community relations have been institutionalized through the police's race relations policy (Metropolitan Toronto Police Services Board 1989) and the Race Relations and Policing Unit of the Ministry of the Solicitor General (set up to implement the recommendations of the 1989 Task Force). But many Black people seriously doubt whether they receive even-handed treatment from the police. Recent demonstrations over the Rodney King verdict in Los Angeles, which coincided with the death of another Black youth at the hands of the Toronto police, show the depths to which police–community relations have sunk.

As Chair of the Police Services Board, Susan Eng accepts that there is a problem and acknowledges the widespread anger and frustration that exists within the Black community. She has reservations, though, about the way radical groups such as the Black Action Defence Committee have expressed those feelings:

> . . . they exaggerate and say things that no one in their right mind would take neither as truth nor as a proper accusation, yet they are showing by those words . . . the level of anger and frustration and fear that the community widely worries about . . . It's a crystallisation of a lot of fear and frustration and we have to respond to that. We cannot just say because [their representatives] exaggerated, it was libellous, or that's slanderous . . . we can't invalidate these fears. (interview with Susan Eng, 28 August 1991)

Yet, as we shall see, this is exactly how the Police Association has conventionally responded to accusations of police racism. From Ms Eng's perspective, the Police Association and its president, Art Lymer, are as much a part of the problem as the diatribes of Dudley Laws and other representatives of the Black Action Defence Committee:

> . . . it's very important that . . . sensible debate in some kind of calmer climate take place. And right now we have . . . it between Dudley Laws and Art Lymer and there's very little in between. (ibid.)

Ms Eng emphasizes the problems that police officers face as part of their normal work:

> [People] . . . have to understand that there are some things that police officers simply have to do. They do have to stop people at three in the morning and ask them where they're going if they don't seem to belong to the neighbourhood. Those are valid policing exercises and the community has got to understand that. (ibid.)

But, she continues:

. . . we have to also not invalidate the experience of people who have been dealt with, where because of the public psyche and the news media and all of this anger, that the one-on-one exchange between a police officer on the beat and the young Black person that he comes across, that that incident is consistently volatile. (ibid.)

While, as we shall see, the Police Federation refuses to acknowledge any hint of institutional racism, the Chair of the Police Services Board is much less defensive:

I think society has changed and the question is whether policing as a culture and as an institution has changed as quickly. No one's asking the police to be better than anybody else. We're just asking them to be as good and as imperfect as anybody else. . . .

[Any] organization that has nearly 6,000 officers and 2,000 civilians and a whole hierarchy of command and a history, a tradition that's constantly thrown up . . . and a $530m budget and so on, has its own basic momentum. It works a certain way. If we thought that we could, by pushing one button, change the entire direction, we're absolute fools. And it isn't good enough to say that if we get rid of this bad apple or that bad apple or a whole bushel of apples that we're going to get rid of the problem. The system produces its own problems. The system has its own work ethic. It has its own culture. It has its own core of values, and it's those things that we have to look upon. (ibid.)

Ms Eng dismisses the significance of "canteen culture" and the "few bad apples" theory of police racism in favour of a more fundamental analysis of the institutional dimensions of police racism, including an analysis of the rôle of White power and privilege:

Well, actually, what you're saying to them is that . . . you're going to have to give up some of your privilege. Isn't that right? Well they don't like that. Those are questions that have to be asked. Those are not the questions that I can now afford to ask publicly in any kind of direct form, but institutionally and slowly and progressively we're going to have to deal with getting the answers to those questions (ibid.).

To emphasize her point, Ms Eng makes an ironic inversion of the common construction of "Black crime" to ask:

Why don't we talk about White crime? For example we've had some examples of serial murderers and all of them have been White males . . . . Well, I think we should get the White community leaders out, don't you, and explain what it is that they've got going on in their midst. Perhaps we should do some statistics based upon White males who commit serial rapes and serial murders. Perhaps there's a genetic predisposition for this kind of behaviour. Maybe it's part of the White privilege (ibid.).

Though made in fun, the comment hints at a refreshing perspective on "race" and crime from someone in such high office. It shows a willingness to question received opinion and a genuine commitment to change that was not always evident among the police officers whom I encountered.

The most brutal, murderous force in North America?

A radically different perspective on police–community relations in Toronto was offered by Mr Dudley Laws, a Jamaican-born immigration consultant who came to Toronto in 1965 and has since earned a reputation as one of the police's most outspoken critics. Described as "Toronto's most infamous radical Black activist" (*Toronto Life*, August 1989), Mr Laws was instrumental in setting up the Black Action Defence Committee in 1988 to co-ordinate public response to the growing number of police shootings of young Black people. He became the subject of a $50,000 law suit, instigated by the Police Association, after describing Toronto's police as "the most brutal, murderous force in North America" (*Share*, 18 April 1991). Despite the controversy that surrounded these remarks, Mr Laws insists that all he and his organization are demanding is fair treatment from the police:

Our purpose is . . . to be a kind of watchdog organisation on police issues and to try to bring about positive changes to the police actions in the community. We do not say bring about a better relationship with the police. What we want is proper policing, equal policing, equal in the sense that what is done in the broader community should be done in our community as well (interview with Dudley Laws, 21 August 1991).

While Mr Laws insists that the problem goes much deeper, he does not imply that all police officers are equally racist:

. . . certainly all police officers are not the same. I mean we have come to that conclusion. Not all of them are capable of shooting somebody. But what is bad about it [is that] they all condone the action. Once the action is committed, everyone is backing up the officer who does the wrong, by saying that he's a good officer . . . and making all kind of excuses for him (ibid.).

Dudley Laws rejects the view that only a few members of Toronto's police force are prejudiced, arguing that, wherever evidence of discriminatory attitudes is found, appropriate disciplinary action should be taken:

. . . the police have a hard task. I mean I know they have to do their job, but the job they have to do is to be done properly. And any police officer who cannot do their job properly . . . should look for another employment. It is as simple as that. (ibid.)

Mr Laws claims that the Police Services Board (formerly the Police Commission), especially under June Rowlands' administration, did not serve as an effective regulatory body, monitoring and disciplining members of the Police Association:

The Police Association has an attitude that we rule, we are our own boss, we rule and we want to rule. There is no discipline at all within the Association themselves or within the police force . . . [T]he Police Association is an entity unto itself which does not have no respect at all in my opinion for the Board of Police Commissioners. (ibid.)

The Black Action Defence Committee refused to give evidence to the 1989 Task Force, claiming that the recommendations of previous inquiries had not been implemented. They became so frustrated with constant disavowals of police racism that they broke off all further negotiations with the police. One particular provocation was a remark by the President of the Police Association that in twenty years on the force he had never witnessed a racist remark by a police officer:

[The Police Association President] was saying he was in the force for, what, twenty odd years and he has never seen or heard a racist remark. And we said why do we come to this conference to talk about better relationships with the police . . . [when] the Police Chief and the Chairperson and the President of the Police Association . . . do not even admit that there is a problem? Before we can deal with the problem, perceived or real, . . . you have to admit that something is not right, you know. (ibid.)

Mr Laws' proposed solution to the problems of policing Toronto is to focus on what people do rather than on what they say:

. . . you can't get rid of racism within society. You may be able to control the actions and attitudes of people who have racist tendencies and one of the ways you can do that is by teaching them about the culture of the people . . . But mainly if they are working in a government institution you have to enforce strict discipline on those people who have racist tendencies or you will never bring about changes because . . . a police officer in Toronto knows that if he goes out there right now and shoots a Black person, the person he kills, even a child, a Black child, that he goes and shoots a Black child, he knows that he'll have one hundred percent support of the Police Association behind him, morally and financially (ibid.).

It is this accusation of institutional racism that the Police Association has found so hard to accept, being prepared only to admit to the possibility of direct racism on the part of a few individual officers.

Black activists, screaming for power?

The organization that represents ordinary rank-and-file members of the Metropolitan Toronto Police Force is the Police Association, a closed-shop, representing 2,200 civilian staff and 5,600 uniformed officers up to the rank of staff-sergeant. Their president, Mr Art Lymer, has been in office since 1988, previously serving as a member of the board of directors since 1977. Born in Liverpool, he emigrated to Canada in 1952. Mr Lymer traces the current deterioration of police–community relations back to the shooting of Buddy Evans in 1980 and is quick to lay the blame at the door of the Black Action Defence Committee:

> I guess in 1980 we had our first shooting of a Black person. And that was called the Buddy Evans case. You know it was a police officer that shot a Black suspect by the name of Buddy Evans. He did so legitimately. His life was being threatened at the time and he was being overpowered by this individual. It resulted in his death. That went by the route of the coroner's inquest. And the coroner's inquest absolved the officer of any blame but it gave the opportunity to the Black activists out there that were screaming for power and saying that you know, our force is racist and everything like that . . . Shortly after that, we had the Albert Johnson shooting. And the Albert Johnson shooting then provoked another . . . opportunity for the Black activists to get media coverage (interview with Art Lymer, 22 August 1991).

Mr Lymer contrasts "responsible groups" such as the Jamaican–Canadian Association, whom he was willing to meet with at any time, with "irresponsible groups" of "Black activists" of whom the Black Action Defence Committee were the chief example:

> . . . they're not responsible people in my opinion. They won't sit down and talk rationally . . . [I]t's my own personal opinion and the opinion of a lot of members of the Black community that Dudley Laws is doing more harm than anybody else, to . . . inflame racial prejudice among members of the White community towards the Black community (ibid.).

As police–community relations in Toronto continued to deteriorate during the 1980s, Mr Lymer made a series of controversial interventions, denying the existence of police racism and reacting fiercely to public criticism of the police. When manslaughter charges were brought against PC David Deviney for the shooting of Lester Donaldson, Mr Lymer accused the Attorney General, Ian Scott, of bowing to political pressure from "a small minority of Black activists" within the Black community (*Toronto Star*, 12 January 1989). He went on to describe the Black Action Defence Committee as "a small group of extremists that does not represent or benefit the black community" (*Globe & Mail*, 14 January 1989). He supported those officers who took industrial action in support of PC Deviney and orchestrated a show of public support from groups such as Citizens Opposed to Police Slander (COPS).

Mr Lymer suggested that Britain was ahead of Canada in dealing with the problems of policing a multicultural society:

> . . . your problem is much more advanced than ours but we're now getting to that position, I would suppose in Metropolitan Toronto, where the UK was maybe about 20 years ago (ibid.).

But, he was adamant about the absence of racially motivated behaviour within the Metropolitan Toronto Police Force:

> . . . we do not have a racially motivated police force you know. There are isolated incidents but . . . we do not have a racist police force (ibid.).

Nonetheless, Mr Lymer has attracted significant criticism for his persistent remarks about "Black crime", suggesting that levels of crime are not in proportion to the size of the Black community. Mr Lymer kept returning to this point:

> . . . some of the people that have come over here from Jamaica . . . are prone to violence, they are very violent. They have very little respect, you know, for life . . . It's the infiltration of drugs and the one main drug is crack and the people that were pushing that in the communities, 98 per cent of them were Blacks. And of the Blacks, I think about 90 per cent of them were from Jamaica (ibid.).

Since the Police Services Board forbids the collection of crime statistics by "race", these remarks are based on very questionable evidence. Significantly, though, they are part of a mindset that does not consider such comments racist.[8] Later in the interview, Mr Lymer returned to this theme in the context of that summer's riots in Nova Scotia:

> . . . anyone from Halifax is a born fighter anyway. They like to drink and fight. . . They're always fighting with each other. It's the same as the Irish used to be, you know. You get a few drinks and "Come on, have a fight", you know (ibid.).

Remarkably, too, Mr Lymer insists that he has never witnessed racist behaviour in all his years service:

> . . . in my 38 years on the force I've never actually witnessed [behaviour] myself that I could say was out and out racist. I'm not saying

that it doesn't happen. It does. And if it's identified, it has to be stopped. And the officer has to be given an opportunity to correct himself, and, if he can't, then fired off the force, because . . . people can have their own prejudices, you can't stop it, but you cannot discriminate (ibid.).

For all their differences, the distinction that Mr Lymer draws here between prejudice and discrimination is not dissimilar from Dudley Laws' insistence that policing practices should be fair, even if individual police officers are prejudiced. However, not all police officers would agree with Mr Lymer's views, as my final interview suggests.

Dudley's a good man

Despite a vigorous employment equity programme, Black police officers remain a small minority of the Metropolitan Toronto Police Force, especially at more senior levels. One such officer, Sergeant Karl Oliver, serves in the police's Inter-Community Relations Unit. In contrast to Mr Lymer's blanket denial of police racism, Sergeant Oliver is much more prepared to admit that problems have arisen and that police–community relations have become politicized as a result:

. . . there have been a few incidents over the past couple of years . . . some [of which] were a bit on the shady side. And those are the incidents that have sparked a lot of these demonstrations and bad feelings. You also have, based on that, . . . some people [who] tend to use these incidents as a means of fostering their own private agenda (interview with Sergeant Karl Oliver, 14 August 1991).

Despite this suggestion of "private agenda", Sergeant Oliver's attitude towards Dudley Laws and the Black Action Defence Committee is remarkably tolerant:

Dudley's a good man. A lot of people don't like Dudley, but . . . Dudley does what he believes in and one thing I can say about Dudley, you can tell that when you talk to him, that Dudley is very frank and forthright . . . [I]f you don't give Dudley a platform, you don't hear from him. You don't hear from Dudley until somebody goes out there and does something stupid. Then of course he does what he has to do by stirring up the hornet's nest and something like that. But if you keep everything on an even keel, you don't hear from Dudley . . . You can't call him an evil. He's a necessary part of the fabric of society . . . . In every society, changes come about because of a few people who are not very popular, who decide to stick their necks out in order to present what they deem to be justice. Now the Black Defence Committee have appointed themselves to do just that. And they have raised certain issues, that if you are honest with yourselves, you'll have to sit back and say well, is there something there that we should be looking into? Rather than dismiss it and say that these people are sensation seekers (ibid.).

Sergeant Oliver is, however, more circumspect about how far organizations such as the Black Action Defence Committee represent the majority of Black opinion:

. . . they haven't got the support and co-operation of the majority of Blacks in Toronto, because most Blacks couldn't care less. As a matter of fact, most of them will tell you point blank that the police are not going far enough in dealing with some of these situations . . . [T]he majority of Blacks and Black parents out there . . . would say if you weren't in that position, in that situation, that location, then you wouldn't have to come into contact with the officer (ibid.).

Sergeant Oliver took particularly strong exception to Mr Lymer's comments about "Black crime", preferring to adopt a more "neutral", colour-blind approach:

I agree with the [Black] community when they become outraged about such stupid statements . . . Crime has nothing to do with race . . . Crime is crime (ibid.).

On the question of institutional racism within the police force, Sergeant Oliver was ambivalent:

I don't think there is a policy. There is not an expressed policy, that is laid down that people should be treated differently . . . Things seem to follow a pattern and there are certain unwritten rules and laws that are in any institution. Nobody tells somebody at IBM or the telephone company or any of these big corporations that a woman is not going to be promoted beyond that management position.

[PAJ: But over time it's always worked out that way.]

That's what happens . . . I mean I've never seen any Blacks super-vising or running a section of this organisation. You know in the 30 years I've been here . . . And they'll come up with all kinds of reasons why it wouldn't work because this one is not willing to accept his instructions and that one's not going to do this and that. Nobody has ever tested it. Nobody's ever tried it. Well, it's just worked out that it's never been done so therefore it's traditional and face it very few senior people come in with their own agenda and their own ways of doing things and you copy from the man who was here before. They always do the same (ibid.).

Sergeant Oliver strongly advocates community-based policing as a solution to Toronto's problems:

> . . . community-based policing has got to be the answer to a lot of the problems. You have to know the people you are policing. You have to know your youths; you have to know your street people. You have to know your winos; you have to know your druggies. If you're working successfully in an area, you have to know them. Not forgetting the fact they're all people. You just do what you have to do. I do what I have to do but when once we understand each other, then that reduces the possibility of confrontation (ibid.).

The four perspectives represented in these interviews offer some interesting insights into the way that "common-sense" and "institutional" discourses combine and play off each other. Each perspective is informed by a distinct set of experiences and is defined in relation to other perspectives to which they are sometimes quite antagonistic. What is perhaps most disturbing is the extent to which different people are operating on the basis of quite different "definitions of the situation", increasing the probability of misunderstanding and the potential for conflict. To what extent can these conflicts be addressed in the language of "identity" and "difference"?

The politics of identity and difference

The material presented here highlights the political salience of current debates about "identity" and "difference". Who you are (and who you are not), who people think you are (and how different from you they imagine themselves to be), can have important repercussions, even deadly consequences. There is clear evidence of a breakdown in communication between the police and some sections of Toronto's Black community. As someone wrote recently to one of Toronto's Black newspapers:

> The police are out there to kill black people. Every black person is considered a pimp or a drug dealer. It's the way this white society tends to look at black people. And because they put us in this category they can murder us wholesale (Contrast, 17 August 1988).

The author's views may be extreme but, once a situation is defined in these confrontational terms, it will have real consequences in terms of people's behaviour. If police officers stereotype all Black men as pimps and drug-dealers, then they are unlikely to respond sensitively to late-night confrontations with Black people, even where the "suspect" is entirely innocent.

But it is not just the police who stereotype Black people in this way. Consider the way that *Maclean's* magazine represented local reaction in Toronto to the Rodney King verdict in Los Angeles and the subsequent "rampage" up Yonge Street in May 1992. *Maclean's* cover depicts the menacing face of an anonymous young Black man over which are superimposed the words: "Young, Black and angry" (see Fig. 8.1). In the subtitle, a particular event ("A Toronto riot") is related to a wider "season of urban tension". Inside the magazine, the editor declares that it is "A time for action": ". . . the violence that ripped through Toronto last week was the result of subtle forms of racism that are endemic to many of Canada's larger cities" (p. 4).

Figure 8.1 *Maclean's* magazine cover, 18 May 1992.

A few pages further on, however, the right-wing columnist Barbara Amiel gives a completely different reading of events. "Racism", her headline reads, was but "an excuse for riots and theft" (p. 15). According to Ms Amiel, the protesters who marched to the US Consulate to demonstrate against the Rodney King verdict and the rioters who made their way down Yonge Street later that night were both equally guilty. Their actions were "informed by a fatally flawed liberal perspective on racism that for the past 30 years has sold blacks in North America the notion that nothing in life is their fault". The King verdict was simply "a handy excuse for helping oneself to stolen goodies". In contrast to "tired rhetoric about systemic racism in Canada", trotted out by "black activists", Ms Amiel insists that "Canadians know themselves, and they know Canadian society is not racist" (p. 15).

Other articles in the same issue suggest that the violent clash on Yonge Street "focuses attention on Canada's racial divide" (p. 24). *Maclean's* journalists debated whether young Blacks could excuse their actions as a justifiable response to the poverty and racism that increasingly "define black urban life" (p. 24). Sensitive reporting on the differences within Toronto's Black population was juxtaposed with more sensational material. On the one hand, *Maclean's* insists that "what appears to some as a single, unified Black presence is actually a mosaic of distinct communities whose members arrived in Canada at various stages over the past four centuries" (p. 27). On the other, it suggests that "for many young Black men, Toronto has become a virtual war zone, presided over by gun-toting entrepreneurs who run the city's trade in crack cocaine" (p. 26). Readers learned that "Much of that underground traffic takes place in the high-rise canyons of the Jane-Finch corridor" – a byword for crime and violence, beyond the comprehension of most law-abiding suburban Canadians.[9]

The photographs that illustrated the "Black and Angry" article show groups of young Black men on street-corners and in other public places (Fig. 8.2). Those that accompanied the following article ("Anatomy of a riot") are even more dramatic, showing three young Black men ("skinheads and disaffected youth", according to the photo caption), smashing a shop window (p. 30). Only one story, a single-page essay by Jules Elder, managing editor of the Black newspaper *Share*, provides a contrast to the dominant view of a lawless, criminalized and apparently homogeneous "Black youth", insisting that "We all share the blame" (p. 32).[10]

How do such dominant representations emerge and what do they tell us about contemporary Canadian society? Canadians pride themselves on their distinctiveness from the United States. Urban crime and its associations with an increasingly alienated Black underclass are widely perceived to be an *American* problem. Clayton Ruby, columnist on the *Globe and Mail*, began his

Figure 8.2 "Black and angry", *Maclean's* magazine, 18 May 1992.

reflections on the Yonge Street disturbances with the phrase "It can't happen here", implying a contrast with the United States. He continued:

Canadians don't have a history of such pervasive, grinding racism and poverty as do Americans. Canadians don't have the gripping certainty of a hopeless future for an entire young generation. Canadians don't have cities so degraded that no one dare live in them or can safely walk the streets. Canadians haven't lost their sense of tolerance and understanding for each other . . . But just look at what has already happened here (5 May 1992).

Ruby goes on to catalogue the deterioration of police–community relations in Winnipeg, Vancouver, Montreal and Toronto, followed by an analysis of "the white face of policing" in which he argued that most police officers have retreated to the comforts of suburban living "where they can be among their own kind", arriving for work "like an occupying army". This rejection of difference in favour of a homogeneous White identity is a worrying trend for urban Canada, signalling a rejection of the multicultural ideal by those who can afford to live in "exclusive" White suburbs. It is a particularly dangerous trend among police officers who have little or no first-hand experience of Toronto's various communities on which to draw when they are faced with situations that call for split-second judgement. In such circumstances, the recognition of difference becomes highly charged and the process of identity-formation takes on immediate political significance.

Conclusion

Before offering any substantive conclusions, I would like to reflect on my position as a White English academic evaluating the problems of another society in situations of heightened social tension. One conventional justification for such research is the comparative dimension that can be brought to bear from such a perspective. But that has been a rather subsidiary concern in this particular chapter.[11] Besides the common problems of cross-cultural research, the current project raises a series of more immediate issues concerning the question of "positionality".

In the course of fieldwork and interviewing in Toronto I came to realize that my own political views were closest to the position outlined by Dudley Laws and the Black Action Defence Committee (though I would not always endorse the way in which BADC has advanced its arguments). My feeling of antagonism towards the Police Association and its refusal to acknowledge the possibility of institutional racism was complicated by their President's personal generosity towards me. Not only did Mr Lymer agree to an interview at very short notice. He also went to considerable lengths to lend me his personal collection of video and audio tapes relating to the period following the police shootings of 1989. This personal dilemma deepened with the announcement in August 1991 that Dudley Laws had been found guilty of assaulting his wife and sentenced to one year's probation (*Toronto Star*, 10 August 1991). My immediate reaction was to regard these events as evidence of police harassment: Mr Laws's wife had not laid charges against her husband, the police had. She had called the police after injuring her back in a minor domestic dispute and the police responded by sending five squad cars to their house – scarcely a normal police response to reports of domestic violence. Dudley Laws's arrest, which was brought to my attention by Mr Lymer, clouded the previously clear picture that I had been forming about police–community relations in Toronto. It was no longer possible to paint a simple picture of "heroes" and "villains"; my sympathies were more divided than I had previously thought.

Similarly, I had not expected Ms Eng to be as candid as she was at interview. I was also flattered at the seriousness with which she listened to my opinions and was probably not as critical in my questioning as I might otherwise have been. These episodes, although trivial at one level, encapsulate many of the issues that arise in contemporary ethnography, giving an immediacy to more abstract debates about the crisis of representation and the politics of position (cf. Jackson 1992b).

My more substantive conclusions are obvious at one level; equivocal at another. There is clear evidence in the interview material that different people are working with quite different "definitions of the situation". For some people (such as Dudley Laws), the evidence of institutional racism is glaringly obvious; for others (such as Art Lymer) it is steadfastly denied. Where these views are held by people in positions of power (such as Mr Lymer) it makes it much harder for those in relatively subordinate positions whose opinions differ (such as Sergeant Oliver) to be heard. Equally obviously, if racism is denied as a routine practice within the police force, it is unlikely to be tackled in any thorough or systematic way. The criticisms of relatively powerless people (such as Dudley Laws) can be ignored by labelling them "extremist", while proposals for radical change by relatively powerful people (like Susan Eng) can be side-stepped by pointing to the existence of formal mechanisms such as employment equity programmes or "race relations" codes such as already exist within the Metropolitan Toronto Police Force.

More equivocally, it is possible to be both optimistic and pessimistic about the future of police–community relations in Toronto. As Dudley Laws remarked:

I think there are a lot of positive things happening in our Black community. We have a lot of young people who are going to school, who are doing very, very well. The cultural aspect like Caribana and the music that we bring to Canada . . . A large percentage of the nurses in the hospitals are Black nurses and I mean the community itself is very strong economically . . . and we have a lot of professional people working in the community too, so it's not that our community is dead and criminalized and all that. I mean it is a really vibrant community with people doing a lot of things. But then you read statistics that the police put together and talk about Blacks this and Blacks that, leads you to believe that nothing else is happening but people committing crimes. (interview with Dudley Laws, 21 August 1991)

The more pessimistic conclusion emerged in reply to my suggestion that Canada was ahead of Britain in the development of multicultural policy and equality rights legislation but behind Britain in relation to some of the policing issues we had been discussing. I suggested that, because of events such as the 1981 riots in Britain, the police had been forced to recognize that they were not policing an increasingly multicultural society very effectively. In sombre mood, Mr Laws replied: "Well, perhaps they are waiting for Brixton or Birmingham". Despite recent events in Halifax, Nova Scotia (*Toronto Star*, 20 July 1991) and in Toronto itself (*Globe and Mail*, 5 May 1992), such violent conflict is still relatively rare in Canada. The liberal conclusion would suggest that recognizing the need for change will help prevent any further deterioration of police–community relations. The more radical conclusion suggests that Blacks have every right to protest, by whatever means necessary, while they continue to be faced with differential policing and institutionalized racism.

Acknowledgements

I would like to thank Jan Penrose and participants at the British Association for Canadian Studies conference in Cambridge (March 1993) for their constructive comments on an earlier draft of this chapter. The Department of Geography at UCL paid for the cost of reproducing the illustrations, for which I am most grateful.

Notes

1. The actual number of incidents is contested and hard to verify. *Maclean's* magazine records that Raymond Lawrence shot and killed by PC Robert Rice in May 1992, was "the 14th black victim of a police shooting in the city since 1978, and the fourth black fatality" (18 May 1992). According to the *Globe and Mail* (5 May 1992), eight Blacks have been shot by police officers in the metropolitan Toronto region in the past four years, four of them killed. My own research (Jackson 1994) indicates that seven Black people have been shot by the police in metropolitan Toronto since 1978 (five since 1988), of whom five have died (three since 1988).
2. Fieldwork was funded by the Canadian High Commission in London as part of an Institutional Research Program (1991–2) on Social Constructions of Race and Ethnicity and via an earlier personal research grant which focused on the cultural politics of Caribana (August–September 1990).

3. The concept of "definition of the situation" originated with the sociologist William Isaac Thomas (1863–1947), an early member of the "Chicago school" of urban sociology (see Janowitz 1966).
4. For a recent discussion of the way that various marginalized groups have sought to exploit the ambiguities of their identity through the use of irony in poetry, fiction and the visual arts, see Hutcheon (1991).
5. For some telling US–Canadian comparisons, see Golberg & Mercer (1986). For an impassioned, well informed account of Toronto's place among North American cities, see Lemon (1984).
6. Ms Eng had clashed with her predecessor on several previous occasions, notably when Ms Rowlands implied that Susan Eng represented a single ethnic community rather than all Toronto's citizens ("Eng seeks Rowlands's apology over ethnic community remark", Globe and Mail, 24 July 1989).
7. Ms Eng had also refused to take the traditional oath of allegiance to the Queen on taking up her appointment, leading the Police Federation to publish a scurrilous cartoon, suggesting that she would make officers swear allegiance to Mickey Mouse (News and Views, July 1991).
8. Here, racism is defined as a set of inter-related ideologies and practices that have significant material consequences for "racialized" groups (Jackson 1987: 3). "Institutional racism" can in turn be defined as policies and practices that systematically reflect and reproduce inequalities between "racialized" groups. Such policies and practices should be judged by their consequences and not by their stated intentions. On the process of "racialization", see Miles (1989) and Jackson (1992a); on "institutional racism", see Williams (1985).
9. These remarks follow the way the British press reported the 1981 riots, creating a mythical "inner city" for which "ordinary people" need feel little responsibility (cf. Burgess 1985).
10. On the ideological construction of the category "Black youth" in Britain, see Solomos (1988).
11. The wider project which I am undertaking with Audrey Kobayashi at McGill University in Montreal does attempt such comparisons with parallel studies of racialized labour, popular culture, police–community relations and the law in Canada and the UK.

References

Burgess, J. A. 1985. News from nowhere: the press, the riots and the myth of the inner city. In Geography, the media and popular culture, J. A. Burgess & J. R. Gold (eds), 199–228. London: Croom Helm.
Goldberg, M. A. & J. Mercer 1986. The myth of the North American city: continentalism challenged. Vancouver: University of British Columbia Press.
Hutcheon, L. 1991. Splitting images: contemporary Canadian ironies. Toronto: Oxford University Press.
Jackson, P. (ed.) 1987. Race and racism: essays in social geography. London: Allen & Unwin.
Jackson, P. 1992a. The racialization of labour in post-war Bradford. Journal of Historical Geography 18, 190–209.
Jackson, P. 1992b. The crisis of representation and the politics of position. Environment and Planning D 9, 131–4.
Jackson, P. 1994. Constructions of criminality: police–community relations in Toronto.

Antipode 26, in press.

Janowitz, M. (ed.) 1966. *W. I. Thomas on social organization and social personality*. Chicago: University of Chicago Press.

Kelner, M. & E. Kallen 1974. The multicultural policy: Canada's response to ethnic diversity. *Journal of Comparative Sociology* 2, 21–34.

Kobayashi, A. 1993. Multiculturalism: representing a Canadian institution. In *Place/culture/representation*, J. S. Duncan & D. Ley (eds), 205–31. New York: Routledge.

Lemon, J. T. 1984. Toronto among North American cities: a historical perspective on the present. In *Forging a consensus*, L. Russell (ed.), 323–51. Toronto: University of Toronto Press.

Metropolitan Toronto Police Services Board 1989. *Race relations policy*. Toronto: Metropolitan Toronto Police Services Board.

Miles, R. 1989. *Racism*. London: Routledge.

Ontario. 1989. *Report of the Task Force on Race Relations and Policing*. Ontario: Solicitor General's Office.

Sewell, J. 1985. *Police: urban policing in Canada*, Toronto: James Lorimer.

Solomos, J. 1988. *Black youth, racism and the state*. Cambridge: Cambridge University Press.

Todd, F. & R. Todd 1992. Ethnic relations and community policing: a Canadian model for Europe? *British Journal of Canadian Studies* 7, 277–89.

Williams, J. 1985. Redefining institutional racism. *Ethnic and Racial Studies* 8, 323–48.

CONCLUSION

Conclusion:
identity and the politics of difference

JAN PENROSE & PETER JACKSON

Each chapter in this book has looked at a specific context in which the application of a social construction perspective can provide new insights into the ways that hegemony is constantly being reproduced and resisted. To conclude the volume, we will try to pull together some of the ideas that have been raised in individual chapters, highlighting their relevance to our overall themes. To do so, we provide an overview of what a social construction perspective can tell us about identity and difference; a consideration of the parallels and intersections of the concepts of "race" and nation and of the ideologies of racism and nationalism; a discussion of the significance of place; and some reflections on the politics of position.

Social construction perspectives on identity and difference

Each of the preceding chapters confirms the importance of challenging assumptions about the "naturalness" of the categories that we use to organize and make sense of the world. The social construction perspective is valuable precisely because it allows apparently immutable categories to·be dissected and critically evaluated. Such a process reveals that much of what is deemed to be "natural" or a matter of "common sense" is deeply rooted in the dominant ideologies of particular societies. By demonstrating the constructedness of these categories, dominant discourses and the interests that they serve can be called into question and radically subverted. Categories that formerly appeared immutable are shown to have assumed different shapes in different historical and geographical contexts – and hence to be amenable to further transformations. In revealing their mutability, categories that were once privileged by being taken for granted can now be questioned as just one of the many dimensions of human difference. By revealing the constructedness of the social categorizations that shape identity and difference, we expand our sensitivity to the politics that these categories engender. At the very least, the rigidity of categories is undermined and the processes which reify them can be exposed and disrupted.

As many of the preceding chapters suggest, a variety of social constructions are in circulation at the same time. Groups with different objectives may even come to share the same constructions as temporary alliances are forged or as subordinate groups work within existing constructions to achieve their separate ends. (The range of support for state-funded Muslim schools in Britain is an example of the former; the nationalist rhetoric of the SNP an example of the latter.) The way that marginalized groups frequently resort to essentialized identities suggests that the relationship between constructionism and essentialism is one of complex intersection rather than diametric opposition. Although largely illusory, fixed social identities have an undeniable potency. As a result, resistance is often couched in terms which do not challenge such dominant modes of representation. Once the constructedness of categories is acknowledged, however, they immediately become negotiable; their neutrality and "naturalness" are undermined.

Each chapter has focused on specific processes of construction. Rather than arguing that one representation should be privileged over any other, the focus has been on the specific contexts in which various representations have come to be advanced. The process of construction is most clearly revealed in moments of crisis (as took place in Sydney when the redevelopment of Redfern during the 1970s gave rise to pressures for low-income Aboriginal housing, or as occurred in New York City when widespread housing abandonment by landlords gave rise to the demand for new forms of tenure, such as limited-equity co-operatives). In each case, crisis (or the perception of crisis) serves as the catalyst in dislodging entrenched constructions, opening the way for alternative readings. This is not to deny the pervasiveness of asymmetrical power relations or the remarkable capacity for hegemony to reassert itself by adopting new forms that continue to deny the emergence of more equitable social relations. Thus, when Australian Aborigines began to have some success in their land-rights struggles, new discourses were employed to frustrate their claims (including forms of cartographic representation that distort their relationship to the land). Likewise, when accused of institutional racism, the Metropolitan Toronto Police Force attempted to discredit their accusers (by calling them unrepresentative) and disputed the evidence with which they were confronted. In each case, "crisis" serves to highlight the socially constructed nature of dominant ways of thinking, intensifying the need for new forms of representation that are less damaging in their human consequences.

Parallels and intersections: "race"/nation, racism/nationalism

The concepts of "race" and nation are deeply entrenched ways of thinking about the world. Both notions are empowered by assumptions about their naturalness and by their tendency to be viewed as unproblematic by those whom they privilege. But there are significant differences too. Whereas "race" is something that members of dominant groups generally use to distinguish others from themselves, nation tends to be used to distinguish themselves from others. Whereas those in power regard nationhood as something they possess but which they deny to others, "race" is regarded as something that applies to others but not to themselves. In each case, it is the dominant group that sets up the oppositions, regarding itself as "normal" and treating subordinate groups as different or "other".

This pattern of application has important implications for the intersection of "race" and nation. The identification of discrete groups of people is central to the construction of nations (as nationalism in Scotland and the United Kingdom reveals) and can be used to legitimize exclusive and selective immigration policies (as has been demonstrated for both the Canadian and British cases). Those who already "possess" the nation can control who is to be admitted within its borders. Where an equation between a distinctive people and a fixed territory or place is part of the vision of the nation, the ascription of "race" becomes a basis for exclusion.

The power to ascribe "race" and to control the nation has wide-ranging consequences for the way in which power is contested within the nation-state. Not only is it difficult for those who have been excluded from the nation because of their alleged "racial" difference to divest themselves of this difference. But the linking of "race" and nation leaves those who have been excluded with little alternative but to use their ascribed difference as a basis of unified resistance. Enforcing the right to ascribe "race" and to control the nation leaves those in power with little scope for exercising tolerance or maintaining equality when they are obliged to defend their position of privilege. Thus, the British government has withdrawn the right of citizenship from many of its former subjects and refused to honour legislation providing state funding for religious schools when to do otherwise would threaten the privilege that the government represents and protects.

Racism and nationalism also have much in common as ideologies. They are usually associated with those whose own "race" and nation are invisible. Thus, problems of "race" are held to occur elsewhere (in inner-city schools) by teachers in Britain's "White highlands", while the English (conveniently thinking of themselves as "British") tend to deny their own nationalism while denigrating the nationalist aspirations of the Scots, Welsh or Irish. But whereas nationalism can be thought of as a liberating ideology by those whose aspirations are currently thwarted, racism is rarely thought of in such a positive light (except where, under another name, it is defended as a means of preserving the "natural" order of society).

Wherever the categories of "race" and nation are in use, the ideologies of racism and nationalism are never far removed. Thus, when racialized groups employ forms of "strategic essentialism", they run the risk of endorsing elements of racist ideology. Similarly, when established nations attempt to defend themselves from the aspirations of would-be nations, they employ a form of nationalist rhetoric and reveal their own deep-rooted nationalism. Such complexities remain to be investigated in depth. That they have been made visible by a social construction approach reinforces our optimism about the potential value of this way of thinking.

The significance of place

The centrality of place in geographical inquiry has been reaffirmed by each of the contributions to this book. However, different chapters have sought to refine our understanding of the significance of place in different ways. Working at a variety of scales, from the nation to the locality, we have demonstrated the importance of geographical context for understanding the construction and application of ideas about "race" and nation. We have also shown how new dimensions of significance emerge when the assumption of homogeneity within particular places is challenged. Place contextualizes the construction of "race" and nation, generating geographically specific ideologies of racism and nationalism.

At the broadest scale, the physical boundaries of a country give tangible expression to hegemonic conceptions of the nation. The space that a country occupies becomes a context for legitimizing and enforcing dominant ideas about "race" and about the relationship between "race" and nation. But, as immigration policies and other processes of nation-building reveal, the conceptual dimensions of place can be as important as its physical manifestations. In other circumstances, conception of space can become overtly political. In Australia, for example, Aboriginal land claims destabilize the nation's vision of itself. In contesting the conceptions of space that define and empower the established nation, Aboriginal land claims challenge the apparent "neutrality" of the hegemonic culture. The assertion that the boundaries of widely recognized places *cannot* be drawn with precision highlights the constructedness of prevailing conceptions which view geographical spaces and places as finite and definite. Part of our research agenda, therefore, must be to understand how specific places are incorporated into specific constructions of "race" and nation and their associated assumptions about the nature and function of space.

Several chapters have pointed the way forwards for this kind of research by showing how hegemonic values set the parameters for contesting space. For example, the hegemonic category of nation can be used to alter the distribution of power (as Scottish nationalists are hoping to do within the UK). But in so doing, the conceptual instrument of a hegemonic vision of world organization is reified, and hegemony is reproduced in a different context. Similarly, other chapters have shown how dominant groups have the power to introduce distinctive categories of space and to limit the scope for resistance to the status quo. This is clearly the case in negotiations surrounding Aboriginal land rights, but it is also true in the case of Muslim campaigns for state-funded schools. In both instances, the artificial separation of sacred spaces from everyday spaces is used to limit the breadth of claims to universal rights. By severing the connection between sacred and everyday spaces, and by declaring that the former is the only authentic repository of a "different" cultural identity, Australian and British authorities have used their power to restrict challenges to the hegemonic culture which they represent. Religious difference may be tolerated, cultural difference will not.

In other instances, hegemonic conceptualizations of place can be subverted to empower the underprivileged. In New York City, for example, the dominant association of "abandonment" with "having no value" provided a space for low-income residents to appropriate unwanted housing and convert it into a valuable resource. The same example shows, however, how spaces of resistance are often only temporary and context-specific. Once they are reinvested with value, their vulnerability to hegemonic control is revived.

Part of the reason for the neglect of low-income housing in New York City was its association with marginalized groups of people: Blacks, the unemployed and women. The hegemonic vision of the value of a specific place cannot be separated from estimations of the value of the people who occupy it. The racialization of place is illustrated in several other examples whether in the conviction that "White" areas do not have a "race" problem or that "Black crime" is concentrated in particular neighbourhoods in Toronto.

Without exception, the chapters in this book confirm that place is always significant. However, its significance is variable and dynamic. As scholars, the places that we choose to study will affect our understanding of the interactions between constructions of place, "race" and nation. This suggests that considerable place-specific research needs to be done alongside our attempts to formulate and refine ideas about processes of social construction. Ironically, for a collection of geographical essays, we may have achieved greater sophistication in our theorization of "race" and nation than we have collectively achieved in theorizing the significance of place. We hope, however, that these essays demonstrate the scope for further research on place by highlighting its centrality in understanding the relationship between "race" and nation.

Position matters: identity and the politics of difference

In exploring specific intersections between the social construction of "race", place and nation, this book has been concerned with the nature of identity. Rather than assuming that identities are fixed and singular, we have shown them to be dynamic and plural. Such a plurality immediately gives rise to a *politics* of identity as groups and individuals become aware of their differences, attach significance to certain dimensions and contest the relevance of other designations.

From the perspective of all of the authors represented here, the struggle for identity is a struggle for power and always takes place within a hegemonic system of social relations. Hegemony sets the context both for the reinforcement of privilege and for resistance to it. Each chapter confirms that the *position* of groups and individuals within the hegemonic system always matters. Collectively, we have shown that at any given place and time positions of hegemony are being employed to exercise and preserve power. This power includes the capacity to set the parameters for negotiation within any given society. It also includes the freedom to define "difference" and to enforce this vision through hegemonic institutions of government, law and education. In a system where "sameness" and conformity are rewarded, the power to define "difference" becomes the power to disadvantage and disempower. It is those who reject this vision of society, or who have been marginalized by it, that are likely to offer the most significance resistance to it. From these positions, they challenge the status quo, either directly through confrontation or indirectly through subversion; in both cases, the underlying objective is a redistribution of power that is capable of engendering increased equality in social relations. Just as resistance often takes a symbolic or ritualistic form so, too, is hegemony most often effected ideologically rather than through direct coercion.

The question of "legitimacy" is clearly a key component in the definition of hegemony and in gauging the effectiveness of different forms of resistance. The book provides many examples where the legitimacy of oppositional strategies is questioned by those in power. These range from Aboriginal representations of their relationship to the land to violent protests over police harassment in Toronto. In each case, it is the hegemonic power that defines whether the form of protest is legitimate, thereby exerting a significant influence on its likely success or failure. Here, too, there are many unanswered questions about the nature of legitimacy that await further research.

By demonstrating the constructedness of hegemonic categorizations, we have emphasized the process through which "difference" comes to be politicized. We are also keenly aware, however, that as academics we are not outside this process of politicization. Developing a critical self-consciousness or reflexivity about our own positions as researchers is fraught with difficulty. We can write ourselves into our accounts in a variety of ways. But a simple statement of the "as a middle-class, White man/woman" kind is clearly inadequate. Our position is ascribed as much as it is chosen, and we may not be fully aware of how all the dimensions of our identities bear upon our research. (The recency with which masculinity and "Whiteness" have become the subject of research is an illustration of this point.)

Our status as scholars places us awkwardly with respect to the hegemonic system which we may wish to resist. From this perspective, all scholars are faced with the choice (whether they recognize it or not), of using their power either to reproduce or to challenge hegemony. Those of us who choose the latter option must also confront the personal contradictions inherent in reproducing the system that we seek to change. For each of the contributors to this book, the act of writing is part of a continuing attempt to contend with these contradictions. As women, some of us are painfully aware of the incongruities of working within a male-dominated academy. As middle class, White students and academics we all confront ingrained assumptions about the alleged neutrality of our social position. Gradually, we are learning to recognize our privilege and to evaluate its impact on our visions the world as it is and as it might become. As members of a particular generation (in our twenties and thirties), we encounter the limitations of our experience as well as the restrictions that our academic positions place on our actions.

As individuals, we must locate ourselves within the intersecting matrix of human identity and difference in order to become aware of our potentially common position. It is through this process of self-location and relocation that each of us experiences first-hand the construction of difference and its centrality to our own identities. Such a reflexive attitude confirms our belief in the positional complexity of human identities and in the constancy of its shifts and realignments. At the same time, our experiences of collaboration on this book and in the construction of a common base of resistance confirm the value of group membership and collective action. In exploring constructions of "race", place and nation, we have been forced to confront the construction of ourselves.

Index

211

54 Dudley
NML

UNIVERSITY OF WOLVERHAMPTON
LIBRARY